D0471220

**Corporate
Bankruptcy
in America**

332.75
Al79c

Corporate Bankruptcy in America

Edward I. Altman
New York University

Heath Lexington Books
D.C. Heath and Company
Lexington, Massachusetts
Toronto   London

WIEBERD LIBRARY
WITHDRAWN
PACIFIC COLLEGE - M.B. SEMINARY
FRESNO, CALIF, 93702
33625

Copyright © 1971 by D. C. Heath and Company

All rights reserved. No part of this publication may be reproduced or transmitted in any form or by any means, electronic or mechanical, including photocopy, recording, or any information storage or retrieval system, without permission in writing from the publisher.

Published simultaneously in Canada.

Printed in the United States of America.

International Standard Book Number: 0-669-75309-2

Library of Congress Catalog Card Number: 79-163187

To my parents, Florence and Sidney Altman

Table of Contents

List of Tables

List of Figures

Foreword

In the midst of the optimism of corporate expansion and merger activity in the late 1960s, Professor Edward Altman was studying the anatomy of corporate failure and bankruptcy. Some dramatic business bankruptcies of major corporations during 1970 have ushered in a broadened wave of business failures. The further development of articles in scholarly journals by Professor Altman and his new management-oriented materials have resulted in the publication of this book on bankruptcies at a very timely juncture.

One of the major contributions of Professor Altman's research was to develop a basis for prediction of corporate failure. By the use of appropriate statistical methods, he was successful in discriminating between firms likely to fail and those likely to avoid financial disaster. His work on prediction of corporate bankruptcy in the manufacturing and railroads sectors provides early warning signals which will afford some opportunity for avoiding failure. This has both managerial and social benefits.

His statistical materials on prediction of bankruptcy are augmented by analysis of macroeconomic forces in the economy which represent broader forces influencing the rate or frequency of business failures. In addition, he investigates methods of avoiding failures by use of mergers and other procedures for strengthening firms.

Professor Altman's studies of investor experience in bankruptcy demonstrate both adverse consequences and wealth conservation opportunities in the bankruptcy process. Through composition of debt obligations and by the reduction of other costs, a firm can make bankruptcy an opportunity for rehabilitation and renewed profitability.

Professor Altman also provides a basis for extending the economic theory of the firm by analysis of the broader economic costs of bankruptcy. He provides a basis for increased understanding of the broader implications of corporate bankruptcy. The comprehensive empirical analyses throughout the book complement the theory extremely well.

Thus, this book is analytical, yet practical. It extends theory and at the same time provides a guide for improved managerial behavior. As such, Professor Altman's book represents a valuable addition to the theory and practice of business finance.

J. Fred Weston

Preface

The last two decades have seen the development of many new and powerful analytical techniques in finance resulting in numerous books and articles on such topics as the capital budgeting decision, cost of capital analysis, valuation analysis, mathematical programming applications, investment portfolio analysis and others. The one thing these subjects have in common is their orientation toward optimization and successful firm performance. Yet, despite these advances, we continually observe negative firm performance often resulting in the ultimate state of affairs—corporate bankruptcy. Corporations have experienced failure ever since charters were first granted, with periodic increases in number and severity. Increased failure activity usually coincides with economic downturns and during the great depression period it claimed the center of discussion and emphasis.

In this long and sometimes stormy history, one cannot help but be struck by the lack of an integrated, analytical framework for bankruptcy discussion. Since the publication of Arthur Stone Dewing's classic text, *Financial Policy of Corporations*, the subject of corporate bankruptcy has been relegated to a descriptive chapter or two, invariably found at the end of a basic business finance textbook. What's more, the topic is rarely discussed in finance courses due to its nonrigorous treatment and the professor's desire to cover the more "positive" subjects. In addition, the last three decades have seen the practical as well as theoretical emphasis in finance shift decidedly toward corporate growth and away from failure.

The start of the 1970s has brought forth a "revival" in the occurrence and practical importance of corporate bankruptcy in America. Failures have increased substantially in all lines of business. During one week in June 1970, three large companies petitioned the courts for protection under the Federal Bankruptcy Act. They included Four Seasons Nursing Centers, Dolly Madison Industries and the grand-daddy failure of them all—Penn Central Transportation Company. Other notable recent 1970-71 failures include King Resources, Beck Industries, Bermac Corp., Farrington Manufacturing, Computer Applications, Remco Co., Roberts Co., Transogram Co., Visual Electronics, and others are on the brink of collapse. Indeed, the Congress of the United States just passed, by the narrowest of margins, a bill to guarantee loans for Lockheed Corp. in order to keep this important defense contractor out of bankruptcy. There also was strong sentiment for establishing an institution similar to the old Reconstruction Finance Corporation to provide emergency loans for companies. Business failures have not occurred only in the United States. Foreign companies of considerable importance like Rolls Royce Ltd. and Upper Cldye Shipbuilders Ltd. have succumbed to severe economic pressures.

The purpose of this book is to provide an analytical framework for discussing the unique business phenomenon, corporate bankruptcy in America. Many of the rigorous techniques developed in recent years will be utilized in this endeavor. Wherever possible, these modern procedures are applied to problems which have heretofore been treated in a descriptive manner. For instance, multivariate statistical analysis methods will be used to investigate the relationship between business failures and other aggregate economic phenomena (Chapter 2), as well as the development of an accurate bankruptcy predictive technique for manufacturing firms (Chapter 3) and railroads (Chapter 7). In addition, such techniques as capital budgeting and portfolio analysis aid in our discussion of the effects of corporate bankruptcy on the various relevant security holders (Chapter 6).

The above types of analysis are complemented by several in-depth case studies in the area of bankruptcy-reorganization mergers (Chapter 5) and other significant failures (Chapter 4, 5, and 7). The introductory chapter and its appendix provide the reader with an institutional background and relevant statistics on bankruptcies in America.

This book is written to serve needs both in the classroom and in the firm. It may be used as a supplementary text in the basic business finance course and as a primary book for those advanced undergraduate and graduate courses in corporation finance, investments and industrial organization where the emphasis is on this relatively specialized subject. In addition, the materials covered should be of particular interest to those students and practitioners who combine the study of law and business application. This is especially important since a special Presidential Commission is now considering revisions to the National Bankruptcy Act. The materials appear to be appropriate for established law curriculums which invariably include courses on bankruptcy and reorganization, as well as the relatively new combined J.D.-M.B.A. programs now prominent in many universities. Business managers in industrial and financial institutions should find the materials on bankruptcy prediction (Chapter 3), accounts receivable, internal control, and commercial credit analysis (Chapter 4), merger implications (Chapter 5) and investment management (Chapter 6) of considerable interest and importance. Finally, it is written for those skeptics who question the very inclusion of bankruptcy analysis within the scope of business finance.

I would like to express my gratitude to the many individuals who aided in the writing of this book. Several talented graduate students including Messrs. Michael Berson, J. Frederick Bush, Dakshinamurthy Dasari, and Raymond Lieberman helped in various stages of the book's development. To my colleagues at New York University, a special note of thanks is extended for their assistance in reading parts of the manuscript and their helpful encouragement. To professors Keith Smith of UCLA and Edward Renshaw of the State University of New York, my sincere appreciation for their aid in the earliest stages of my interest in corporate bankruptcy. Miss Rowena Wyant of Dun & Bradstreet and Mr. Jack Stutman of Quittner, Stutman, Treister and Glatt both provided valuable information and data for which I am grateful. I would like also to publicly thank those women who unselfishly spent long hours in typing the manuscript—specifically, Nora Burke, Beatrice Ospina and Lee Silman.

There is one person, however, without whose continuous enthusiasm and assistance this book would never have been completed. Professor J. Fred Weston of UCLA read and made helpful comments on the earlier drafts of the manuscript as well as providing the type of encouragement and inspiration so crucial to someone writing his first book. Of equal importance is my gratitude to my wife Elaine who not only coped wonderfully with the eccentricities of an author writing on bankruptcy but also did an exceptional editing job on the manuscript.

1

Bankruptcy in Perspective

Business failures, including the corporate bankruptcy phenomenon, are sobering economic realities reflecting the uniqueness of the American way of corporate death. The subject of this book has received relatively little attention of late from business practitioners and theorists with their major preoccupation concerning policies and techniques designed to achieve corporate success. In addition, the bankruptcy process is generally viewed (1) by economists as a technical problem of limited theoretic import; (2) by businessmen as a course of action to be considered only when all other alternatives fail, and then left to legal specialists; (3) by most legal authorities as a subject of creditor and owner priorities; and (4) by political scientists as an inevitable but necessary evil of the capitalist system. In a review of past analytical treatment given to corporate bankruptcy, one cannot help but conclude that there remains a large vacuum to fill. This book is an attempt to fill a portion of that void.

Most concerned individuals view the unsuccessful business venture as a negative economic event both to the principals of the unfortunate entity and to society in general. In addition to the obvious and usually quantifiable costs to employees, creditors, and owners of the debtor, there usually are serious second order effects borne by the community at large. The larger the bankrupt's interface with others, the more profound the effect. Suppliers suffer reduced demand, customers are often inconvenienced even if alternative goods and/or services are available, and the public in general is often forced to shoulder a portion of overall bankruptcy costs due to increased tax burdens. The latter is implicit in the case of direct government subsidies and tax abatements granted to large public interest or essential service corporations on the verge of bankruptcy or to firms which are temporarily exempt from paying their financial obligations to creditors and government due to the protection afforded by the Federal Bankruptcy Act. Recent examples of these types of societal burdens are the Lockheed Aircraft—Rolls Royce fiasco, the Penn Central bankruptcy debacle and foreign expropriation of American owned facilities. In these cases, the public is presently asked, and will no doubt continue, to bear a portion of the costs attributable to the microeconomic problems of privately owned companies.

On the other hand, there are arguments for the direct and indirect benefits of corporate failure. Schumpeter argued for business failure's cleansing effect on competition and innovation.[a] Economic theorists and public servants alike often

---

[a]Schumpeter's theory of innovation incorporates the concept of "creative destruction" leading to temporary spurts of business failures and slackening entrepreneurial activity.[1]

1

cite the competitive environment for its weeding out of inefficient and poorly managed entities in order to perpetuate a healthy vibrant economy. The so-called competitive equilibrium is achieved through the continuous entrance and exit of firms in particular industries. Finally, the same bankruptcy process which protects the company from creditor and government claims can, at the same time, enable a firm to become rehabilitated and lead to greater long-run returns to all parties involved.[b]

The remainder of this chapter will be devoted to definitions and background material relevant to corporate bankruptcy. Various types and degrees of corporate problems are discussed, evolutionary statutes and developments reviewed, and statistical data presented in order to provide the proper framework for further discussion.

Defining Corporate Problems

The unsuccessful business enterprise has been defined in numerous ways in order to depict the formal process confronting the firm and/or to economically categorize the problems involved. Three generic terms which are commonly found in the literature are failure, insolvency and bankruptcy. Sometimes these states are used interchangeably by writers and we will attempt to illustrate their similarities and differences.

Failure, by economic criteria, represents the situation where the realized rate of return on invested capital, with allowances for risk considerations, is significantly and continually lower than prevailing rates on similar investments. Somewhat different economic criteria have also been cited, including insufficient revenues to cover costs and situations where the average return on investment is below the firm's cost of capital. These economic situations make no positive statements as to the existence or discontinuance of the entity. Normative decisions to discontinue operations are based on expected returns and the ability of the firm to cover its variable costs. It should be noted that a company may be an economic failure for many years and yet, due to the absence or near absence of legally enforceable debt, it is never unable to meet its current obligations. When the company can no longer meet the legally enforceable demands of its creditors, it is sometimes called a *legal failure*. The term legal is somewhat misleading because the condition, as just described, may exist without formal court involvement.

Finally, the term failure has been adopted by Dun & Bradstreet (D & B)—a leading supplier of relevant statistics on unsuccessful enterprises—in order to describe various conditions of business problems.[c] In actuality, business failures

---

[b]This line of reasoning will be examined in subsequent discussions.

[c]Business failures include those businesses that ceased operations following assignment or bankruptcy; ceased with loss to creditors after such actions as execution, foreclosure, or attachment; voluntarily withdrew leaving unpaid obligations, were involved in court actions such as receivership, reorganization, or arrangement; or voluntarily compromised with creditors.[2]

as defined by D & B, are only a fraction of those enterprises which are discontinued each year. Table 1-1 shows, for selected years, the number of enterprises started and discontinued each year, with the number and percentage of failures also listed.

Insolvency is another term depicting negative firm performance and is generally used in a more technical fashion. In fact, the state of *technical insolvency* exists when a firm cannot meet its current obligations signifying a lack of liquidity. Another term used to depict the same situation is *insolvency in an equity sense.*[3] Walter discussed the measurement of technical solvency and advanced the theory that net cash flows relative to current liabilities should be the primary criterion used to evaluate technical solvency and not traditional working capital measurements.[d] Technical insolvency may be a temporary condition, although it often is the immediate cause of formal bankruptcy declaration.

Insolvency in a bankruptcy sense is a more critical condition and indicates a chronic rather than temporary illness. A firm finds itself in this situation when its total liabilities exceed a fair valuation of its total assets. The real net worth of the firm is, therefore, negative. The irony of the above insolvency condition is that technical insolvency is easily detectable, while the more serious condition requires a comprehensive valuation analysis which is usually not undertaken until asset *liquidation* is contemplated. Indicators of potential insolvency in an equity sense usually involve the firms leverage ratios and earning power.[e] Insolvency, as it relates to the formal bankruptcy process, is defined explicitly in Chapter 1, clause 19 of the National Bankruptcy Act.

Finally, we come to bankruptcy itself. One type of bankruptcy is described above and refers to the net worth position of an enterprise. A second, more observable type is the formal declaration of bankruptcy by a firm in a federal district court accompanied by a petition to either liquidate its assets or attempt a recovery program. The latter procedure is legally referred to as *bankruptcy-reorganization* and is the subject of discussion in the next section. The judicial reorganization is a formal procedure which is usually the last measure in a series of remedies attempted in the treatment of a sick company.

The theory of reorganization in bankruptcy is basically sound and, as mentioned earlier, has potential economic and social benefits. The process is designed to enable the financially troubled firm to continue in existence and maintain whatever goodwill it still possesses rather than liquidate its assets for the benefit of its creditors. Justification of this attempt is in the belief that continued existence will manifest itself into a healthy going concern operation

---

[d]He emphasized the use of cash flow analysis to determine obligations and sources and applications of funds analysis in the overall assessment of insolvency.[4]

[e]Fisher utilized a variation of the familiar debt/equity ratio in his corporate bond study. A slightly different measure is examined in this volume, see Chapter 3. Gordon utilizes the term "financial distress" to indicate the situation when a firm's earning power falls to some point where there is a nontrivial probability that it will no longer be able to meet the interest and principal payments on the outstanding debt. Under these circumstances, the company's bonds will sell at yields materially above prevailing interest rates to otherwise similar corporations.[5]

worth more than the value of its assets sold in the marketplace. Since this rehabilitation process often requires several years, the time value of money should be considered explicitly through a discounted cash flow procedure. If, in fact, economically productive assets continue to contribute to society's supply of goods and services, above and beyond their opportunity costs, the process of reorganization has been of benefit, to say nothing of the continued employment of the firm's employees. These benefits should be weighed against the costs of bankruptcy including the opportunity cost of the receipts realizable from liquidation of these same assets. Other groups of interested and relevant parties are the firm's creditors and owners. The experience of these parties is of paramount importance in the evaluation of the bankruptcy-reorganization process and subsequent chapters in this book will investigate their experience. Regardless of the experience of the various interested parties, the primary responsibility of the reorganization process is to relieve the burden of the debtor's immediate liabilities and realign the capital structure so that the same problems will not recur in the foreseeable future.

Evolution of the Bankruptcy Process in the United States

The United States Congress has the power, under the federal Constitution, to establish uniform laws regulating bankruptcy. By virtue of this authority, various acts and amendments have been passed starting with the Bankruptcy Act of 1898. Since that time, there have been several new bankruptcy acts passed and,

Table 1-1

Business Population Changes and Failures, Selected Years, 1950-1964

(in thousands)

Year	Operating Businesses	New Enterprises[a]	Discontinued Enterprises	Business Failures[b]	Failures/ Discontinuances
1950	4008	348	290	9.2	3.2%
1955	4286	408	314	11.0	3.5
1960	4660	443	386	15.4	4.0
1964	4930	479	411	13.5	3.3
1960-1964 (Annual Average)	4750	445	394	15.2	3.9

Source: *Survey of Current Business: Business Statistics, 1965 ed.*, U.S. Dept. of Commerce, Office of Business Economics, pp. 10-11. Unfortunately, the population totals are reported only through 1962; the 1963 and 1964 estimates are provided by J. Cohen and S. Robbins, *The Financial Manager*, (New York: Harper & Row, 1966), p. 862.

[a]Annual Totals.

[b]*Failure Record Through 1969*, Dun & Bradstreet, Inc., p. 1. These are actual totals.

in 1970, a new bill was passed authorizing a two-year investigation of ways to improve the procedure. This section will review the highlights of previous bankruptcy statutes and provide an institutional background for the more analytical discussions in subsequent chapters.

Equity Receiverships

The original Bankruptcy Act of 1898 provided only for a company's liquidation and contained no provisions allowing corporations to reorganize and thereby remain in existence. The latter process was, however, effected through equity receiverships. Although the basic theory of corporate reorganization (discussed earlier) is sound, the equity receivership procedure proved to be ineffective. It was developed to prevent disruptive seizures of property by dissatisfied creditors who were able to obtain a lien on specific properties of the financially troubled concern. Receivers were appointed by the courts to manage the corporate property during financial reorganization. This procedure presented serious problems, however, and was essentially replaced by the Bankruptcy Acts of 1933 and 1934. Receivership in equity is not the same as receivership in bankruptcy. In the latter case, a Receiver is a court agent who administers the bankrupt's assets until a trustee is appointed. While receivership is still available to companies, it has been almost entirely replaced by reorganization under the Bankruptcy Act.[6]

Equity-receivership was extremely time consuming and costly as well as being susceptible to severe injustices. The courts had little control over the reorganization plan and the committees set up to protect security holder interests were usually made up of powerful corporate insiders who used the process to further their own interests. The initiative for equity receivership was usually taken by the company in conjunction with some friendly creditor. There was no provision made for independent, objective review of the plans which were invariably drawn up by a biased committee or friendly receiver. Since ratification required majority creditor support, it usually meant that powerful dissenters were paid off in cash in order to solicit their support. This led to charges of unfairness and long delays. Because of these disadvantages, the procedure proved ineffective especially when the number of receiverships skyrocketed during the depression years.

Chandler Act of 1938

In 1933, a new Bankruptcy Act with a special Section 77 (for railroad reorganizations) was hastily drawn up and enacted. The following year Section 77B was enacted which provided for general corporate reoganizations. The Act was shortlived and in 1938, a comprehensive revision of the Act was adopted by

Congress and called the Chandler Act.[f] This Act was the result of the joint efforts of the National Bankruptcy Conference, the Security and Exchange Commission, which had embarked on its own study of reorganization practices, and various other interested committees and associations.

Chapter XI

For our purposes, the two most relevant chapters of the Chandler Act are those related to corporate Bankruptcy and subsequent attempts at reorganization.[8] Chapter XI applies only to the unsecured creditors of corporations and removes the necessity to get all creditor types to agree on a plan of action. A Chapter XI arrangement is a voluntary proceeding which can be initiated by corporate or noncorporate persons. The Court has the power to appoint an independent trustee or receiver to manage the corporate property or, in many instances, to permit the old management team to continue its control during the proceedings. The bankrupt's petition for reorganization usually contains a preliminary plan for financial relief. The prospect of continued management control and reduced financial obligations makes Chapter XI particularly attractive to the present management. During the proceedings, a referee will call the creditors together and go over the proposed plan and any new amendments which are proposed. If a majority in number and amount of each class of unsecured creditors consent to the plan, the court may confirm the arrangement and make it binding on all creditors. Usually, the plan provides for a scaled-down creditor claim (composition of claims), and/or extension of payment over time. New financial instruments may be issued to creditors in lieu of their old claims.

In addition to the advantage noted above, Chapter XI places the bankrupt's assets strictly in the custody of the court and makes them free from any prior pending bankruptcy proceeding. Too, the debtor can borrow new funds which have preference over all unsecured indebtedness. Although the interest rate on such new credit is expectedly high, it still enables the embarrassed firm to secure an important new source of financing. As in all corporate reorganizations, the assets are protected by the Court during these proceedings. Also the duration of Chapter XI arrangements, if successful, is relatively short and, since administrative expenses are a function of time, less costly than proceedings which involve all security holders. Successful out-of-court settlements, however, are usually even less costly. Finally, the arrangement is binding in all states of the country.

---

[f]The Act, named for Representative Walter Chandler, contained 143 chapters and 125 sections. Chapters I-VII of the Act deal with personal bankruptcies and provide for liquidation, distribution, and discharge of the bankrupt. Chapter VIII provides for agricultural settlements usually through composition of claims. Chapter IX deals with city, town, and municipality readjustments. Chapter XII, XIII & XIV provide for mortgage readjustments on real property, wage earners' plans, and Maritime Commission liens, respectively.[7]

Chapter X

The least common but most important type of corporate bankruptcy-reorganization is the Chapter X proceeding. The importance of this bankruptcy form is clearly illustrated by the dollar amount of liabilities involved, the size and importance of the petitioning companies, and the fact that most of the empirical data utilized in subsequent discussions involve Chapter X bankrupts.

Chapter X proceedings apply, in effect, to all publicly held corporations, except railroads, and to those which have secured creditors. The bankruptcy process can be initiated voluntarily by the debtor or involuntarily by three or more creditors with total claims of $5,000 or more. It was generally felt that the 1934 Act (Section 77B) was too liberal to the small creditors since only $1,000 in claims were required.[9] The bankruptcy petition must contain a statement as to why adequate relief cannot be obtained under Chapter XI.[10] This was to make Chapter X proceedings unavailable to corporations having simple debt and capital structures. On the other hand, the court has the right (and has exercised it on several occasions),[g] to refuse to allow a Chapter XI proceeding and to require that the reorganization be processed under Chapter X. This is usually the case where a substantial public interest is deemed by present the Court or the SEC, and the firm had originally filed a Chapter XI voluntary petition. In most cases, a Chapter XI will be preferred by the debtor because Chapter X automatically provides for the appointment of an independent, disinterested trustee(s) to assume control of the company for the duration of the bankruptcy proceeding.[h]

The independent trustee is charged with the development and submission of a reorganization plan which is "fair and feasible" to all of the parties involved. The Interstate Commerce Commission is charged with this task in the case of railroad bankruptcies. Invariably, this plan involves all of the creditors as well as the preferred and common stockholders. This important trustee task is in addition to the day-to-day management responsibilities, although he usually delegates the latter authority to the old management or to a new management team. New management is often installed since management incompetence, in one form or another, is by far the most common cause of corporate failures. In most contemporary Chapter X bankruptcies, the Trustee is aided by various experts in the development and presentation of reorganization plans as well as by committees representing the various creditors and stockholders. At the outset,

---

[g]The SEC has on particular occasions filed motions in Chapter XI proceedings to force companies into Ch. X. The reason for this motion is that Chapter XI cannot adequately handle the case where a substantial public interest is involved. Cases where this has occurred are Dejay Stores, Davega Stores, Bzura Chemical Co., and Yuba Consolidated Industries.

[h]Actually the Act provides for the appointment of the independent trustee in every case in which indebtedness amounts to $250,000 or more. Where the indebtedness is less than $250,000, the judge may either continue the debtor in possession or appoint a disinterested trustee. The only prescribed qualification of the trustee, in addition to disinterestedness, is competence to perform his duties.

the creditors, indenture trustees and stockholders are permitted to file answers controverting the allegations of a voluntary or involuntary petition. Under the previous section 77B, individual creditors and stockholders were required to act in concert with others holding claims in order to reach a specified amount or percentage of claims. Under the Chandler Act, these restrictions are removed and any interested party may file an answer. Therefore, while bankruptcy initiation action is curtailed by the 1938 Act, the ability to answer is enhanced.

Another extremely important participant in Chapter X proceedings is the SEC. Although the Commission does not possess any decision-making authority, its involvement, via the SEC Advisory Reports is a powerful objective force in the entire process. The SEC is charged with rendering its Advisory Report if the debtor's liabilities exceed $3 million, but the Court can ask for SEC assistance regardless of liability size. These reports usually take the form of a critical evaluation of the reorganization plan submitted by the Trustee and an opinion as to fairness and feasibility of the plan. This typically involves a comprehensive valuation of the debtor's existing assets in comparison with the various claims against the assets. In the event of a discrepancy between the SEC evaluation and that of the Trustee, the former usually suggests alternative guidelines. Ultimately, the decision as to (1) whether the firm will be permitted to reorganize; and (2) the submission of the plan for final acceptance, rests with the Federal Judge.

The law provides that the reorganization plan, after approval by the Court, is to be submitted to each class of creditor and stockholder for final approval. Final ratification requires approval of two-thirds of each class of stockholder. Of course if the plan, as accepted by the Court, completely eliminates a particular class, such as the common stockholders, then this excluded group has no vote in the final ratification. Common stockholders will be eliminated where the firm is deemed insolvent in a bankruptcy sense—where the liabilities exceed a fair valuation of the assets. Whether or not the old stockholders are permitted to participate in the reorganized enterprise, the plan invariably entails a restructuring of the old capital accounts as well as plans for improving the productivity of the debtor.

Now that we have specified the important participants and regulations involved with a Chapter X proceeding, let us review the entire process briefly. The best condensed summary of the various bankruptcy procedures and their many aspects is found in Weston and Brigham[11] and is reproduced in Table 1-2.

(1) Corporation, creditor(s), or indenture trustee files a petition in a Federal District Court.
(2) If the Court agrees that a bankruptcy-reorganization is possible, an independent trustee(s) is assigned by the Court.
(3) The trustee, with whatever assistance he deems necessary, operates the business and develops a reorganization plan.
(4) The plan is submitted to all interested parties, including the SEC in most cases, and time is given for comments on the proposed plan.

Table 1-2
Summary of Financial Rehabilitation Procedures

Function	Equity Receivership	Chapter X	Chapter XI	Section 77 (1933)
1. Initiation of proceedings	1. Friendly creditor petitions court for appointment of receiver	1. a. Voluntary by debtor b. Involuntary—3 or more creditors with claims totaling $5,000 or more	1. a. Voluntary only b. Noncorporate and corporate c. Affects only unsecured creditors	1. a. Railroads only b. Voluntary c. Involuntary by creditors representing 5% or more if total indebtedness
2. Custody of property	2. Court appoints receiver to a. Take title to property b. Attempt rehabilitation	2. Court appoints disinterested trustee (mandatory if debts over $250,000) a. Cannot be officer or employee b. Co-trustee from previous management to aid in operation	2. Court may or may not appoint receiver or trustee	2. Trustees who act as operating managers
3. Creditor protection	3. Each class of creditors forms a protective committee to represent it	3. Committees representing each class of creditors and stockholders are formed	3. Court conducts meetings; may use advisory creditors' committee	3. Committee for each class of creditor

(continued on next page)

Table 1-2 (*Continued*)

Function	Equity Receivership	Chapter X	Chapter XI	Section 77 (1933)
Reorganization plan	4. Protective committees form a joint reorganization committee to formulate plan	4. a. Trustee, creditors, or creditors' committee prepares plan; confers with committees b. Court hearings on the plan c. SEC renders advisory report (mandatory if debts exceed $3,000,000)	4. Debtor proposes arrangement	4. Presented by a. Trustee, or b. Debtor, or c. Holders of 10% or more of each class of security
5. Court review	5. Court fixes price	5. Court approves plan if a. Fair b. Feasible	5. Court holds hearings	5. a. Hearings before Interstate Commerce Commission b. ICC submits plan to court c. Court approval
6. Reorganization plan	6. Provides for a. Foreclosure sale b. Formation of new corporation to take over property c. Raise cash to pay off dissenters d. Underwriting agreement to sell additional securities	6. Provides for a. Provision for exchange of securities b. Provision for selection of new management c. Adequate means for execution of plan	6. Composition –claims of unsecured creditors scaled down, or extension in time of payment, or both	6. Same as Chapter X

e. Voting trust to provide uninterrupted management during rehabilitation	7. All claimants must approve	7. Two-thirds of each class of creditors by value; majority of stockholders (unless total liabilities exceed total assets)	7. Majority in number and amount of each class	7. Same as Chapter X

7. Approval	8. Reorganization committee is usually only bidder at foreclosure sale
	  a. Can make best utilization of assets
	  b. May use claims at face value
	  c. New corporation formed and receiver dismissed by court
		8. Court confirms plan. Additional securities may be sold with the aid of investment bankers	8. Receiver, trustee, or disbursing agent to carry out arrangement	8. Plan executed by ICC

8. Execution of plan				

Source: J.F. Weston & E. Brigham, *Managerial Finance*, 2nd Ed., pp. 724-26.

(5) After a comprehensive evaluation of the plan and the comments, the Judge will either approve the plan and submit it for final ratification, or send it back for alterations. The process continues until Court Approval.

(6) Final voting on the plan by the relevant creditors and stockholders.

Liquidation

When, either through a court petition or a Trustee decision, it is deemed that there is no hope for rehabilitation or if prospects are so dim as to make further efforts, costs and time unreasonable, the only remaining alternative will be liquidation. Economically, liquidation is justified when the value of the assets sold individually exceeds the capitalized value of the assets in the marketplace. Usually, the key variable is time. For instance, it may be estimated that the *absolute* economic value of the firm will exceed the liquidation value but the realization of the economic benefits are subject to uncertainty, due to time and subjective probability estimates resulting in a lower *discounted* value. In this case, final liquidation may take the form of an assignment or a formal bankruptcy liquidation.

An assignment is a private method where assets are assigned to a Trustee, usually selected by the creditors, to be liquidated by him. The net liquidation value realized is equal to the funds received less the creditor claims against the company. Rarely are the funds sufficient to pay off all creditors in full. All creditors must agree to the settlement. Since the assignment is generally handled in good faith, it is customary for the creditors to release the debtor from further liability. This process is usually faster and less costly than the more rigid bankruptcy procedure but it is not usually feasible when the debtor has a complicated liability and capital structure.

Before 1933, the Bankruptcy Act only provided for liquidation. The expanded Act (1938) continued to provide for the orderly liquidation of an insolvent debtor under court supervision. The process may be voluntary (petition filed by the debtor) or involuntary (petition filed by creditors where the debtor owes $1000 or more, the petitioning creditors have claims in excess of $500, and the debtor has committed an act of bankruptcy within four months of the petition[12]). Regardless of who files the petition, liquidations are handled by referees who oversee the operation until a Trustee is appointed. The latter liquidates the assets, makes a final accounting and pays the liquidating dividends—all subject to referee approval. Priorities for dividend receipt usually entail unpaid wages and taxes followed by secured creditors and general or unsecured claims last.

The liquidation fate is primarily observed in the small firm. The large bankrupt firm is more likely to be reorganized and/or merged into another entity (see Chapter 5 for a discussion of merger-reorganizations). Sometimes, however, the basis for merger terms while a corporation is in bankruptcy is the net liquidating value of the bankrupt company and not its capitalized income worth. This was precisely the basis for negotiation at the Interstate Commerce Commission hearings on the Penn Central–New York, New Haven and Hartford R.R. merger in 1968.[i]

Current Proposal for Change

Since the enactment of the original National Bankruptcy Act in 1898, there has been only one major revision–the 1938 Chandler Act. The 1946 amendment to the Chandler Act merely changed the financial status of the bankruptcy referees and established a fund in the Treasury to pay for the referee salary and office expenses. A recent resolution in the House of Representatives (June 23, 1969) proposed to create a special commission to study the bankruptcy laws of the United States.[j] The following reasons were presented in this resolution to show the need for a revision to the Bankruptcy Act.

(1) In the 30 years since the last major revision, there has probably been even greater change in the social and economic conditions of the country than in the 40 years prior to the enactment of that 1938 act.
(2) Population has increased by 70 million people, while installment credit has skyrocketed from about $4 billion to $80 billion. The number of total bankruptcies has risen to an annual rate of more than 200,000 from a rate of 110,000 in 1960. By far, the major increase has been in personal bankruptcies.
(3) More than one quarter of the referees in bankruptcy have problems in the administration of their duties and have made suggestions for substantial improvement in the Act.
(4) There is little understanding by the federal government and the commercial community in evaluating the need to update the technical aspects of the Act.

The proposal charges the new commission (composed of nine members representing various interested parties) to submit a report and recommendations to the President and Congress within two years (July, 1972). While it is probable that the provisions of the Bankruptcy Act will be changed primarily in the

[i]The author participated in these hearings and presented evidence for establishing a discounted value for liquidation realizable funds, [Finance Docket submitted on behalf of Bond Trustee of N.Y., New Haven & Hartford R.R. before ICC, Oct. 21, 1968, pp. 75-80]. The final decision on this amount is still pending (1971) due to continuous appeals. The entire Penn Central situation is discussed in Chapter 7.

[j]S.J.Rs. 88, 91st Congress, 1st Session, July 24, 1970 proposed to create this special commission. An accompanying report from the Committee on the Judiciary, Report No. 91-240, strongly endorsed the proposal. This writer is presently serving as an advisor to the Commission on the Bankruptcy Laws of the United States. Charles Seligson, a member of this Commission, enumerated some current problems in "Major Problems for Consideration By the Commission on the Bankruptcy Laws of the United States," *American Bankruptcy Law Journal*, Winter, 1971, pp. 73-112.

personal bankruptcy sector, recent dramatic events in the corporate area may lead to significant changes here also.

The bankruptcy process can be improved in the corporate area as well as the personal sector. Specific proposals for change in the corporate area will possibly originate from the Security and Exchange Commission, since this agency is perhaps the most interested and well-informed *potential* member of the Commission to study the Bankruptcy laws. Finally, members of the economic community can and should play an important advisory role in the future structuring of the nation's bankruptcy process. The analysis in this book will provide a foundation for evaluating recommendations for change and for assessing the present structure of the bankruptcy process.

Business Failure and Bankruptcy Statistics

The final section of this introductory chapter explores the scope and magnitude of business failures and bankruptcies in America. Table 1-1 showed that the number of new businesses tends to exceed discontinuances each year by a small margin but that the aggregate flow is considerable. Failure statistics have been compiled by Dun & Bradstreet, Inc. since 1857 and Table 1-3 presents selected yearly statistics since that date. In addition, yearly failure rate and average liability statistics along with real GNP data are plotted in Figure 1-1. This chart strongly suggests that failure rate experience cannot be explained by long-term secular trends, but more than likely by cyclical forces and other macroeconomic factors.[k]

In the last decade (1960s), the failure rate was fairly stable over most of the period, with a noticeable decline in 1968 and 1969. During late 1969 and 1970, however, business failures rose considerably. Total failures in 1970 increased 17 percent, and the failure rate 19 percent, over the prior year. In the first four months of 1971, this rate has increased 10 percent over the comparable 1970 period. The association between reduced (and slightly negative) economic growth and increased failures is glaring. Dollar liabilities in 1970 swelled to an all time high of almost $1.9 billion. This total was almost $750 million greater than 1969—an incredible increase of over 65 percent. The 1970 failure rate figure of 44 per 10,000 firms was still considerably below the highest post World War II rate of 64 in 1961, yet total liabilities and the average failure liability in 1970 far exceeded 1961 statistics. The lowest postwar rate was 5 per 10,000 firms in 1946, but this exceptionally low rate increased continuously during the next four years as the nation's economy adjusted to peace-time conditions. The highest failure rate in the twentieth century, of course, occurred during the depression years—154 in 1932.

The trend in total failure liabilities, unlike failure rates, is noticeably up in the

---

[k]A multivariate statistical model, consisting of several aggregate economic series, is specified in Chapter 2 in order to explain aggregate failure rate and liability experience.

Table 1-3
Historical Failure Rate Experience of United States Businesses

Year(s)	Number (Average Number) of Failures	Average Failure Rate*	Average Liability Per Failure
1857-1968 (112)	1,258,141 (11,233)	87	$ 28,292
1900-1968 (69)	942,447 (13,659)	70	32,889
1946-1968 (23)	255,041 (11,089)	42	61,101
1959-1968 (10)	138,805 (13,881)	54	84,724
1961	17,075	64	63,843
1965	13,514	53	97,800
1966	13,061	52	106,091
1967	12,364	49	102,332
1968	9,636	39	97,654
1969	9,154	37	124,767
1970	10,748	44	175,638

*Per 10,000 listed concerns.

Source: Commercial Failures in the United States, Dun & Bradstreet, Inc., Business Economics Department, p. 1.

last 25 years due to increased levels of prices—reflecting higher asset and liability values—and lately, in the noticeable increase in million-dollar bankruptcies. The latter rose to a record 279 in 1970. While there are no doubt more million-dollar asset companies than ever before, their increased failure rate points toward greater failure vulnerability on the part of larger firms and perhaps also to increased bankruptcy acceptability. Whether this trend will persist as the economy rebounds is highly unlikely, but the less tangible issue of acceptability is worth surveillance. Table 1-4 lists the most important corporate bankruptcies in 1970 and 1971 and shows that a firm cannot feel immune from bankruptcy simply because of its size.

The larger firm vulnerability issue is clouded by the observation that many of these companies are not permitted to fail. Except in the event of fraud, or where the failing company is simply too large, we rarely observed in the decades before 1970 firms of over $25 million in total assets actually going bankrupt.[1] In many

---

[1] The Penn Central case is an example of an ailing company that was simply too large to be absorbed into another firm. Of course, there were other reasons for its unfortunate fate (see Chapter 7). The $25 million asset figure is arbitrary and based on the author's experience.

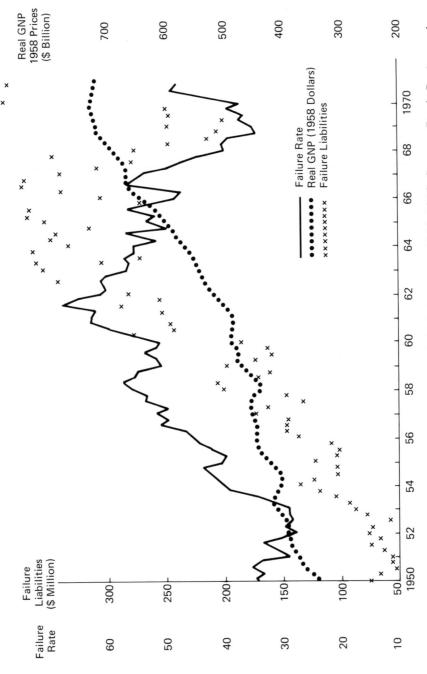

Figure 1-1. Quarterly Failure Rate, Liability and GNP Statistics, 1950–1970. Source: *Dun's Review* and *Federal Reserve Bulletin* (monthly), 1950–1970.

Table 1-4
Large Corporate Bankruptcies In America, By Asset Size, 1970 and 1971

1970 Bankruptcies	1969 Assets**
Penn Central Transportation Company	4,700.0
Boston & Maine Railroad	224.1
Lehigh Valley Railroad	173.8
Beck Industries	156.9
Dolly Madison Industries	92.4
Four Seasons Nursing Centers	37.7
Roberts Company	36.8
Visual Electronics	24.3
Bishop Industries	16.3
Milo Electronics	13.0
National Radio Company	10.2
RIC International Industries, Inc.	10.2
GF Industries, Inc.	9.6
Century Geophysical Corp.	8.9
1971 Bankruptcies*	**1970 Assets**
King Resources Company	176.7
Bermac Corporation	102.3
Farrington Manufacturing Company	37.6
Computer Applications	28.9
Remco Industries	25.1
Transogram Inc.	21.5
Cle-ware Industries	20.0
Executive House Inc.	13.6

*Through July, 1971
**In millions of dollars

cases, the financially troubled firm can expect to be wooed by a highly liquid and/or managerially rich firm, usually resulting in a merger or absorption before insolvency in a bankruptcy sense occurs.

Aggregate Bankruptcy Statistics

The previously cited statistics dealt with business failures, which is a much broader categorization than corporate bankruptcy. Legal bankruptcy is the climax of a series of unfortunate events in the lifespan of a firm. In the event of subsequent liquidation, the climactic bankruptcy petition marks the end of the normal existence of the firm; where reorganization follows, bankruptcy can be viewed as a necessary step for the continued existence of the firm. Tables 1-5 and 1-6 present a statistical summary of the bankruptcy activity in the United States from 1940-1970. Filings include all petitions filed in the Federal District Courts and reported to the Administrative Office of the United States Courts.

The columns in Tables 1-5 and 1-6 that we are primarily concerned with are the Chapter X and Chapter XI filings and total bankruptcy filings. Curiously enough, total business bankruptcies consistently exceed the total of business failures reported in Table 1-3.[m] The number of bankruptcy filings has remained remarkably stable since 1961, although these 1969 statistics are not complete and probably will show a significant increase. Prior to 1961, the trend in bankruptcies from the end of World War II was steadily upward. Within the business sector, the occupations of the most frequent bankrupts are not perfectly clear. We must interpret the category of "Others in Business" (Table 1-6) since this category accounts for the highest percentage of all bankruptcy filings. Financial and real estate concerns make up the bulk of the "others"—with the latter sector probably accounting for most of the bankrupts. In recent years, merchants, manufacturers, and professionals, in that order, are the next most active contributors toward bankruptcy. A more complete breakdown of failures within the retail and manufacturing industries is found in the Dun & Bradstreet statistics.[n]

The most common type of bankruptcy petition, by far, is the voluntary straight bankruptcy. This includes, for the most part, individual employee filings and is of no further interest for us. Chapter X and XI filings are of primary interest and require some additional comment. It is clear that if we observe the number of Chapter X bankruptcy proceedings and compare this figure with all business bankruptcies, the results imply that Chapter X is an insignificant feature of the Bankruptcy Act. In fact, in the last decade, the number of Chapter X's as a percentage of total business bankruptcies has varied between 0.49 percent (1962) and 0.79 percent (1963).[o] This conclusion, however, is erroneous since the average firm size and importance of the Chapter X proceedings far outweighs every other type of petition. Since total aggregate statistics on the size of the Chapter X liabilities are not available, we can only speak in qualitative terms.[p]

---

[m]The reason for this discrepancy is that the business failures reported by Dun & Bradstreet include only those firms registered in their Reference Book and does not cover all business enterprises. Specific types of firms not covered by the failure statistics, but included in the bankruptcy data, are financial enterprises, real estate companies, railroads and terminals, amusements, professions and farmers.

[n]In recent years, the retail firms with the highest propensity to fail were books and stationary, woman's ready to wear, toys and hobby crafts, furniture & furnishings, and children's clothing. In the manufacturing sector, the leaders were the furniture, transport equipment, electric machinrnery, leather and shoe industries, and textiles.[13]

[o]Including 1969 and 1970 statistics, the all-time high for Chapter X filings was 1948 when they accounted for 2.7% of all bankruptcy filings. The highest absolute number of Chapter X filings was 320 in 1940.

[p]An educated guess would be that Chapter X bankruptcies account for between 20 and 25 percent of the total bankruptcy liabilities.

19

Table 1-5
Filings by Chapter of the Bankruptcy Act

Fiscal Year	Total	Voluntary straight bankruptcy	Involuntary straight bankruptcy	Ch IX	Ch X	Ch XI	Ch XII	Ch XIII	Ch XV
1940	52,577	43,902	1,752	117	320	990	149	3,247	6
1941	56,332	47,578	1,491	19	269	769	71	4,433	0
1942	52,109	44,366	1,295	43	183	520	52	4,100	0
1943	34,711	30,913	649	13	114	205	22	2,007	5
1944	19,533	17,629	277	5	68	58	10	1,249	0
1945	12,862	11,101	264	8	72	41	5	1,248	0
1946	10,196	8,293	268	7	54	79	1	1,371	1
1947	13,170	9,657	697	7	96	291	7	2,354	0
1948	18,510	13,546	1,029	7	137	442	20	3,315	0
1949	26,021	18,882	1,240	2	149	531	17	5,111	4
1950	33,392	25,263	1,369	4	134	583	31	6,007	0
1951	35,193	26,594	1,099	3	88	459	22	6,924	2
1952	34,873	25,890	1,059	15	74	413	21	7,397	1
1953	40,087	29,815	1,064	0	86	437	15	8,670	0
1954	53,136	41,335	1,398	2	104	649	12	9,634	1
1955	59,404	47,650	1,249	1	73	547	19	9,864	1
1956	62,086	50,655	1,240	1	40	597	15	9,535	2
1957	73,761	60,335	1,189	0	65	599	24	11,549	0
1958	91,668	76,048	1,417	2	67	720	23	13,391	0
1959	100,672	85,502	1,288	3	78	787	21	12,993	0
1960	110,034	94,414	1,296	0	90	622	12	13,599	1
1961	146,643	124,386	1,444	0	112	947	31	19,723	0
1962	147,780	122,499	1,382	1	77	903	37	22,880	1
1963	155,493	128,405	1,409	0	128	1,188	33	24,329	0
1964	171,719	141,828	1,339	0	125	1,088	47	27,292	0
1965	180,323	149,820	1,317	0	88	1,022	49	28,027	0
1966	192,354	161,840	1,165	0	93	909	75	28,261	0
1967	208,329	173,884	1,254	1	125	1,033	68	31,963	1
1968	197,811	164,592	1,017	3	112	953	69	31,065	0
* 1969	184,930	154,054	963	0	70	867	66	28,910	0
1970	194,399	161,366	1,085	0	115	1,262	58	30,510	0

*Through September 30, 1969.

Source: *Table of Bankruptcy Statistics*, Administrative Office of the President, Washington, D.C., 1970 and 1971 supplement.

Table 1-6
Bankruptcy Cases Filed by Occupations in the Business Sector

Fiscal Year	Total Bankruptcy Case Filings	Non-Business	Business Total	Merchants	Manufacturers	Farmers	Professionals	Others
1940	52,577	39,073	13,248	35.1%	7.0%	20.2%	6.0%	31.7%
1941	56,335	44,713	11,619	36.8	6.6	20.4	6.4	29.8
1942	52,109	42,251	9,858	34.3	5.1	20.8	5.9	33.9
1943	34,711	28,782	5,929	29.9	4.8	19.4	6.7	39.2
1944	19,533	16,752	2,781	19.9	6.5	18.4	7.6	47.6
1945	12,862	11,051	1,811	15.8	8.4	16.8	8.4	50.6
1946	10,196	8,566	1,630	14.5	12.3	16.0	6.9	50.3
1947	13,170	10,234	2,936	21.5	20.3	6.2	3.8	48.2
1948	18,510	13,537	4,973	26.9	16.2	3.4	2.3	51.2
1949	26,021	19,144	6,877	28.6	12.4	3.4	2.3	53.3
1950	33,392	25,040	8,352	30.7	9.6	3.5	1.5	54.7
1951	35,193	27,806	7,387	31.9	7.0	2.8	1.7	56.6
1952	34,873	28,331	6,542	35.4	8.1	3.0	2.0	51.5
1953	40,087	33,315	6,772	35.5	7.6	3.2	2.1	51.6
1954	53,136	44,248	8,888	35.9	8.4	3.6	1.7	50.4
1955	59,404	50,219	9,185	36.1	8.2	4.2	2.4	49.1
1956	62,086	52,608	9,478	33.3	7.7	4.2	2.2	52.6
1957	73,761	63,617	10,144	31.2	6.6	4.0	2.0	56.2
1958	91,668	80,265	11,403	30.7	6.7	2.9	2.5	57.2
1959	100,672	88,943	11,729	29.0	5.4	3.5	3.7	58.4
1960	110,034	97,750	12,284	25.7	5.1	3.7	4.0	61.5
1961	146,643	131,402	15,241	27.8	5.2	3.6	4.1	59.3
1962	147,780	132,125	15,655	27.4	4.7	3.5	5.0	59.4
1963	155,493	139,190	16,303	26.2	5.3	3.4	4.6	60.5
1964	171,719	155,209	16,510	30.7	5.0	3.4	4.8	56.1
1965	180,323	163,413	16,910	28.7	5.0	3.5	4.6	58.2
1966	192,354	175,924	16,430	28.5	4.5	3.4	3.8	59.8
1967	208,329	191,729	16,600	29.7	4.4	2.7	4.2	59.0
1968	197,811	181,266	16,545	27.6	4.5	3.4	6.6	57.9
1969	184,930	169,500	15,430	25.7	4.4	3.9	8.4	57.6

Source: *Table of Bankruptcy Statistics*, Administrative Office of the President, Washington, D.C., 1970.

The importance of reorganizing a Chapter X debtor in terms of its asset, employment, and maintenance of capital contributions to society is perhaps the most important consequence of the National Bankruptcy Acts.

Chapter XI arrangements rank second in importance, but these too have occurred relatively infrequently. Since 1960, the percentage of Chapter XI bankruptcies of total filings has varied between 5.1% in 1960 to 7.3% in 1963. This latter figure is almost the highest in any recorded year; 7.7% in 1948 is the Chapter XI leader.

Age of Business Failures

One of the most outstanding and seemingly irrevocable failure statistics is the high propensity on the part of young firms to fail. The longer a company survives, generally other things being equal, the smaller becomes the probability of failure.[14] The reasons for this are fairly obvious. The new firm usually has an immediate competitive disadvantage relative to established firms in a particular field or industry. This disadvantage is more than likely highlighted in the marketing activities of the firm, whatever the product may be. A second major factor combines the effects of competitive inferiority with the ability of the firm to withstand financial and economic problems. In the large, well-established corporation the appearance of temporary business recessions usually does not present a threat to the very existence of the firm because of its adequate reserves accumulated through the years. These firms have much greater access to the money and capital markets than do young companies. A new firm is also usually a small firm and must rely on sources of capital which typically possess only limited amounts of funds. From this discussion, it would appear that the age variable, or a proxy for age, would be a prime measure to utilize in a bankruptcy prediction model. Subsequent analysis in Chapter 3 will investigate this potential.

The above reasons account for the fact that the majority of those firms which fail do so within the first five years of their existence. Table 1-7 presents failure data by age in various broad industry classifications for the year 1969.[q] Approximatley one-third of all failures occur in the first three years, 53 percent in the first five years and over 77 percent in the first ten years. It appears that the retail industry has the highest early-age failure rate, with the wholesale and manufacturing industries possessing the highest late failure rate. An interesting observation is that within the manufacturing industry's sector, a relatively high early and late failure rate exists. Perhaps this is due to competitive forces which are most severe to the new firm, due to relative plant size and marketing factors, and to the old firm (over 10 years in existence) due to technology problems.

A further aspect of company age and its relationship to failure potential is the

---

[q]1969 is the latest year of available data and appears to be representative of contemporary failure statistics.

trend in this relationship. With the exception of the late 1940s and early 1950s, the percentage of all firms which fail in the first five years of their existence has fluctuated very little—between 53.0% and 58.9%. In the last decade, in fact, the failure rate by age has been almost constant throughout the age spectrum. There has been absolutely no noticeable trend in failure rates by age although the latest year's data (1969) saw the failure rate level in the first five years fall to 53.2 percent of all failures, which is the lowest percentage in the post-World War II period.

Causes of Business Failures

A comprehensive analysis of fundamental and typical causes of commercial failures is not attempted in this volume. The implications of earlier studies, however, will be briefly summarized. One major finding of previous studies is the

Table 1-7
Age of Business Failures by Functions in 1969

Age in Years	Manufacturing	Wholesale	Retail	Construction	Commercial Service	All Concerns
< 1	2.0%	2.4%	2.9%	1.4%	2.5%	2.4%
2	11.9	8.6	18.3	8.6	11.4	13.7
3	11.8	11.4	18.9	11.8	16.0	15.3
Total Three Years or Less	25.7	22.4	40.1	21.8	29.9	31.4
4	11.9	11.7	12.6	11.0	12.7	12.1
5	9.7	7.5	9.7	10.1	11.4	9.7
Total Five Years or Less	47.3	41.6	62.4	42.9	54.0	53.2
6	7.4	7.1	6.7	8.4	7.5	7.2
7	4.6	6.3	4.8	8.1	6.3	5.6
8	4.1	6.2	3.7	6.0	3.9	4.4
9	3.2	4.2	3.4	5.2	4.1	3.8
10	2.8	2.8	2.9	4.3	5.5	3.4
Total Six-Ten Years	22.1	26.6	21.5	32.0	27.3	24.4
> 10	30.6	31.8	16.1	25.1	18.7	22.4
Total	100.0%	100.0%	100.0%	100.0%	100.0%	100.0%

Source: *Table in Failure Record Through 1969*, Dun & Bradstreet, New York, p. 9.

wide variety of causes of business failures.[15] These same analyses have asserted that failures are preventable and that the consequent burden on the economy could be lessened. My own studies, however, suggest that analysis of failure causes will not provide a sound basis for preventing them.

The statistical studies I have conducted, and the discussion of their implications—presented in Chapters 2, 3, and 4—emphasize the detection of impending crisis sufficiently in advance so that corrective action can be taken. These two approaches—enumerating the varied causes of failure and specifying a predictive model—are not necessarily inconsistent. An effective early warning system permits analysis of underlying causal variables which may contribute to reducing the incidence of failure. The latter can be accomplished through corrective action which involves eliminating fundamental causes of failure. Merely enumerating the causes, however, is but a minor step in the direction of reducing the costly consequences of failure. Perhaps, the primary benefit from a careful enumeration of failure causes is the potential increased ability of the analyst to utilize this information in his search for early signals (variables) of failure.

We further observe marked similarities in failure causes from year to year and from economic period to period. The Department of Commerce study in 1932 reported that the major causes of bankruptcy were inefficient management, unwise use and extension of credit, adverse domestic and personal factors, and dishonesty and fraud.[16] Dewing wrote of four fundamental economic causes of failure: (1) competition; (2) unprofitable expansion; (3) cessation of public demand; and (4) excess payment of capital charges.[17] Finally, Dun & Bradstreet regularly tabulates and reports failure causes. Their latest report shows that over 90 percent of all failures result from one type of management inefficiency or another. Table 1-8 breaks down this list into its components as well as presenting the remaining other causes. Also listed are selected 1932 statistics.

It should be noted that the causes and percentages listed are based on the opinions of informed creditors and from credit reports and not from the owners themselves. Naturally, one would expect that the managers' or the owners' enumeration would look quite different.[r] The true answer to the question—"What was the primary cause of failure"—is probably much closer to the creditor opinion, although even here there is undoubtedly some bias built into the results.

The two causes least susceptible to prior detection are fraud and disaster. No discussion is necessary regarding disasters which include such episodic events as fire, flood, burglary and strikes. In the event of fraud, the enterprise is usually being presented as healthy and vibrant until the fraud is detected and further investigations ensue. The opinion that contemporary large firms simply do not go bankrupt from traditional economic causes is reinforced when we observe

---

[r]The Sadd and Williams study reported that in one particular industry (real estate) the cause "inefficient management" was cited three times more frequently by the creditors than by the owners. In every other industry, this relative discrepancy was also observed.

that fraud is a leading cause of bankruptcy in the large firm today.[s] If serious fraud is detected, the one remaining course of action which enables continued existence is often bankruptcy-reorganization whereby the assets are protected while the trustee "cleans house."

Conclusion

The preceding descriptive discussion should form the basis for subsequent analysis. Before we move to more analytical material, it might prove helpful to present a practical hypothetical bankruptcy case which delves into much of the aforementioned concepts. Appendix A provides such a case study.

Table 1-8
Business Failures by Cause in 1969 and 1932[a]

Causes	Manufacturing	Wholesale	Retail	Construction	Commercial Service	All Concerns
Lack of or Unbalanced Experience	36.6	24.5	46.8	42.0	37.5	41.5
Incompetence	55.2 (87.5)[b]	54.9 (58.0)[b]	40.3 (54.8)[b]	46.7 (58.9)[b]	44.1 (48.2)[b]	45.6 (51.7)[b]
Neglect	2.0	3.3	2.8	3.2	2.9	2.8
Fraud	1.1 (50.0)[c]	2.0 (56.0)[c]	1.1 (27.1)[c]	0.9 (33.1)[c]	0.9 (25.0)[c]	1.2 (28.7)[c]
Disaster	1.7	2.3	1.8	0.3	0.5	1.4
Unknown	3.4	4.3	7.2	6.9	14.1	7.1
Total	100.0%	100.0%	100.0%	100.0%	100.0%	100.0%

[a]Percentages in brackets refer to 1932 compilation from Sadd and Williams, pp. 14-16. These percentages do not add up to 100%.
[b]Refers to the category "Inefficient Management."
[c]Includes "dishonesty" category.
Source: 1969 Statistics from Dun & Bradstreet, pp. 11-12.

[s]Recent examples of this are Westec Corporation, Fifth Avenue Coach Lines and Yale Express. It should be noted, however, that fraud was not necessarily the main cause of failure in these cases, but perhaps a contributing force.

Appendix A: Illustrative Bankruptcy Case—
The Avenues of Escape*

Reliable Manufacturing Corporation finds itself unable to pay its current liabilities, and several of its creditors are threatening legal action. The balance sheet of Reliable indicates that its assets exceed liabilities by $200,000. However, included in its assets are good will, research and development, and certain prepaid expenses carried at a total valuation of $225,000.

Reliable owes Fidelity Bank $25,000 on an unsecured loan but has $10,000 on deposit with the bank in its commercial account. The company occupies premises pursuant to a 15-year lease with rent payable at $2,000 per month. The lease will expire in five years.

Mr. J.P. Smith is president of Reliable, and he and his wife are the sole stockholders. When Reliable was incorporated about five years ago, Smith and his wife subscribed for 2,500 shares of stock at $10 par value and paid cash thereof. At the time of incorporation, Smith loaned the corporation $225,000 on a long-term loan, all of which loan is unpaid.

Reliable owns a parcel of unimproved real property subject to a first deed of trust in favor of Commercial Realty Company. There appears to be an equity of about $50,000 in the real property, but due to Reliable's financial condition, it has been unable to maintain the payments to Commercial Realty or the real estate taxes thereon. Commercial Realty has recently filed a notice of default under the deed of trust.

Within the last two months, Reliable has made some substantial payments to certain of its creditors, including Fidelity Bank. The indebtedness owing to Fidelity Bank was personally guaranteed by Smith and his wife. The unsecured creditors of Reliable are made up as follows: approximately 50 creditors whose claims are under $100; approximately 200 creditors whose claims are in excess of $100 but less than $5,000; and 30 creditors whose claims are each in excess of $5,000, approximately one-half of which are out-of-state creditors. Reliable also owes the following taxes: $10,000 to the Internal Revenue Service for withholding taxes, and $5,000 to the State of Illinois for employment taxes and sales and use taxes. (See Table A-1.)

Included in the assets of Reliable are inventory carried at a cost of $50,000, equipment carried at a cost of $100,000, and $125,000 in accounts receivable deemed collectible. None of these assets are in any way encumbered. (See Table A-2.)

Reliable is unable to make any payments on past indebtedness at this time. The firm, which has sustained substantial losses since incorporation, is placing great hope on a pending patent for a new manufacturing process and feels that

*Facts and figures for this case were provided generously by Mr. Jack Stutman of Quittner, Stutman, Treister and Glatt.

Table A-1
Financial Statement: Reliable Manufacturing Corporation, March 31, 1971

Assets		
Current Assets:		
Cash – Fidelity Bank	$ 10,000	
Accounts Receivable	125,000	
Finished Inventory (cost)	50,000	
Work in process and raw materials	75,000	
Total Current Assets:		$260,000
Other Assets:		
Land (unimproved)	$100,000	
Fixtures and equipment	100,000	
Leasehold improvements	30,000	
(1) Research and development	175,000	
Prepaid expenses	25,000	
Good will	25,000	
Total Other Assets		$455,000
Total Assets:		$715,000

(1) Expended in connection with patent pending.

given nine months to a year, it can turn around and emerge as a profitable company. There is a possibility that a well-established national manufacturing company might be interested in acquiring the assets or stock of Reliable, chiefly because of the value of its new patent.

Questions for Discussion –
Avenues of Escape Case

1. On the basis of the prepared statement of facts and the financial statement of Reliable Manufacturing Corporation, what avenues of escape or approach are generally available to the debtor and/or its creditors?
2. Are the alternatives of Chapter X, XII or XIII available to the debtor?
3. Based upon the statement of facts and financial statement, which is the most favorable way for the debtor to proceed in solving its creditor problems?
4. Please discuss the balance sheet from the debtor's point of view with respect to the assets.
5. Please discuss the balance sheet from the creditor's point of view with respect to the assets.

Table A-1 *(Continued)*
Financial Statement: Reliable Manufacturing Corporation

Liabilities			
Current Liabilities:			
Note payable – Fidelity Bank		$ 25,000	
Accounts Payable		200,000	
Taxes Payable – U.S.		10,000	
Taxes Payable – State of Illinois		5,000	
Portion long term debt to Commercial			
Realty Co. within one year		10,000	
Total Current Liabilities:			$250,000
Other Liabilities:			
Note payable officer (Smith)		$225,000	
Liens on real estate (Commercial Realty Co.)	$50,000		
Less: Current portion shown above	10,000		
		40,000	
Total Other Liabilities:			$265,000
Capital stock		25,000	
Capital Surplus		225,000	
Retained Earnings		(50,000)	
Net Worth			200,000
Total Liabilities and Net Worth:			$715,000

Creditors by Number and Amount	
50 creditors have claims of $100 or less totalling	$ 3,000
200 creditors have claims of $100 to $5,000 totalling	37,000
30 creditors have claims over $5,000 totalling	160,000
280 creditors	$200,000

6. Please discuss current, then other liabilities, from the debtor's point of view.
7. Please discuss current, then other liabilities, from the creditor's point of view.
8. What about subordination of principal's claim from the debtor's point of view?
9. What about subordination of principal's claim from the creditors' point of view?
10. What do you think the creditors will get on liquidation if Smith's claim is *not* subordinated? If it is subordinated?

11. We have previously indicated that the informal method was the debtor's best approach toward solution of its problems. On the assumption that you would commence the informal method by calling a creditors' meeting, who would you invite and what type of proposal would be made?
12. What are the weaknesses of the informal method?
13. Should the debtor be asked to leave the room at any time during the discussion? How about the election of a creditors' committee?
14. Explain the mechanics of a debtor working with the creditors' committee.
15. Let us assume that we feel Smith is not answering candidly or cooperatively. How can we shape him up outside of a court proceeding?
16. Would an assignment cure (1) lack of candor or cooperation; or (2) preferences? What about Chapter XI or bankruptcy as a cure?
17. What would make you go into a Chapter XI?
18. What risks do suppliers have in a Chapter XI?
19. What control does a debtor have in Chapter proceedings, vis a vis, the receiver, unsecured creditors, and secured creditors?
20. What are the various factors involved in getting a plan confirmed?
    (1) How much time can you get?
    (2) Treatment of expenses of administration and priority claims.
21. What about recalcitrant creditors? What about a hostile receiver or hostile court? How do you handle this?
22. Please discuss the jurisdiction of the court in a Chapter XI or straight bankruptcy proceeding.

**Answers to Questions: Avenues
of Escape Case**

Answer to Question 1. Reliable may attempt to resolve its problems with creditors independent of the Bankruptcy Act by informally seeking creditor cooperation to a program providing for extended payment and/or composition (settlement) of its unsecured indebtedness. Such an informal program may start out with a moratorium. If the goal of Reliable is rehabilitation and if an informal proceeding will not succeed because of creditor opposition or other reasons, Reliable can seek its rehabilitation through a Chapter XI proceeding. If events develop which indicate that a liquidation is in order, that liquidation can be accomplished informally through the device of an assignment for the benefit of creditors or through a straight bankruptcy proceeding, creditors have a right to force bankruptcy, upon the requisite conditions being met, through an involuntary petition. Reliable, if it became a voluntary or involuntary bankrupt, could convert its proceeding to one under Chapter XI.

Answer to Question 2. Chapter XII is not available to Reliable by reason of the fact that Reliable is a corporation. Chapter XII is primarily a device intended for real estate reorganizations and is available only to an individual or copartnerships. Chapter XIII deals with wage earners. A wage earner is defined as an individual whose principal income is derived from wages, salary or commissions. Reliable, obviously, does not fit in this category. Chapter X is technically available to Reliable. However, one generally thinks of Chapter X as a device for the reorganization of a corporation substantially larger than Reliable with public stock holders or bond holders. As the facts indicate, Reliable is a "mama-papa" corporation with all its stock being owned by Smith and his wife. In a Chapter XI proceeding, a debtor has a good measure of control over its destiny. In Chapter X, with some exceptions, the affairs of the debtor corporation are administered by an independent trustee. A plan or reorganization is promulgated through the trustee. Choosing between Chapter X and Chapter XI, Reliable's principals would much prefer the Chapter XI route.

Answer to Question 3. The debtor's choice would be the informal method. Some of the reasons for preferring the informal method are:

A. That method is generally thought to be less costly to the debtor than a proceeding under Chapter XI.
B. The restrictions on the debtor's operation in an informal proceeding are usually far less than those encountered in Chapter XI. Should the debtor desire to maintain an operation in Chapter XI, in all likelihood the Chapter XI court would appoint a receiver.
C. Reliable's lease to its business premises may contain a so-called "bankruptcy clause." A Chapter XI proceeding might threaten the viability of that lease, whereas the informal proceeding would probably not trigger the bankruptcy clause.
D. The advent of a Chapter XI proceeding might jeopardize the debtor's ability to attract future business. Such proceeding might also jeopardize the debtor's existing contracts. The likelihood of jeopardy to present and future business would be less in the informal proceeding. The bankruptcy stigma regardless of its inherent qualities, is often very costly.

Answer to Question 4. It is the debtor's obligation to suggest to its creditors what might be realized from its assets should a liquidation, either bankruptcy or otherwise, be required. Taking that approach, the following appears:

A. While cash on hand is reflected at $10,000, that cash is located at the Fidelity Bank. As appears on the liability side, the debtor owes Fidelity Bank $25,000. Fidelity could offset this $10,000 in cash against the obligation.
B. In a liquidation, the likelihood is that there will be a substantial diminution in accounts receivable shown on the balance sheet at $125,000. It is not untypical for account debtors, when they become aware of an insolvency situation, to think upon all sorts of excuses for not paying. Further, undoubtedly, there are warranty problems involved with regard to the items manufactured by Reliable. If Reliable is out of business with a resulting

termination of its ability to service its warranty obligations, its account debtors will have justification for being slow to pay or not to pay at all.

C. Finished inventory shown at $50,000 on the balance sheet, if disposed of in bulk in a liquidation, will bring substantially less than that amount.

D. Work in process and raw materials scheduled at $75,000 will probably be sold for scrap and bring so many cents on the pound.

E. Land which is reflected at $100,000 is subject to a $60,000 mortgage. A keynote of a liquidating type proceeding is the swift conversion of assets to cash. A sale of the land will reduce its $40,000 equity through commission payable to a broker and through escrow fees. Further, a rapid sale would probably require the acceptance of something less than the price which the land would bring if it were held for a long enough time to find the right buyer.

F. As appears in the statement of facts, fixtures and equipment valued at $100,000 are carried at cost. These fixtures and equipment are unencumbered. They have obviously been used and depreciated. Sold under the hammer, unless they are in unique demand, such fixtures and equipment will produce substantially less than $100,000 in cash realization.

G. Leasehold improvements of $30,000 are not generally a realizable asset in a liquidation. If Reliable ceases to operate and terminates its lease, its landlord will probably obtain all the benefits of Reliable's leasehold improvements.

H. Research and development shown at $175,000 is generally a zero asset in a liquidation. In this instance, research and development is represented by a patent pending. The value of that patent pending is too uncertain to be counted as an asset of consequence.

I. Prepaid expenses are generally a book entry with no salvage value in a liquidation.

J. Insofar as good will is concerned, it is obvious that this type of so-called asset terminates when the business ceases to operate and undergoes a liquidation.

Answer to Question 5. Approaching the assets from a creditor standpoint, a caveat to be remembered is that debtors generally tend to understate their asset realization in offering a liquidation approach to creditors. The debtor's analysis is very likely correct insofar as it relates to a cash offset by the Fidelity Bank. With regard to accounts receivable, vigorous pursuit of same in a liquidation could yield substantial recovery. As appears in the statement of facts, the accounts receivable on the balance sheet are deemed collectable. The realization from finished inventory, work in process and raw materials can be enhanced beyond that suggested by the debtor if the liquidation is carefully and intelligently handled. The same would hold true with regard to the debtor's land, fixtures and equipment. While the debtor tends to belittle the worth of the patent pending, this asset should be carefully investigated. It may well be that the debtor's expenditure of $175,000 can be substantially recovered by an intelligent disposition of the patent pending. Insofar as prepaid expenses are concerned, it is conceivable that some of these expenses may be in the nature of deposits with utilities and the like which could be recovered. The debtor's analysis of leasehold improvements and good will in a liquidation is quite correct with one possible exception. The debtor's lease should be carefully reviewed both to determine whether it is an economically good lease and whether that lease contains a solid bankruptcy clause. If, perchance, the property leased by the debtor is worth substantially more than $2,000 per month and if, perchance, the lease does not contain an effective bankruptcy clause, the lease and the leasehold improvements thereon can be assigned, by a trustee in bankruptcy, to a third party for affirmative dollars. Moreover, realization from a liquidation if that liquidation is by way of bankruptcy, can be enhanced by recoveries made available by the Bankruptcy Act. By way of example, the statement of facts indicates that within the last two months Reliable made substantial payments to certain of its creditors. If it can be demonstrated that these payments constitute voidable preferences, judgments can be obtained against such creditors and moneys recovered thereby.

Answer to Question 6. With regard to liabilities in the event of a liquidation, the following appears to be the case:

A. The note obligation to Fidelity Bank would be reduced to $15,000 after that bank offsets the debtor's cash on hand.
B. The cash funds realized through liquidation would, before unsecured creditors see a penny of same, be subjected to the costs of the liquidating proceeding plus the $15,000 in tax obligations to the United States and State of Illinois. These categories of charges come right off the top.
C. The $60,000 obligation owing Commercial Realty Co. would in all likelihood be satisfied through a sale of the real property asset.
D. Whatever dollars remain following payment of administrative costs and taxes would be prorated among $425,000 worth of debt, $215,000 being owed to the trade and $225,000 being owed to Smith. Keep in mind also that Reliable's premises are being leased at the rate of $24,000 per year. That lease will not expire for another five years. Accordingly, Reliable's liability in the event of liquidation will undoubtedly be augmented by a substantial claim from the landlord.

Answer to Question 7. From a creditor standpoint, the analysis of the liability side of the balance sheet by debtor's counsel is correct with a number of important limitations. First and foremost, creditors would take the position that the note payable to Smith of $225,000 should be subordinated until such time as all other creditors have been paid in full. A bankruptcy court has the power to impose a subordination if the circumstances so justify. As appears from the statement of facts, the debtor's initial capitalization was but $25,000. Contemporaneously with its organization, Smith, the debtor's principal, advanced it $225,000. Investigation might indicate that the debtor was not adequately capitalized for its business purposes and that the moneys advanced to it by Smith by way of loan were in fact tax motivated and were really nothing more than a further contribution to the debtor's capital. With regard to the liability to the landlord, in straight bankruptcy, his claim would be limited to a maximum of one year's prospective rent ($24,000). In a Chapter XI proceeding, the landlord's claim, assuming a termination of lease, cannot exceed a maximum of three year's rent reserved in the lease.

Answer to Question 8. Obviously, in the liquidation analysis, it is very important for the debtor to contend that the note payable to Smith of $225,000 will participate on a parity with other creditors. The debtor would argue that $25,000 did constitute sufficient capitalization and that the $225,000 advanced was a legitimate loan. How long the debtor was in business is a factor to be considered in determining the adequacy of the initial capitalization. While the facts do not so indicate, if the debtor has operated for a long period of time, such operation would tend to demonstrate that $25,000 was good and sufficient capital. At best, the concept of subordinating an insider's claim is a lawsuit. Lawsuits take time and their results are uncertain.

Answer to Question 9. As is obvious, the claim of Smith comprises 50% or more of the debtor's unsecured liability. Subordination of that claim will double unsecured creditors realization in the event of bankruptcy. Should the debtor seek an informal arrangement with its creditors where an extended payment program is offered, creditors, as the price for going along with such a program, would insist upon the subordination of Smith's claim pending full payment to them.

Answer to Question 10.

A. Based on an educated guess, somewhere in the range of 18% to 20%, predicated upon the following: cash—nil; accounts receivable—$75,000; finished inventory—$25,000; work in process and raw materials—$7,500; land—$13,000; fixtures and equipment—$33,000. These asset items total $153,500. Allow 25% ($38,375) for administrative costs and discount $15,000 for taxes. The balance is approximately $100,000. Figure unsecured claims including Smith at $500,000.
B. If Smith's claim is subordinated, the claims of the unsecured creditors are computed at $275,000. Therefore, these creditors could expect to receive approximately 36%.

Answer to Question 11. Sound planning would include *all* creditors. Discrimination among creditors based upon the size of their claims is unwise. A creditor who is not invited to a meeting because his claim is not deemed to be of sufficient amount can get very recalcitrant. One attachment can conceivably spell the end of an informal proceeding and require the institution of a Chapter XI. Based upon the statement of facts and the financial data, it is best to first seek a moratorium. As appears in the statement of facts, Reliable can meet current obligations on a current basis, but at present it lacks the wherewithal to make any reduction in its past due debt. The company should also seek to enter into an extension agreement with creditors which would contemplate payments tied to anticipated profits on an installment basis. It would also seem wise to agree to council with a creditors' committee with regard to how heavy payments should be and when they should commence. Reliable's patent pending may attract third party interest. Depending upon what the third party has in mind, the situation may be one which will ultimately lend itself to a cash settlement or perhaps even a stock plan.

Answer to Question 12. To make the informal proceeding work, almost unanimous creditor cooperation is required. A recalcitrant consequential creditor who refused to go along can force a Chapter XI proceeding. As a rule, there is no practical way in the informal proceeding to avoid questioned transactions made by the debtor. By way of example, under the law of the State of California, there is nothing wrong with making a preference to an unsecured creditor. In a bankruptcy proceeding, preferential transfers made within four months of the filing date can be recovered. The statement of facts indicate that Commercial Realty, the creditor holding the trust deed on Reliable's land, has filed notice of default. Without timely repayment of past due amounts to Commercial, or Commercial's voluntary consent to abate its foreclosure, there is no other way to stop such foreclosure. Upon a showing of equity, as here appears, the bankruptcy court would very likely restrain the Commercial foreclosure for a reasonable period of time so as to permit realization on the equity in question. The informal method offers no way to enforce subordination of the Smith claim short of Smith's voluntary consent.

Answer to Question 13. It is typical during informal creditors' meetings that the debtor, his counsel and other persons in interest leave the room during the course of the discussion. The reason is apparent. When the debtor is present, creditors at the meeting may be reluctant to discuss information in their possession which bears critically upon the debtor or its future. With the debtor out of the room, a freer atmosphere ensues which is more productive to the generation of information which may be critical to the debtor or its operation. Election of a creditors' committee at the informal meeting is very general practice. It is not uncommon for debtors to affirmatively request that such a committee be chosen. The creditors' committee will act for the benefit of creditors generally and will be in a position to make decisions with the debtor which creditors generally will be likely to accept. It would be unwieldy to call a general creditors' meeting each time important problems arise which require resolution. Also, it is not unusual for a creditors' committee or members thereof to give the debtor valuable advice with regard to the improvement of its business operation.

Answer to Question 14. The typical relationship between a debtor and creditors' committee is one involving meetings at periodic intervals with a submission by the debtor to the committee of operating reports. Usually, meetings between the debtor and a committee are more frequent at the inception of a moratorium and extension proceeding. As the debtor makes progress and the committee grows more confident of the debtor's management, the meetings become more infrequent. Occasionally, a creditors' committee will in turn be divided into subcommittees containing individual creditors who are adept in given areas of the debtor's problems, such as financing, operations, sales, etc.

Answer to Question 15. Typically, an extension arrangement between a debtor and his creditors is documented by an extension agreement. There are generally provisions in the extension agreement which require certain standards of conduct from the debtor and its management. These provisions generally provide that if the debtor or management does not perform up to standard, creditors have the right to terminate the extension arrangement. Assuming this type of extension agreement, Smith can probably best be shaped up by suggesting to him the potential of a termination of the informal proceeding.

Answer to Question 16. An assignment for the benefit of creditors does not cure a lack of candor or cooperation. As previously mentioned, preferences, with limited exception, can only be avoided in bankruptcy proceedings. Accordingly, the assignment is not a device to be utilized if major preferences exist. With regard to lack of candor or cooperation, when the assignment is made, the debtor should turn over to his assignee all of his business books and records. Such books and records can reveal what the debtor may be hiding. If the evils that are hidden cannot be cured in the assignment, creditors can resort to bankruptcy, the assignment being an act of bankruptcy. In an assignment the assignee, usually with the guidance of creditors, directs the show. However, frequently a debtor's cooperation is required to maximize assets. There is nothing the assignee can do to compel this. The bankruptcy Act, in Section 7, imposes a substantial number of duties on a bankrupt. If cooperation is required, bankruptcy may be the place to go.

Answer to Question 17. Among the primary factors that would make one go into a Chapter XI are the following:

A. A major attachment which the creditor will not release.
B. The failure of a major creditor or group of creditors to go along with the informal program imposed. In Chapter XI, majority in number and amount of creditors consenting to a plan binds recalcitrant creditors.
C. Difficulty of obtaining financing. In Chapter XI, the bankruptcy court may authorize the borrowing of funds with the grant of a debtor or receiver's certificate to the lending creditor. This certificate creates a prior obligation to

the creditor which is generally secured by a lien on the equities in the debtor estate.

Answer to Question 18. Suppliers of goods in a Chapter XI proceeding are treated as class 1 priority creditors—administrative claimants. Accordingly, Chapter XI obligations incurred to suppliers must be paid before any moneys are made available to lesser priorities and unsecured creditors. The risk to a Chapter XI supplier is that the proceeding will fail with a resulting adjudication in bankruptcy. In the ensuing bankruptcy proceedings, the administrative obligations of the new proceeding are paid before payments can be made to the unpaid Chapter XI suppliers. Accordingly, if the costs of the ensuing proceeding are substantial and the assets on hand are minimal, the Chapter XI supplier may receive a percentage of his obligation or even nothing.

Answer to Question 19. In a Chapter XI proceeding, the debtor may occupy two functions. He may be both a debtor and a debtor in possession. As a debtor in possession, he would have all the powers of a receiver or trustee in bankruptcy including the preservation of assets and the institution of litigation. Where a receiver is appointed, such powers generally pass to him, although there is some gray area as to just how far a receiver may go without the debtor's cooperation. The function of a debtor, as distinguished from debtor in possession, in the Chapter XI proceeding is primarily to propose and obtain confirmation of a plan of arrangement. Proposal of the plan is exclusively the debtor's right, albeit he may consult with his receiver and creditors. Normally and within the limits of his duties, a receiver in a Chapter XI proceeding will attempt not to act inconsistently with the debtor's concept for a plan. As previously suggested, secured creditors can be denied foreclosure or reclamation of their assets in Chapter XI upon a showing of equity. Unsecured creditors have an important voice in Chapter XI proceedings. The debtor's control over unsecured creditors is primarily limited to binding dissidents to a plan upon obtaining consent to such plan from a majority in number and amount of such creditors.

Answer to Question 20. To confirm a plan of arrangement, the debtor needs the requisite consent to such plan from a majority in number and amount of his creditors. He also needs the deposit which is fixed by the bankruptcy court as a precondition to obtaining confirmation. The deposit basically includes the total dollars required for administrative costs and priority claims. If creditors are to receive cash upon confirmation, the cash to be received is to be included in the deposit. Apart from the above factors, before a plan can be confirmed, the primary things that the court must find are that the plan is in the best interests of creditors and is feasible. "Feasible" primarily means that it appears that the plan proposed by the debtor is workable. "Best interests of creditors" generally means that through the debtor's plan of arrangement, creditors will be receiving more in the way of economic consideration than they would receive in some other way—such as by liquidation. The other major factor which must be found by the court is that the debtor has not committed any acts which would be a bar to the discharge of a bankrupt. A confirmed plan of arrangement operates in the same way as a discharge in bankruptcy. There is really no way to predict how much time a debtor will be allowed by the court in confirming a plan. Basically, each case must be taken on its own facts. If the court can see the possibility of a constructive result being achieved, the court will be liberal in the grant of time. As previously noted, administrative expenses and priority claims must be provided for (or expressly waived) before a plan can be confirmed.

Answer to Question 21. When the debtor obtains consents from a majority of both number and amount of its unsecured creditors to its plan of arrangement, recalcitrant and nonconsenting creditors are bound thereby. However, the recalcitrant creditors, even though outvoted, have the right to oppose the debtor's plan by contending by way of example that it is not feasible; that it is not in the best interest of creditors; and that the debtor has committed an act sufficient to bar the discharge of a bankrupt. If the court is hostile to the debtor's Chapter XI proceeding, the only solution the debtor has is to attempt to remove the Referee for prejudice. That is not a matter which is readily achieved. The problem of the hostile receiver is also difficult of solution. If the receiver has committed acts of sufficient flagrancy to warrant his termination, the debtor can bring these acts to the court's attention and the court will act accordingly. Beyond such conduct, the debtor must learn to live with his receiver. Different courts attach different weight to the attitudes and recommendations of the receiver.

Answer to Question 22. The jurisdiction of the bankruptcy court in Chapter XI and straight bankruptcy matters is a subject of exceeding complexity. Generally speaking, the jurisdiction of the Chapter XI court over the debtor and its assets is nationwide whereas the jurisdiction of the bankruptcy court over the bankrupt and his assets is statewide. In bankruptcy, ancillary proceedings are available to permit jurisdiction over property located in other states. Insofar as controversies relating to the status of property is concerned, bankruptcy jurisdiction is generally predicated upon possession in the bankrupt (actual or constructive) as of the filing date. Chapter XI jurisdiction in this regard is broader. Title to the involved property, in addition to actual or constructive possession, will give the Chapter XI court jurisdiction. Of course, in any controversy affecting either a bankrupt or Chapter XI estate, the court can acquire jurisdiction if the respondent raises no objection to the bankruptcy court's jurisdiction.

2

Aggregate Influences on Business Failures

In the latter months of 1970 and the ensuing start of 1971, the United States economy experienced two economic phenomena of a vastly different, and seemingly inconsistent, nature. The nation's money GNP rose above the one trillion dollar level and, at the same time, the number of business failures—especially large companies—reached such proportions that one could scarcely peruse financial and economic periodicals without observing a commentary on the import of some bankrupt entity.[a] This remarkable occurrence comes after thirty years of apparent neglect of business failures on the part of business theorists and practitioners. After the great depression of the thirties and the consequent rash of failures both large and small, the subject of bankruptcy and its relationship to other economic phenomena was usually relegated to a single chapter at the end of basic business finance textbooks and to monthly summary statistics recorded in *Dun's Review*. This is in marked contrast to the prominence given the subject by authors before the second World War. One classic textbook devotes approximately one-third of its second volume (of over 1,000 pages) to corporate bankruptcy and reorganization.[1]

Even in these prior works, however, the attention given to the relationship between other aggregate economic phenomena and business failures was scanty and usually summed up by the generalization that failures and economic growth are negatively correlated. Bankruptcy was treated as essentially a microeconomic phenomenon and emphasis placed at that level. The one exception to this predominant micro-oriented approach is the work of the National Bureau of Economic Research since 1920 in the area of business cycle analysis. The Bureau has carefully observed and analyzed a large number of aggregate economic series and subsequently classified them into one of three general groupings of economic indicators; leading, coincident, and lagging series relative to their business reference cycle. Two of the series analyzed are business failures and failure liabilities.[2] Their work has on occasion prompted others to investigate the failure occurrence, especially its relationship to corporate profits.[3] For many years, it was generally concluded that the business failure liability series was a fairly consistent and rather lengthy leading business cycle indicator (ranging up to 27 months), generally giving earlier notice of approaching recessions than of

[a]Indeed, the American Finance Association saw fit to devote one entire session at its 1970 annual meeting to the subject of the Penn Central bankruptcy in particular and to business failures in general.

expansions.[b] Total business failures, however, are found to be a leading indicator only prior to business peaks while displaying roughly coincident patterns at the troughs. In all cases, the relationship between failures and general business activity is inverse. A significant conclusion of prior works is that large business failures occur prior to failure of smaller firms, thereby causing the failure liabilities series to lead the number of failures series.[c]

The primary purpose of this chapter is to examine aggregate economic influences on business failure experience in the post World-War II period. While most analysts have traditionally categorized the causes of business failures as either "fundamental" (the root causes) or "immediate" (the last event preceding failure), their frame of reference has always been *internal* to the unfortunate firm. It will be argued that certain aggregate measures of macroeconomic conditions are closely associated with the immediate causes and help to transform the marginal enterprise into a bankrupt. We will rely upon economic theory and the work of the National Bureau in order to specify the appropriate relationships.

The subsequent analysis, however, differs from business cycle study in that relationships will be examined on a continuous quarterly basis, regardless of the economic health of the nation, rather than on the more restrictive basis of limiting the analysis to business cycle turning points. To this end, we utilize a quarterly, first difference regression model covering numerous economic cycles during the post World War II period. Relatively simple lead and lag adjustments are also introduced in order to specify the most significant timing relationships between the various economic series and business failure rates and liabilities.

Model Development

Although business failures are essentially microeconomic phenomena caused by unique firm situations, the aggregate number of business failures is likely influenced by other aggregate data which reflect, to a great extent, a summation of individual economic unit activity. The following general group classifications are specified as containing potentially helpful explanatory variables when related to the failure rate and failure liability experience of American business entities: (a) economic growth series; (b) money market conditions; and (c) investor expectations.

---

[b]The consistency of failure liabilities as a leading indicator has been questioned of late with the dropping of this indicator from the short list (primary indicator list) to the long list. The latter contains nonclassified as well as classified series.[4]

[c]The major reason given for this lead-lag relationship is that the larger firms dominate the failure liabilities series. This line of reasoning is clearly an example of the situation where explanation and theory follow empirical observation. An equally good case could be made for large firms failing, on the average, *after* smaller ones because of the former's ability to withstand economic and financial problems for a longer period of time. Certainly, this is true for the very large firms, i.e., firms possessing liabilities over $25 million.

Economic Growth

As noted earlier, general interest in business failures is usually heightened in periods of economic stress probably due to the very increase in failures. If this be the case, we could expect that low or negative economic growth is associated with increasing levels of failures and failure liabilities. As the economy struggles along, the marginal firm is subjected to more extreme pressures on its existence than during periods of high growth. Sales and earnings of individual business enterprises are directly related to overall business activity and for this reason, we should expect a significant negative correlation between series which reflect the economic growth of our country and business failures. This is not necessarily true, however, on a continuous basis. As the nation continues to grow and sales activity expands, many new—and sometimes marginal firms—are enticed into existence. As we saw earlier in Chapter 1, the propensity to fail is greatest for firms in their formative stages of development and a temporary influx of firms caused by optimistic economic activity could lead to an increase in failures in subsequent periods. The timing of the influx of new firms, however, might coincide with dampened economic growth as the economy begins to slow down, and the subsequent *increase* in failures coincident with economic *expansion*. This relationship is illustrated in Figure 2-1. Here, we depict increasing economic growth climaxed at point 1, followed by an increase in the net formation of companies reaching its peak at point 2, followed by a rise in failures peaking at point 3. The latter point, however, is coincident with a *new* business expansion and thereby would give results opposite to our *a priori* expectations. These interrelationships, however, are based upon fairly regular and homogeneous

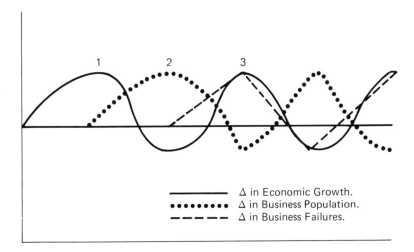

Figure 2-1. Dynamic Elements of Time Series Movements: An Illustration.

periods of expansion and recession which are rarely the case. In addition, when we seek to explain the nation's failure *rate*, the number of enterprises is implicitly considered.[d] We present the above hypothetical series of events merely as an illustration of the possible dynamic elements involved in a continuous series analysis. It is not felt, however, that this sequence will manifest to such an extent as to lead us to change our *a priori* expectation of an inverse relationship between economic growth and business failures.

The two primary series chosen to reflect actual economic growth are real GNP and Corporate Profits. Both are aggregate series indicating the sales and profit experience of the individual entities of the economy. While GNP data reflects more than just business activity, it has traditionally been utilized as a barometer of the nation's economic health. The relationship between corporate profits and failure rates is perhaps more direct and has been the subject of concern in the literature on several occasions.[6] The theory is quite straightforward linking changes in profits of companies to failures; a fall in profits or an increase in negative profits could be critical to the marginal entity. Both aggregate GNP and corporate profits series have been examined extensively by the National Bureau, with GNP consistently classified as a roughly coincident indicator and the corporate profit series originally designated as a primary leading indicator (and later reclassified to the coincident category).[7] At a later point, we will discuss our empirical findings, including a surprising result concerning the relative explanatory powers of the two aggregate economic growth series—real GNP and profits.

Money Market Conditions

One of the more lively current economic debates concerns the effect that the nation's money supply has on the economy. While most economists conclude that "money matters," the extent of this monetary influence is not clear. In the case of the potential failing firm, the argument is clear—money, or more correctly credit, most certainly does matter. A typical chain of events leading to a failure situation begins with operating difficulties manifested in losses and/or deteriorating market share. This condition is often aggravated by relatively high financial leverage capital structures. Sources of funds from the capital markets are either unavailable or extremely costly to firms whose solvency is threatened. As long as the firm has adequate internal liquidity or can acquire credit from financial institutions to meet its short-term obligations, it will almost never be motivated to declare bankruptcy. It is only when cash runs out and credit is no longer available do we witness management's fateful decision.

The credit-availability doctrine and an allied theory of credit discrimination

---

[d]The most comprehensive series depicting failures of American businesses is reported by Dun & Bradstreet and one of their measures is called the Failure Rate. This is a measure of the number of failures per 10,000 listed corporations.[5]

against smaller[8] and poorer risk firms (both concepts to which we subscribe) hypothesize that during periods of tight money, we can expect credit to be rationed amongst the best credit risks, thereby adding a further impetus to the marginal firm's demise. While the empirical evidence remains uncertain as to the exact amount of discrimination on the part of financial institutions, we should look at this monetary phenomenon from the demand for loanable funds and the supply side. It is likely that large firms are more sensitive to economic expansions in that their demand for loans will increase substantially regardless of the commercial loan offer rate. If at the same time, the monetary authorities are restricting the supply of money in order to combat inflationary pressures (present or expected), then the *proportion* of loanable funds provided to the best risk and largest companies will increase relative to the smaller, poorer risk companies. Since the great majority of failures are small firms (only 1.2 percent of all failures in 1968 had liabilities over 1 million), the so-called small business credit rationing effect, which is alleged to occur during tight money conditions, is potentially an important influence on the total failure experience of American businesses. The hypothesized relationship between credit availability and business failures is therefore inverse.

Measures which are expected to reflect credit and liquidity conditions are the nation's money supply (demand deposits plus currency), free reserves, and interest rates (Moody's Aaa rate). Credit conditions are affected by the combined forces of supply and demand for funds as well as the monetary policy presently being pursued by the Federal Reserve System. The use of the money supply as an indicator of monetary policy has been sanctioned by an increasing number of eminent economists, although their chosen measures of money are not always in accord with one another.[9] In this book, we will attempt to observe a further economic consequence of adjusting the money supply. Heretofore mentioned reasons for attempting to adjust the supply of money and credit concern overall economic growth goals, the containment of price inflation, and sometimes, balance of payments problems. Certainly, a related item to the overall consequences of shifts in money supply is the costs, (or gains) of increasing (decreasing) business failures.

The two other measures of money market conditions which we examine, free reserves and interest rates, are probably less consistent in their relationship to credit conditions. Both may be considered as transmitters of Federal Reserve actions. While we chose Moody's Aaa rate, we might have utilized the Baa or some other rate to reflect credit conditions. Since interest rates tend to move together, however, the choice of one rate is probably as good as another. In addition, we examine the differential (Baa-Aaa) as a separate variable.

Investor Expectations

The potential failing firm is less likely to take the necessary steps of failure declaration if the future appears optimistic. This is logical whether the optimism is manifest internally or from forces external to the firm. One sector of external influence is investment community expectations which are reflected in the prices it is willing to pay for financial asset ownership. The relationship between common stock prices and business failures is predicated on both empirical and theoretical grounds. Empirically, business cycle analysts have consistently reported that business failures and stock prices are both leading indicators of cyclical turning points. The fact that we observe these two aggregate series moving together periodically, with both indicating changes in future economic activity, is interesting but not necessarily indicative of a causal relationship with each other. Both are likely to be related to a third factor—expected economic conditions—and, therefore, their mutual association is not clearly direct.

A case could be made for a more direct relationship between stock prices and failures if we consider the definition of insolvency in a bankruptcy sense as the situation where the firm's liabilities exceed the economic value of its assets. An accurate indicator of just how much of a fall in asset value is necessary before this insolvency situation is manifest is the market value of the firm's equity as a percentage of its total debt (MV/TD). A company whose (MV/TD) ratio is 25 percent indicates that asset values can only fall 20 percent before insolvency is theoretically manifest. That is, if the book value of liabilities is $20 million and there are 1 million shares of common stock outstanding with a market price of $5 per share and we assume that the economic value of the assets is therefore equal to $25 million, these assets can *fall* in value by no more than $5 million (a decrease of 20 percent) before liabilities will exceed assets.

The argument here is that market value, in a rather accurate way, reflects economic value. A drop in the growth of the overall stock price index is indicative of depressed investor expectations and usually affects almost all firms. It can be crucial, however, to the marginal enterprise. In a rising stock market environment, the marginal firms' securities might still have some tangible positive price, but with the onset of a bear market, the price level is more apt to fall to some nil level which more accurately reflects the dire situation. The failure symptoms may have been present within the firm for some time. Therefore, the drop in stock price to some negligible value, along with other failure symptoms, is the immediate cause of failure. *Ceteris paribus*, this is more likely to occur in a bear market than in favorable stock market conditions. Not only are investors unwilling to supply desperately needed funds to the potential bankrupt, but the realization of the critical nature of the firm's problems are now painfully clear.

A counterargument to this line of reasoning could be presented in view of an increasingly common recent phenomenon—corporate mergers between financially sick firms whose equity price is depressed, and some aggressive company. If this merger occurs prior to formal declaration of bankruptcy by the weak firm, the aggregate failure series is denied a worthy and likely member. The relative tradeoffs between failure declaration and mergers in low or negative stock market growth conditions is not clear. It is not likely, however, that the tradeoffs are symmetrical in favorable market price growth conditions and we expect that failures and stock price growth are negatively correlated.

In order to reflect overall stock market performance, we utilize Standard and Poor's Composite Index of Stock Prices (S & P). The major reasons for this choice are the relative comprehensiveness of this index and the availability of quarterly observations during the entire post World-War II period. Since most firms that fail are not listed corporations, the use of the S & P Index is a proxy for investor expectations. Also, the S & P Index is the one utilized by the National Bureau in their economic indicator analysis.

A second type of investor expectation variable which may have some relationship with business failures is a type of risk-premium measure. All financial instruments, except the so-called risk-free assets, contain an element of financial risk which is reflected in the yield that investors require. The difference between this yield and the risk free rate could be called the risk premium. The more risky the security, the greater the risk premium. Although we do observe a stable ordinal relationship between rates of return on various risky assets over time, this by no means implies that the *yield differential* between various risk securities is numerically stable. On the contrary, we find this differential fluctuating continuously over time. Aside from general interest rate conditions, it is felt that the rate differentials reflect investor expectations as to the ability of fixed income security issuers to repay their debts. Therefore, we find greater fluctuations in yield in the relatively high-risk securities.

The above phenomenon is possibly reflected in the relationship between the yield on the highest grade corporate fixed-income bonds and the yield on more speculative risky bonds. We have chosen the differential between Moody's Aaa and Baa bonds.[e] During stable times, we hypothesize that this differential is relatively small and it increases as investors become less optimistic as to the ability of some firms to fulfill their financial obligations. While the credit risk component of *all* rates is expected to rise as future conditions become less certain, the expected increase in this component of the rate on more risky securities is greater. Therefore, the absolute differential should increase during periods, or perhaps slightly before periods, of increased uncertainty. Since we also expect to experience an increase in failure rates in these same periods, the hypothesized relationship between our risk-premium variable and the failure series is *positive*.

Variable Interrelationships

Thus far, we have hypothesized that business failures will be affected by changes in economic conditions, including credit availability changes and investor expectations. The actual variables embodied in these general classifications, however, have also displayed somewhat consistent historical relationships to one

---

[e]The Aaa rating is reserved for those companies judged to be of the best quality. They carry the smallest degree of investment risk. Baa bonds are considered lower medium-grade obligations. Such bonds lack outstanding investment characteristics and have speculative characteristics as well.

another. Empirically, money supply changes have usually led stock price movements which, in turn, lead business cycle changes. We might therefore postulate that changing money supply conditions precede all of the other variables, including failure rates. Recent reports have stated that the lead of declining monetary growth over peak stock prices and economic conditions is sizeable (up to 12 months), but has shortened considerably in recent years.[10] Its lead over the corresponding troughs, however, is quite short and it too is possibly decreasing. As a result, leads of up to four quarters, as well as coincident data, are tested for the money supply series.

Recent studies have further documented the statistically significant influence that the money supply has on economic activity[11]—part of which is the failure rate experience of American business. These results, if valid, however, create new problems in our analysis, as well as providing a strong and predictable explanatory variable. Both the Anderson-Jordan and Keran studies emphasize that monetary influences have significant impact on economic activity over the business cycle. They utilize quarterly first difference regression techniques which are similar to the approach of this analysis. The problem lies in the fact that GNP and money supply will both be specified here as independent variables. Therefore, while a strong case is made for their potential individual effect on failures, it appears that the two are also significantly related to each other. This problem, referred to as statistical multicollinearity, is potentially serious because it can cloud the specific quantitative association between the dependable variable and each respective independent variable. Therefore, tests will be performed, in the next section, to determine the statistical interrelationships between our explanatory variables.

Dependent Variable(s)

The subsequent empirical study differs from prior works in several respects—some of which are noted above. In addition, the choice of our failure series is somewhat different. Instead of total failing businesses, we will concentrate primarily on the *failure rate* (Dun & Bradstreet's measure of failures per 10,000 listed concerns). The rate is a relative measure of failures and adjusts for other phenomena, e.g., the growth in the number of firms. (A regression which includes this economic variable—number of enterprises—is examined in the following section.) The failure rate is a directly observable statistic regardless of the time period we are concerned with and it is perhaps the best ex-post measure of the propensity of firms to fail. Regressions are also run with the failure liability series as our dependent variable. The latter measure is of interest due to its inclusion in the National Bureau's studies and because it is one of the few directly observable measures of failure costs.

Structure of the Model

The structure of our proposed model is a quarterly, first-difference, regression model covering observations from 1947-1970, inclusive. Quarterly data provide us with observations within the various business cycles, as well as the relatively few peaks and troughs experienced in the post-World War period. While the analysis of peak and trough relationships is extremely important, especially for government fiscal and monetary policy decisions, it does not provide us with the comprehensive investigation potential which is inherent in a more continuous time series analysis.

Since we are interested in the influence of various aggregate measures on changes in failure rates and failure liabilities, we have chosen a first difference format. The specific structure of the model is of the form:

$\triangle$ Failure Rate

or $\quad = \mathrm{f}\left(\triangle X_1, \triangle X_2, \triangle X_3, \ldots, \triangle X_n\right)$

$\triangle$ Failure Liabilities

Where

$$\begin{array}{c} \triangle \text{ Failure Rate} \\ \text{or} \\ \triangle \text{ Failure Liabilities} \end{array} = \begin{array}{l} \text{Quarterly change in Dun \& Bradstreet's Failure/} \\ \text{Rate or Failure Liabilities Series.} \end{array}$$

$\triangle X_1 - \triangle X_n = $ Quarterly change in Various Aggregate Economic Series.

This structure focuses on how changes in the independent variables affect the change in the dependent variable. Also note that we are interested in absolute changes in our variables, which is comparable to the National Bureau's analysis of changes in its economic indicators.

As noted earlier, we also include various lead and lag specifications for our independent variables. Guidelines for establishing these timing relationships are derived from historical empirical observations and judgment on the part of the author. For instance, the relevant variables, or closely associated ones, are listed in Table 2-1 with their median monthly lead time observations taken from the latest business cycle study.[12]

Table 2-1
Estimated Monthly Median Lead Times

(1)	Failure Liabilities	−7
(2)	GNP	0
(3)	S. & P. Index	−4
(4)	Money & Credit Flows	−9
(5)	Formation of Business Enterprises	−6
(6)	Corporate Profits	−5

Based on these *median* lead times, we might expect failure rates to be roughly coincident with (3), (5), and (6), slightly lagging to (4) and slightly leading to (2). Since the above guidelines are median results, covering peaks and troughs going back to the early 1900s, we can only view them as indicators and not exact specifications. In addition, the recent experience of the failure liabilities series has been unstable and makes consistent specification over the entire sample period (96 observations) somewhat difficult. In the empirical analysis, lags of up to four quarters and leads of up to two quarters will be examined.

Empirical Evidence

From the original list of potential explanatory variables, including various lead-lag combinations, the final specification for our *failure-rate* equation is of the form:

$$\triangle F.R. = a_0 + a_1 \triangle GNP_{t+1} + a_2 \triangle SP_t + a_3 \triangle MS_t + e$$

where,[13]

$\triangle F.R.$	=	Change in the Failure Rate in Quarter t.
$\triangle GNP_{t+1}$	=	Change in GNP in Quarter $t + 1$.
$\triangle SP_t$	=	Change in Standard & Poor Index of Common Stock Prices in Quarter t.
$\triangle MS_t$	=	Change in Money Supply in Quarter t.
e	=	Error term.

Failure-Rate Results

Statistical results for this equation and an almost identical one, substituting GNP_t for GNP_{t+1}, are presented in Table 2-2. The table also includes results for two subperiod regressions.

The parameters, a_1 (a_1'), a_2 and a_3 indicate the statistical effect of the various aggregate economic factors on the failure rate, and a_0 is a proxy for the trend of all other influences. Since failure rates were at their historical lows immediately after World War II, the remaining factor is not unexpectedly positive. The first subperiod regression (1947-1958) indicates a greater positive trend in other factor influences than in the second subperiod (1959-1970).[f] The overall standard error of estimate (2.70 compared to the intercept term, 1.83), however, indicates that the trend coefficient, a_0, is not statistically significant. Simply correlating failure rate with time during the 24-year period results in the equation,

---

[f]The subperiods, 1947-58 and 1959-70, are arbitrarily selected. Both consist of 12 years of data, 48 quarters, with the earlier period containing 3 minor economic recessions and the later period 2 recessions and one "minirecession."

Table 2-2
Failure-Rate Results

Equation: (Observations)	Constant Term (a_o)	Change GNP_{t+1} ($ billions) (a_1)	Change GNP ($ billions) (a_1')	Change SP_t (Index) (a_2)	Change MS_t ($ billions) (a_3)	Standard Error of Estimate	F Ratio	Adjusted R^2	D-W
I									
1947–1970 (96)	1.83	−0.137b (−2.41)		−0.128c (−1.64)	−0.598a (−2.56)	2.70	7.97a	.19	2.24
I′									
1947–1970 (96)	1.81		−0.126b (−2.40)	−0.165b (−1.96)	−0.623a (−2.69)	2.70	7.95a	.18	2.35
II									
1947–1958 (48)	1.93	−0.093c (−1.64)		−0.009 (−0.15)	−1.092a (−2.76)	2.15	5.30a	.22	2.24
II′									
1947–1958 (48)	1.94		−0.119b (−1.97)	−0.003 (−0.28)	−0.944b (−2.31)	2.11	5.96a	.24	2.22
III									
1959–1970 (48)	1.73	−0.183b (−1.97)		−0.149 (−1.42)	−0.415 (−1.31)	3.20	4.00b	.11	2.32
III′									
1959–1970 (48)	1.54		−0.122 (−1.53)	−0.190c (−1.74)	−0.495c (−1.64)	3.25	3.40b	.10	2.44

Table 2-2 contains regression coefficients for the independent variables with respective t values in parentheses; R^2 = percent variation in failure rates explained by independent variables—adjusted for degrees of freedom; F ratio = ratio of explained to unexplained variance adjusted for degrees of freedom; D-W = Durbin Watson Statistic.

[a]Significant at .01 level.
[b]Significant at .05 level.
[c]Significant at .10 level.

$$Y = 4.81 - 0.049 \text{ (time)} \quad R_2 = 0.001$$
$$(-0.37) \qquad \text{s.e.} = 36.1$$

giving further evidence to the lack of a significant trend in the American failure rate.

The overall empirical results, although not highly statistically impressive, are indeed revealing and for the most part conform with our *a priori* expectations. The R^2 of .19 indicates that a considerable proportion of the *change* in the *first differences* of failure rates is explained by *changes* in the independent variables examined. Keep in mind that we are dealing with first differences and we would expect our statistical explanatory power to suffer under this structure. In addition, we repeat that the failure of a business is basically a microeconomic phenomenon and in the above model we are examining those aggregate economic influences on failure situations.

An important result is that every sign of the independent variables in the equations of Table 2-1 conforms with expectations. That is, we observe that the change in failure rate is *inversely* associated with changes in GNP, stock prices, and money supply. The regression coefficients of equation I or I´are significant at the .01 or .05 level (with one exception), and the overall equation is significant at the .01 level (*f*-value). We do observe, however, that the stock price variable coefficient displays inconsistent amounts and significance in the two subperiod regressions. Although we still believe that stock price activity is negatively correlated with failures, we have little confidence in the long-run statistical regression coefficient. The major statistical problem with these two variables took place in the late 1940s and 1950s when both aggregate measures were adjusting to peace-time conditions. In recent years, we observe a more significant relationship.

A particularly interesting and somewhat surprising result concerns the timing specification of our independent variables. We examined various lead-lag relationships in order to determine the highest statistical correlation—on a multivariate basis—between the variables. Prior expectations were that changes in GNP would lag failure-rate changes, but that money supply changes would lead our dependent variable. Stock price changes were expected to be roughly coincident with failures. The results, however, show that the greatest statistical significance is achieved either when all of the variables are specified in a coincident pattern (all in the same quarter, equation I´) or when our GNP variable is specified in $t + 1$ (equation I). The latter specification illustrates failure-rate change leading GNP change by one quarter. Statistically, there is little to choose between equations I and I´, with the former slightly more significant on an overall basis, while the latter's independent variables, particularly the regression coefficient of MS_t, slightly more significant on an individual basis. As will be shown later in Table 2-4, the $\triangle GNP_{t+1}$ variable has a slightly greater negative relationship with failure-rate change than the $\triangle GNP_t$ variable (−0.36 to −0.32) and thus we choose to give equation I slightly more prominence. In addition, this specification is more in line with our prior expectations.

Although it is difficult to capture the exact lead-lag pattern when dealing with average relationships over a relatively long continuous time series study, we are nevertheless surprised by the predominant coincident end result. We conclude, therefore, that aggregate failure rates are negatively related on a roughly coincident basis with GNP, stock price and money supply movements.

Since the independent variables do not have the same measurement characteristics and equivalent dimension and variability magnitudes, further investigation is necessary to determine their relative explanatory contributions. Our GNP variable is a flow concept measuring changes in billions of dollars; the S & P data is a stock variable measuring changes in an index; the money supply is another stock variable showing changes in billions of dollars. Therefore, we adjust their respective regression coefficients and calculate beta coefficients, illustrated in Table 2-2. This table indicates that the most important explanatory variable is the change in money supply, followed closely by GNP and stock price change variables, respectively. The same rankings are indicated by the partial correlation coefficients, also noted in Table 2-3.

We are careful not to state explicitly that the independent variables are all direct causal mechanisms of business failure-rate experience. While it is firmly believed that aggregate economic activity, investor expectations and credit conditions are strongly associated with failure data, one must not forget that the de-facto failure status is largely a unique firm decision. Also, we cannot state with total certainty that our dependent variables do not in some way contribute to the value of our independent variable.[g] There appears, however, to be little reason to believe that the failure activity of marginal concerns affects aggregate economic growth and monetary policy and we can under normal circumstances, visualize a relatively small effect on investor expectations.[h]

Excluded Variables

As mentioned earlier, we examined several other variables including two that we expected to make a significant contribution toward explaining failure rates—corporate profits and our risk premium variable. The former, however, was overshadowed by the GNP variable, as discussed in the next section, and the latter (Baa - Aaa rates) showed statistically insignificant correlation with the failure series, although the sign of their association (positive) was as expected.

---

[g]This involves a critical condition which is necessary in a single equation approach. The regression coefficients are meaningful only if the independent variables are statistically and economically exogeneous and thereby not simultaneously determined by the failure activity of individual firms. If this assumption is not satisfied, the dual-causality argument against the single equation approach is valid and a simultaneous equation format is required.

[h]We have observed, however, that when large, publicly held firms which are listed on a major stock exchange fail, there can be very definite effects on the short-term market movements for all firms. In the Penn-Central case, the bankruptcy of a $5-billion firm had severe repercussions in the money markets as well as in the stock market (see Chapter 7). Failures of large, listed firms are relatively rare, however.

Table 2-3
Relative Importance of Individual Factors Affecting Failure Rates, 1947-1970

Independent Variable	Beta[1] Coefficient	Partial Correlation Coefficient[2]
	Equation I	
$\triangle GNP_{t+1}$	−0.246	−0.25
$\triangle SP_t$	−0.141	−0.15
$\triangle MS_t$	−0.251	−0.26
	Equation I '	
$\triangle GNP_t$	−0.215	−0.25
$\triangle SP_t$	−0.182	−0.20
$\triangle MS_t$	−0.218	−0.27

[1]Beta coefficients standardize the regression coefficients by multiplying each variable's regression coefficient by the standard deviation of the variable divided by the standard deviation of the dependent variable.
[2]Coefficient of partial correlation measures the correlation between the dependent variable and each of the several independent factors, while eliminating the effect of the remaining independent factors.

That is, as the interest rate differential increases, indicating greater required rates of return on more risky debt securities, the failure rate also increases. The regression including the risk-premium variable is:

$$\triangle F.R. = 1.6 - .11\ (\triangle GNP_t) - .14\ (\triangle SP_t) - .60\ (\triangle MS_t) + 4.1\ (\triangle Baa - Aaa)$$

$$(-2.06) \qquad (-1.63) \qquad (-2.63) \qquad (+1.26)$$
$$F = 6.32 \qquad R^2 = .183 \qquad\qquad\qquad D\text{-}W = 2.31$$

GNP vs. Corporate Profits

The inclusion of the GNP change variable was surprising in that it proved to be a more significant explanatory variable than the change in corporate profits. Prior studies have consistently emphasized the associate importance between corporate profits and failures.[14] Logically, conditions which lead to a change in corporate profits are also related to changes in failures, since a drop in profits to the marginal firm can often be critical to its existence. While similar reasoning can be applied to the association between overall economic activity and failures, it was initially felt that corporate profits would reflect this relationship more clearly. Yet, statistical results indicate that the more significant relationship is with GNP regardless of its timing. Table 2-4 illustrates this finding through simple correlation coefficient comparisons. The correlation coefficients for both GNP_t and GNP_{t+1} are considerably higher than the best corporate profit results. It is true that the studies by Zarnowitz and Lerner, and Anderson examined failure liabilities and not rates, but our conclusions seem to hold for liabilities as well. That is, the GNP series retain their higher correlation with the liability series. One possible explanation for the lower corporate profit correlation is that the profit series is dominated by large firms, which rarely fail, while the failure rate is affected by all firms, regardless of size, as well as unincorporated enterprises.

As mentioned earlier, we observe in Table 2-4 that $\triangle GNP_t + 1$ has a slightly greater inverse relationship to failure rate change and it is only because of the interactions with the other independent variables that we included both equation I and I'. The coincident pattern between failure rates and the other two independent variables, MS_t and SP_t, is clearly illustrated.

The correlation matrix for the three independent variables from equations I and I' is reproduced in Table 2-4. Recall that we cautioned about the collinearity problem especially between money supply (MS_t) and GNP (GNP_t) changes. The correlations do not, however, show any cause for alarm with the highest single correlation $(r = .31$ or $R^2 = .096)$ between MS_t and $GNP_t + 1$—considerably lower than prior studies had concluded.[i]

Table 2-4
Simple Correlation Coefficients between Failure Rates and Other Variables, 1947-1970

Dependent Variables	Independent Variables				
	Change GNP_t	Change GNP_{t+1}	Change GNP_{t+2}	Change GNP_{t+4}	
△ Failure Rate	−.32	−.36	−.19	.07	
△ Failure Liabilities	−.16	−.18	−.09	−.07	
	Change CP_t	Change CP_{t+1}	Change CP_{t+2}	Change CP_{t+4}	Change CP_{t-2}
△ Failure Rate	−.25	−.17	.00	.14	−.21
△ Failure Liabilities	−.14	−.08	−.06	−.02	−.16
	Change MS_t	Change MS_{t-1}	Change MS_{t-2}	Change MS_{t+1}	
△ Failure Rate	−.33	−.20	−.17	−.18	
	Change SP_t	Change SP_{t+1}	Change SP_{t+2}	Change SP_{t+4}	Change SP_{t-1}
△ Failure Rate	−.23	.03	.14	.17	−.21

CP   = Corporate Profits
Source = Correlation Matrix

---

[i]The statistical relationship between money supply and GNP changes was much higher in these two studies than it is in our experience; possibly this is because of the timing specification differences.

A Final Empirical Note on Failure Rates

During the early stages of this empirical investigation of aggregate influences on business failures, another independent variable was thought to have significant explanatory power—the *number* of enterprises in the economic system. The theoretical relationship between rates of business failures and the size of our system is not obvious. One might hypothesize that as the nation's economic growth increases, the number of enterprises will also increase due to optimistic expectations. Many of these new firms may be of a marginal nature and susceptible to early failure. Statistics indicate that approximately one-third of all firms which fail do so in the first three years of their existence, but that only about two percent fail in the first year. In order to explore the potential influence of the number of enterprises on failure rates, we included this variable with the aforementioned set of independent variables with the following result,

$$\triangle F.R. = 1.8 - .14 \, (\triangle GNP_t + 1) - .13 \, (\triangle SP_t) - .65 \, (\triangle NS_t) + .18 \, (\triangle NE_t)$$

$$(-2.84) \qquad (-1.65) \quad (-2.71) \qquad (+5.76)$$

$$R^2 = .417$$

With $\triangle NE_t$ = Change in the number of enterprises in quarter t.
T-values are in parentheses.

The overall results are indeed much improved over those reported in Table 2-2, but the validity of the model is open to serious question. The primary reason for this is that the failure *rate* already adjusts for the size of the economic system by its amount *per 10,000 listed concerns*. The extremely high

Table 2-5
Correlation Coefficient Matrix - Equations I and I ' (Table 2-2)

Equation I		$\triangle GNP_{t+1}$	$\triangle SP_t$	$\triangle MS_t$
	$\triangle GNP_{t+1}$	1.00	0.28	0.31
	$\triangle SP_t$		1.00	0.07
	$\triangle MS_t$			1.00
Equation I '		$\triangle GNP_t$	$\triangle SP_t$	$\triangle MS_t$
	$\triangle GNP_t$	1.00	0.12	0.26
	$\triangle SP_t$		1.00	0.07
	$\triangle MS_t$			1.00

significance of NE_t is quite probably a statistical artifact to a significant degree, and subject to considerable question. Therefore, we do not include it in our primary equation (Table 2-2), but we thought it important enough to present these results parenthetically.

Failure Liability Results

Compared to the failure-rate results, the statistical findings of the failure liability regressions are less impressive. Results for several liability regressions are illustrated in Table 2-6. The liability series was tested using both absolute dollars and liabilities adjusted for price level changes (GNP deflator). Results were essentially identical. Equation IV contains the same variables as the primary failure-*rate* equation (Table 2-2). Although the overall regression is barely significant, we note that only the stock price variable $(\triangle SP_t)$, and to an extent the $\triangle GNP$ variable, is individually significant. The signs of each independent variable, however, do conform to prior expectations. Therefore, it is observed that the change in failure liabilities is inversely associated with roughly coincident changes in GNP, stock price, and the money supply. A second specification (equation V) includes the number of enterprises variable (NE_t) and increases the overall significance slightly. Therefore, we observe that the number of enterprises is *positively* associated with failure liability changes and conforms to expectations. That is to say, as the sheer size of our economic system grows, we expect that the number of failures and failure liabilities will increase also, *ceteris paribus*. Since failure liability data are in absolute dollars, we do not encounter the aforementioned statistical problem relating to the number of enterprises variable (NE_t) as we did in the failure-rate analysis. One further interesting implication related to the failure liability empirical results is the lack of explanatory importance of the money supply variable.

One of the costs to society resulting from business failures is the loss to creditors of all or part of the debtor's outstanding liabilities. Based on the earlier failure-rate results, we might conclude that a tight monetary policy and the consequent reduction in the money supply is a contributory factor to this social cost. We *cannot*, however, reach this conclusion based upon the empirical findings. The money supply variable is insignificant by itself and, in fact, if we exclude this variable from Equation V, we observe results shown in Equation VI. Not only is the partial r of MS_t nil, but the overall R^2 increases along with the F ratio when we exclude the money supply variable. A reason which might explain this occurrence relates back to the discriminatory nature of tight money against small, marginal firms and the nature of this new dependent variable—failure liabilities. That is to say, the failure liability series is dominated by the relatively small number of large firms that fail.[j] Since there is some evidence that tight money affects the small firm more severely than the larger, the effect of changes

[j]For example, the average firm failure liability in 1969 was slightly over $100,000, yet only 21 percent of all failures had liabilities in excess of $100,000.[15]

Table 2-6
Failure Liability Model, 1947–1970

Equations: (Observations)	($ Thousands) (S.E.)*	($ Billions) ΔGNP_{t+1}	(Index) ΔSP_t	($ Billions) ΔMS_t	(000 Firms) ΔNE_t	F Ratio	Adjusted R^2	D-W
–IV–								
1947–1970	11.14	−0.916[c]	−2.552[b]	−2.194		4.49[a]	0.10	2.82
(96)	(34.12)*	(−1.76)	(−2.24)	(−0.75)				
–V–								
1947–1970	10.53	−0.663	−3.470[a]	−1.870	0.070[c]	3.70[b]	0.11	2.84
(96)	(32.42)*	(−1.26)	(−2.74)	(−0.53)	(1.68)			
–VI–								
1947–1970	9.80	−0.824	−3.695		0.071	4.88[a]	0.12	2.83
(96)	(29.40)*	(−1.44)	(−3.11)[a]		(1.74)[c]			

Table 2-6 contains the regression coefficients for the independent variables with respective t values in parentheses.

R^2 = Percent Variation in failure rates explained by independent variables – adjusted for degrees of freedom.

F ratio - Ratio of explained to unexplained variance adjusted for degrees of freedom.

D-W - Durbin Watson Statistic.

[a]Significant at .01 level.
[b]Significant at .05 level.
[c]Significant at .10 level.
*S.E. = Standard error of estimate.

in monetary policy possibly will not show up in the liability data. This lack of monetary influence on liability data is consistent nonetheless with its significant effect on changes in the failure rate.

Summary and Implications

The purpose of this analysis was to examine the influence of aggregate economic factors on business failure experience. The post-World War II period was chosen as our sample period. Findings indicate that a firm's propensity to fail is heightened during periods of reduced economic growth, stock market performance and money supply conditions. Failure rate changes tend to lead changes in aggregate GNP performance (but just slightly), indicating that the rate of failures may have some utility as a leading indicator. We also observe the roughly coincident pattern of change between failure rates and two other aggregate series—stock prices and money supply.

Similar regression models examining aggregate influences on failure liabilities proved to be less significant. Failure liabilities appear to be inversely related to economic growth and common stock activity and positively related to firm population. These associations, however, were not very consistent nor significant. Money supply changes were not found to influence failure liabilities. This is attributed to the fact that failure liability data are dominated by large firms, but credit condition changes have their major impact on small, marginal firms. Future research in this area might be more revealing if the failure liability series was stratified as to various firm sizes and the economic influences could be examined against a more discrete classification of firms. Presently, aggregate numbers and percents of total failures by size are available but not in adequate form for meaningful analysis. Overall, we have found little evidence to classify business failure liabilities as a leading economic indicator. It should be noted, however, that the primary purpose of this analysis was not an economic indicator investigation.

In both the failure rate and failure liability regressions, the change in GNP performance was more closely associated with failures than the seemingly more direct aggregate economic variable—corporate profit changes. Since GNP totals contain many diverse economic ingredients, as well as corporate related figures, the answer to this occurrence lies in the makeup of GNP data. Based on the findings, we question the use of overall corporate profit data as the most important link with the failure experience of business entities in the United States.

Finally, we make two suggestions which derive from this study. The first concerns microeconomic policy decisions. If a firm finds its existence in a tenuous state and the aggregate economic conditions indicate increased failure pressures, then drastic preventive measures should be implemented—if possible and if deemed desirable. For instance, the alternative to eventual failure and perhaps liquidation may be to seek a merger with a sound company or perhaps to declare bankruptcy and reorganize under the National Bankruptcy Act. The latter decision, if made early enough, may salvage whatever economic worth is left in the firm's assets. Second, the results of this study highlight the potential to combine selected aggregate economic variables with the unique micro-economic characteristics of specific firms in order to more efficiently explain and predict individual business failures. The results of such analysis have obvious relevance to external credit allocation as well as to internal management considerations. The purpose of the next chapter will be to examine a procedure to predict corporate bankruptcy utilizing microdata only.

3

Predicting Corporate Bankruptcy

At this point, the emphasis of the book shifts to the individual companies which have become business failures and comprise the aggregate list of failures studied earlier. Although we have shown that aggregate economic conditions, exogenous to the individual firm, may contribute to its eventual failure, it should be made clear that in almost all cases, the fault lies within the confines of the firm itself. The purposes of this chapter are twofold. First, those unique characteristics of business failures are examined in order to specify and quantify the variables which are effective indicators and/or predictors of corporate bankruptcy. By doing so, we also hope to highlight the analytic as well as the practical value inherent in the use of financial ratios. Specifically, a set of financial and economic ratios will be investigated in a bankruptcy prediction context wherein a multiple discriminant statistical methodology is employed.[1] Through this exercise, we will explore not only the quantifiable characteristics of potential bankrupts but also the utility of a much maligned technique of financial analysis—ratio analysis.

Academicians seem to be moving toward the elimination of ratio analysis as an analytical technique in assessing the performance of the business enterprise. Theorists downgrade arbitrary rules of thumb (such as company ratio comparisons) widely used by practitioners. Since attacks on the relevance of ratio analysis emanate from many esteemed members of the scholarly world, does this mean that ratio analysis is limited to the world of "nuts and bolts"? Or, has the significance of such an approach been unattractively garbed and therefore unfairly handicapped? Can we bridge the gap, rather than sever the link, between traditional ratio analysis and the more rigorous statistical techniques which have become popular among academicians in recent years? Along with our primary interest, corporate bankruptcy, we also will be concerned with an assessment of ratio analysis as an analytical technique.

First, a brief review of the development of traditional ratio analysis as a technique for investigating corporate performance is presented. Following this review, criticism of the traditional utility of ratios is discussed and a different statistical technique called multiple discriminant analysis (MDA) is introduced. The emphasis will be on the compatibility of ratio analysis and this more modern statistical technique (MDA); together it will be shown that they can be an extremely efficient predictor of corporate bankruptcy. After the various techniques are explained, the chapter's content will center on a discriminant model whereby an initial sample of sixty-six manufacturing firms is utilized to establish a criterion which discriminates between companies in two mutually exclusive groups: bankrupt and nonbankrupt firms. Finally, we examine the model's predictive ability on several completely different holdout samples of companies and illustrate how the technique can be utilized without the continual use of an electronic computer.

Traditional Ratio Analysis

The detection of company operating and financial difficulties is a subject which has been particularly susceptible to financial ratio analysis. Prior to the development of quantitative measures of company performance, agencies were established to supply a qualitative type of information assessing the credit-worthiness of particular merchants.[2] (For instance, the forerunner of well-known Dun & Bradstreet, Inc. was organized in 1849 in Cincinnati, Ohio, in order to provide independent credit investigations.) Formal aggregate studies concerned with portents of business failure were evident in the 1930s. A study at that time[3] and several later ones concluded that failing firms exhibit significantly different ratio measurements than continuing entities.[4] In addition, another study was concerned with ratios of large asset-size corporations that experienced difficulties in meeting their fixed indebtedness obligations.[5] A recent study involved the analysis of financial ratios in a bankruptcy-prediction context.[6] This latter work compared a list of ratios individually for failed firms and a matched sample of nonfailed firms. Observed evidence for five years prior to failure was cited as conclusive that ratio analysis can be useful in the prediction of failure.

The aforementioned studies imply a definite potential of ratios as predictors of bankruptcy. In general, ratios measuring profitability, liquidity, and solvency prevailed as the most significant indicators. The order of their importance is not clear since almost every study cited a different ratio as being the most effective indication of impending problems.

The previous discussion cited several studies devoted to the analysis of a firm's condition prior to financial difficulties. Although these works established certain important generalizations regarding the performance and trends of particular measurements, the adaptation of their results for assessing bankruptcy potential of firms, both theoretically and practically, is questionable. (At this point, we use bankruptcy in its most general sense, meaning simply business failure.) In almost every case, the methodology was essentially univariate in nature and emphasis was placed on individual signals of impending problems.[7] Ratio analysis presented in this fashion is susceptible to faulty interpretation and is potentially confusing. For instance, a firm with a poor profitability and/or solvency record may be regarded as a potential bankrupt. However, because of its above average liquidity, the situation may not be considered serious. The potential ambiguity as to the relative performance of several firms is clearly evident. The crux of the shortcomings inherent in any univariate analysis lies therein. An appropriate extension of the previously cited studies, therefore, is to build upon their findings and to combine several measures into a meaningful predictive model. In so doing, the highlights of ratio analysis as an analytical technique will be emphasized rather than downgraded. The question becomes, which ratios are most important in detecting bankruptcy potential, what weights should be attached to those selected ratios, and how should the weights be objectively established.

Multiple Discriminant Analysis

After careful consideration of the nature of the problem and of the purpose of this analysis, we chose a multiple discriminant analysis (MDA) as the appropriate statistical technique. Although not as popular as regression analysis, MDA has been utilized in a variety of disciplines since its first application in the 1930s.[8] During those earlier years, MDA was used mainly in the biological and behavioral sciences.[9] In the last few years, this new technique has become increasingly popular in the practical business world as well as in academia. Recently, this method has been applied successfully to financial problems such as consumer credit evaluation[10] and investment classification. For instance in the latter area, Walter utilized an MDA model to classify high and low price earnings ratio firms,[11] and Smith applied the technique in the classification of firms into standard investment categories.[12] Of primary relevance to the subject of this book is the study by Pifer and Meyer whereby financial ratios of various statistical forms were utilized within a framework similar to MDA in order to predict commercial bank failures.[13]

MDA is a statistical technique used to classify an observation into one of several *a priori* groupings dependent upon the observation's individual characteristics. It is used primarily to classify and/or make predictions in problems where the dependent variable appears in qualitative form, e.g., male or female, bankrupt or nonbankrupt. Therefore, the first step is to establish explicit group classifications. The number of original groups can be two or more.

After the groups are established, data are collected for the objects in the groups; MDA then attempts to derive a linear combination of these characteristics which "best" discriminates between the groups. If a particular object, for instance, a corporation, has characteristics (financial ratios) which can be quantified for all of the companies in the analysis, the MDA determines a set of discriminant coefficients. When these coefficients are applied to the actual ratio, a basis for classification into one of the mutually exclusive groupings exists. The MDA technique has the advantage of considering an entire profile of characteristics common to the relevant firms, as well as the interaction of these properties. A univariate study, on the other hand, can only consider the measurements used for group assignments one at a time.

Another advantage of MDA is the reduction of the analyst's space dimensionality, i.e., from the number of different independent variables to $G - 1$ dimension(s), where G equals the number of original *a priori* groups.[14] This analysis is concerned with two groups, consisting of bankrupt firms on the one hand, and of nonbankrupt firms on the other. Therefore, the analysis is transformed into its simplest form: one dimension. The discriminant function of the form $Z = v_1 x_1 + v_2 x_2 + \ldots + v_n x_n$ transforms the individual variable values to a single discriminant score or Z value which is then used to classify the object

where,
$v_1, v_2, \ldots, v_n$ = Discriminant coefficients
$x_1, x_2, \ldots, x_n$ = Independent variables

The MDA computes the discriminant coefficients, v_j while the independent variables x_j are the actual values

where,
$j = 1, 2, \ldots, n.$

When utilizing a comprehensive list of financial ratios in assessing a firm's bankruptcy potential, there is reason to believe that some of the measurements will have a high degree of correlation or collinearity with each other. While this aspect necessitates careful selection of the predictive variables (ratios), it also has the advantage of yielding a model with a relatively small number of selected measurements which has the potential of conveying a great deal of information. This information might very well indicate differences between groups, but whether or not these differences are significant and meaningful is a more important aspect of the analysis. To be sure, there are differences between bankrupt firms and healthy ones; but are these differences of a magnitude to facilitate the development of an accurate prediction model?

Perhaps the primary advantage of MDA in dealing with classification problems is the potential of analyzing the entire variable profile of the object simultaneously rather than sequentially examining its individual characteristics. Just as linear and integer programming have improved upon traditional techniques in capital budgeting, the MDA approach to traditional ratio analysis has the potential to reformulate the problem correctly. Specifically, combinations of ratios can be analyzed together in order to remove possible ambiguities and misclassifications observed in earlier traditional studies.

Development of the Model

Sample Selection

The initial sample is composed of sixty-six corporations with thirty-three firms in each of the two groups. The bankrupt group (1) are manufacturers that filed a bankruptcy petition under Chapter X of the National Bankruptcy Act during the period 1946-1965.[a] The mean asset size of these firms is $6.4 million, with a range of between $0.7 million and $25.9 million. Recognizing that this group is not completely homogeneous (due to industry and size differences), we attempted to make a careful selection of nonbankrupt firms. Group 2 consisted of a paired sample of manufacturing firms chosen on a stratified random basis. The firms are stratified by industry and by size, with the asset size range restricted to between $1–$25 million.[b] Firms in Group 2 were still in existence in 1966. Also, the data collected are from the same years as those compiled for the bankrupt firms. For the initial sample test, the data are derived from financial statements dated one annual reporting period prior to bankruptcy.[c]

An important issue is to determine the asset-size group to be sampled. The decision to eliminate both the small firms (under $1 million in total assets) and the very large companies from the initial sample essentially is due to the asset range of the firms in Group 1. In addition, the incidence of bankruptcy in the large asset-size firm is quite rare today, while the absence of comprehensive data negated the representation of small firms. A frequent argument is that financial ratios, by their very nature, have the effect of deflating statistics by size, and that therefore a good deal of the size effect is eliminated. To choose Group 1 firms in a restricted size range is not feasible, while selecting firms for Group 2 at random seemed unwise. However, tests performed subsequent to the original sample do not use size as a means of stratification.[d]

Variable Selection

After the initial groups are defined and firms selected, balance sheet and income statement data are collected. Because of the large number of variables found to be significant indicators of corporate problems in past studies, a list of twenty-two potentially helpful variables (ratios) is compiled for evaluation. The variables are classified into five standard ratio categories, including liquidity, profitability, leverage, solvency and activity ratios. The ratios are chosen on the

[a]The choice of a twenty-year period is not the best procedure since average ratios do shift over time. Ideally, we would prefer to examine a list of ratios in time period t in order to make predictions about other firms in the following period ($t + 1$). Unfortunately, it was not possible to do this because of data limitations. However, the number of bankruptcies was approximately evenly distributed over the twenty-year period for both the original and the secondary samples.

[b]The mean asset size of the firms in Group 2 ($9.6 million) was slightly greater than that of Group 1, but matching exact asset size of the two groups seemed unnecessary.

[c]The data were derived from Moody's Industrial Manuals and selected Annual Reports. The average lead time of the financial statements was approximately seven and one-half months prior to bankruptcy.

[d]One of these tests included only firms that experienced operating losses (secondary sample of nonbankrupt firms).

basis of their (1) popularity in the literature;[e] (2) potential relevancy to the study; and (3) a few "new" ratios initiated in this analysis.

From the original list of twenty-two variables, five variables are selected as doing the best overall job together in the prediction of corporate bankruptcy.[f] This profile did not contain the most significant variables measured independently. This would not necessarily improve upon the univariate, traditional analysis described earlier. The contribution of the entire profile is evaluated, and since this process is essentially iterative, there is no claim regarding the optimality of the resulting discriminant function. The function, however, does the best job among the alternatives which include numerous computer runs analyzing different ratio-profiles.

In order to arrive at a final profile of variables, the following procedures are utilized: (1) Observation of the statistical significance of various alternative functions including determination of the relative contributions of each independent variable; (2) evaluation of intercorrelations between the relevant variables; (3) observation of the predictive accuracy of the various profiles; and (4) judgment of the analyst.

The final discriminant function is as follows:

$$\text{(I)} \quad Z = .012X_1 + .014X_2 + .033X_3 + .006X_4 + .999X_5$$

where,

X_1 = Working Capital/Total Assets
X_2 = Retained Earnings/Total Assets
X_3 = Earnings before Interest and Taxes/Total Assets
X_4 = Market Value Equity/Book Value of Total Debt
X_5 = Sales/Total Assets
Z = Overall Index

X_1 —**Working Capital/Total Assets**. The Working Capital/Total assets ratio, frequently found in studies of corporate problems, is a measure of the net liquid assets of the firm relative to the total capitalization. Working capital is defined as the difference between current assets and current liabilities. Liquidity and size characteristics are explicitly considered. Ordinarily, a firm experiencing consistent operating losses will have shrinking current assets in relation to total assets. Of the three liquidity ratios evaluated, this one proved to be the most valuable.[g]

---

[e]The first Beaver study concluded that the cash flow to debt ratio was the best single ratio predictor. The ratio was not considered here because of the lack of consistent appearance of precise depreciation data. The results obtained, however, are superior to the results Beaver attained with his single best ratio.[15]

[f]The MDA computer program used in this study was developed by W. Cooley and P. Lohnes. The data are organized in blocked format; the bankrupt firms' data first followed by the nonbankrupt firms'.

[g]Two other liquidity ratios were the current ratio and the quick ratio. The Working Capital/Total Assets ratio showed greater statistical significance both on a univariate and multivariate basis.

Inclusion of this variable is consistent with the Merwin study which rated the net working capital to total asset ratio as the best indicator of ultimate discontinuance.[16]

X_2 –**Retained Earnings/Total Assets.**[h] This measure of cumulative profitability over time was cited earlier as one of the "new" ratios. The age of a firm is implicitly considered in this ratio. For example, a relatively young firm will probably show a low RE/TA ratio because it has not had time to build up its cumulative profits. Therefore, it may be argued that the young firm is somewhat discriminated against in this analysis, and its chance of being classified as bankrupt is relatively higher than another, older firm, *ceteris paribus*. But, this is precisely the situation in the real world. The incidence of failure is much higher in a firm's earlier years.[17]

X_3 –**Earnings before Interest and Taxes/Total Assets.** This ratio is calculated by dividing the total assets of a firm into its earnings before interest and tax reductions. In essence, it is a measure of the true productivity of the firm's assets, abstracting from any tax or leverage factors. Since a firm's ultimate existence is based on the earning power of its assets, this ratio appears to be particularly appropriate for studies dealing with corporate failure. Furthermore, insolvency in a bankruptcy sense occurs when the total liabilities exceed a fair valuation of the firm's assets with value determined by the earning power of the assets.

X_4 –**Market Value of Equity/Book Value of Total Debt.** Equity is measured by the combined market value of all shares of stock, preferred and common, while debt includes both current and long term. The measure shows how much the firm's assets can decline in value (measured by market value of equity plus debt) before the liabilities exceed the assets and the firm becomes insolvent. For example, a company with a market value of its equity of $1,000 and debt of $500 could experience a two-thirds drop in asset value before insolvency. However, the same firm with $250 in equity will be insolvent if assets drop only one-third in value. This ratio adds a market value dimension which other failure studies did not consider.[i] It also appears to be a more effective predictor of bankruptcy than a similar, more commonly used ratio: Net Worth/Total Debt (book values).

---

[h]Retained earnings is the account which reports the total amount of reinvested earnings and/or losses of a firm over its entire life. The account is also referred to as earned surplus. It should be noted that the Retained Earnings account is subject to manipulation via corporate quasireorganizations and stock dividend declarations. While these occurrences are not evident in this study, it is conceivable that a bias would be created by a substantial reorganization or stock dividend.

[i]The reciprocal of X_4 is the familiar Debt/Equity ratio often used as a measure of financial leverage. X_4 is a slightly modified version of one of the variables used effectively by Fisher in a study of corporate bond interest rate differentials.[18]

X_5 –**Sales/Total Assets.** The capital-turnover ratio is a standard financial ratio illustrating the sales generating ability of the firm's assets. It is one measure of management's capacity in dealing with competitive conditions. This final ratio is quite important because, as indicated below, it is the least significant ratio on an individual basis. In fact, based on the statistical significance measure, it would not have appeared at all. However, because of its unique relationship to other variables in the model, the Sales/Total Assets ratio ranks second in its contribution to the overall discriminating ability of the model.

A Clarification

The reader is cautioned to utilize the model in the appropriate manner. Due to the original computer formatting arrangement, variables X_1 through X_4 must be calculated as absolute percentage values. For instance, the firm whose net working capital to total assets (X_1) is ten percent should be included as 10.0% and not .10. Only variable X_5 (sales to total assets) should be expressed in a different manner, i.e., a S/TA ratio of 200% should be included as 2.0. The practical analyst may have been concerned by the extremely high relative discriminant coefficient of X_5. This seeming irregularity is solely due to the format of the different variables. Table 3-1 illustrates the proper specification and form for each of the five independent variables.

To test the individual discriminating ability of the variables, an "F" test is performed. This test relates the difference between the average values of the ratios in each group to the variability (or spread) of values of the ratios within each group. Variable means measured at one financial statement prior to bankruptcy and the resulting "F" statistics are presented in Table 3-1.

Variables X_1 through X_4 are all significant at the .001 level, indicating extremely significant differences in these variables between groups. Variable X_5 does not show a significant difference between groups and the reason for its inclusion in the variable profile is not apparent as yet. On a strictly univariate level, all of the ratios indicate higher values for the nonbankrupt firms. Also, the discriminant coefficients of Equation I display positive signs, which is what one would expect. Therefore, the greater a firm's bankruptcy potential, the lower its discriminant score.

One useful technique in arriving at the final variable profile is to determine the relative contribution of each variable to the total discriminating power of the function. The relevant statistic is observed as a scaled vector. Since the actual variable measurement units are not all comparable to each other, simple observation of the discriminant coefficients is misleading. The adjusted coefficients shown in Table 3-2 enable us to evaluate each variable's contribution on a relative basis.

The scaled vectors indicate that the large contributors to group separation of the discriminant function are X_3, X_5, and X_4, respectively. The profitability ratio contributes the most, which is not surprising if one considers that the incidence of bankruptcy in a firm that is earning a profit is almost nil. What is surprising, however, is the second highest contribution of X_5 (Sales/Total Assets). Recall that this ratio was insignificant on a univariate basis; the multivariate context is responsible for illuminating the importance of X_5.[19] A probable reason for this unexpected result is the high negative correlation $(-.78)$ we observe between X_3 and X_5 in the bankruptcy group. The negative correlation is also evident in subsequent bankrupt group samples.

In a recent evaluation of the discriminant function, Cochran concluded that most correlations between variables in past studies were positive and that, by and large, negative correlations are more helpful than positive correlations in adding new information to the function.[20] The logic behind the high negative correlation in the bankrupt group is that as firms suffer losses and deteriorate toward failure, their assets are not replaced as much as they were in healthier times. Also, the cumulative losses have further reduced the asset size through debits to Retained Earnings. The asset-size reduction apparently dominates any sales movements.

Table 3-1
Variable Means and Test of Significance

Variable	Bankrupt Group Mean	Nonbankrupt Group Mean	F Ratio
	n = 33	n = 33	
X_1	$-\ 6.1\%$	41.4%	32.60*
X_2	-62.6%	35.5%	58.86*
X_3	-31.8%	15.4%	26.56*
X_4	40.1%	247.7%	33.26*
X_5	1.5%	1.9%	2.84

*Significant at the .001 level.

$$F_{1,60}\ (.001) = 12.00$$
$$F_{1,60}\ (.01)\ =\ 7.00$$
$$F_{1,60}\ (.05)\ =\ 4.00$$

Table 3-2
Relative Contribution of the Variables

Variable	Scaled Vector	Ranking
X_1	3.29	5
X_2	6.04	4
X_3	9.89	1
X_4	7.42	3
X_5	8.41	2

A different argument, but one not necessarily inconsistent with the above, concerns a similar ratio to X_5 —Net Sales to Tangible Net Worth. If the latter ratio is excessive, the firm is often referred to as a poor credit risk due to insufficient capital to support sales. Companies with moderate or even below average sales generating power (i.e., low asset turnover, X_5) might very well possess an extremely high Net Sales/Net Worth ratio if the Net Worth has been reduced substantially due to cumulative operating losses. This ratio, and other net worth ratios, are not considered here because of computational and interpretive difficulties arising when negative net worth totals are present.

It is clear that four of the five variables display significant differences between groups, but the importance of MDA is its ability to separate groups using multivariate measures. A test to determine the overall discriminating power of the model is the common F-value which is the ratio of the sums-of-squares between-groups to the within-groups sums-of-squares. When this ratio is maximized, it has the effect of spreading the means (centroids) of the groups apart and, simultaneously, reducing dispersion of the individual points (firm Z values) about their respective group means. Logically, this test (commonly called the "F" test) is appropriate because one of the objectives of the MDA is to identify and to utilize those variables which best discriminate *between* groups and which are most similar *within* groups.

The group means, or centroids, of the original two-group sample are

$$\text{Group } 1 = -0.29 \qquad F = 20.7$$
$$\text{Group } 2 = +5.02 \qquad F_{5,60}(.01) = 3.84$$

The significance test therefore *rejects* the null hypothesis that the observations come from the same population. With the conclusion that *a priori* groups are significantly different, further discriminatory analysis is possible.

Once the values of the discriminant coefficients are estimated, it is possible to calculate discriminant scores for each observation in the sample, or any firm, and to assign the observations to one of the groups based on this score. The essence of the procedure is to compare the profile of an individual firm with that of the alternative groupings. The comparisons are measured by a chi-square value and assignments are made upon the relative proximity of the firm's score to the various group centroids.

Empirical Results

At the outset, it might be helpful to illustrate the format for presenting the results. In the multigroup case, results are shown in a classification chart or accuracy-matrix. Table 3-3 shows how the chart is set up.

The actual group membership is equivalent to the *a priori* groupings and the model attempts to classify these firms correctly. At this stage, the model is basically explanatory. When new companies are classified, the nature of the model is predictive.

Table 3-3
Classification Results Format

	Predicted Group Membership	
Actual Group Membership	Bankrupt	Nonbankrupt
Bankrupt	H	M_1
Nonbankrupt	M_2	H

The Hs stand for correct classifications (Hits) and the Ms stand for misclassifications (Misses). M_1 represents a Type I error and M_2 a Type II error. The sum of the diagonal elements equals the total correct "hits," and when divided into the total number of firms classified (sixty-six in the case of the initial sample), yields the measure of success of the MDA in classifying firms, that is, the percent of firms correctly classified.

The final criterion used to establish the best model was to observe its accuracy in predicting bankruptcy. A series of six tests was performed.

(1) Initial Sample (Group 1)

The initial sample of 33 firms in each of the two groups is examined using data compiled one financial statement prior to bankruptcy. Since the discriminant coefficients and the group distributions are derived from this sample, a high degree of successful classification is expected. This should occur because the firms are classified using a discriminant function which, in fact, is based upon the individual measurements of these same firms. The classification matrix for the original sample is shown in Table 3-4.

The model is extremely accurate in classifying 95 percent of the total sample correctly. The *Type I error* proved to be only 6 percent, while the *Type II error* was even better at 3 percent. The results, therefore, are encouraging, but the obvious upward bias should be kept in mind and further validation techniques are appropriate.

Table 3-4
Classification Results, Original Sample

						Predicted	
					Actual	Group 1	Group 2
					Group 1	31	2
					Group 2	1	32
	Number Correct	Percent Correct	Percent Error	n			
Type I	31	94	6	33			
Type II	32	97	3	33			
Total	63	95	5	66			

(2) Results Two Statements prior to Bankruptcy

The second test is made to observe the discriminating ability of the model for firms using data compiled two statements prior to bankruptcy. The two-year period is an exaggeration since the average lead time for the correctly classified firms is approximately twenty months, with two firms having a thirteen month lead. The results are shown in Table 3-5. The reduction in accuracy is understandable because impending bankruptcy is more remote and the indications are less clear. Nevertheless, 72 percent correct assignment is evidence that bankruptcy can be predicted two years prior to the event. The Type II error is slightly larger (6 percent vs. 3 percent) in this test, but still it is extremely accurate. Further tests will be applied below to determine the accuracy of predicting bankruptcy as much as five years prior to the actual event.

(3) Potential Bias and Validation Techniques

When the firms used to determine the discriminant coefficients are reclassified, the resulting accuracy is biased upward by (a) sampling errors in the original sample; and (b) search bias. The latter bias is inherent in the process of reducing the original set of variables (twenty-two) to the best variable profile (five). The possibility of bias due to intensive searching is inherent in any empirical study. While a subset of variables is effective in the initial sample, there is no guarantee that it will be effective for the population in general.

The importance of secondary sample testing cannot be overemphasized and it appears appropriate to apply these measures at this stage. A method suggested by Frank et al.[21] for testing the extent of the aforementioned search bias was applied to the initial sample. The essence of this test is to estimate parameters for the model using only a subset of the original sample, and then to classify the remainder of the sample based on the parameters established. A simple t-test is

Table 3-5
Classification Results, Two Statements Prior to Bankruptcy

					Predicted	
				Actual	Group 1 (Bankrupt)	Group 2 (Nonbankrupt)
				Group 1	23	9
				Group 2	2	31
	Number Correct	Percent Correct	Percent Error	n		
Type I	23	72	28	32		
Type II	31	94	6	33		
Total	54	83	17	65		

then applied to test the significance of the results. Five different replications of the suggested method of choosing subsets (sixteen firms) of the original sample are tested, with results listed in Table 3-6. (The five replications include: (1) random sampling; (2) choosing every other firm starting with firm number one; (3) starting with firm number two; (4) choosing firms 1-16; and (5) firms 17-32.)

The test results reject the hypothesis that there is no difference between the groups and substantiate that the model does, in fact, possess discriminating power on observations other than those used to establish the parameters of the model. Therefore, any search bias does not appear significant.

(4) Secondary Sample of Bankrupt Firms

In order to test the model rigorously for both bankrupt and nonbankrupt firms, two new samples are introduced. The first contains a new sample of twenty-five bankrupt firms whose asset-size range is the same as that of the initial bankrupt group. On the basis of the parameters established in the discriminant model to classify firms in this secondary sample, the predictive accuracy for this sample as of one statement prior to bankruptcy is described in Table 3-7.

The results here are surprising in that one would not usually expect a secondary sample's results to be superior to the initial discriminant sample (96 percent vs. 94 percent). Two possible reasons are that the upward bias normally present in the initial sample tests is not manifested in this investigation, and/or the model, as stated before, is something less than optimal.

Table 3-6
Accuracy of Classifying a Secondary Sample

Replication	Percent of Correct Classifications	Value of t
1	91.2	4.8*
2	91.2	4.8*
3	97.0	5.5*
4	97.0	4.5*
5	91.2	4.8*
Average	93.5	5.1*

Total number of observations per replication (n) 34

*Significant at the .001 level.

$$t = \frac{\text{proportion correct} - .5}{\sqrt{\frac{.5(1-5)}{n}}}$$

(5) Secondary Sample of Nonbankrupt Firms

Up to this point, the sample companies were chosen either by their bankruptcy status (Group 1) or by their similarity to Group 1 in all aspects except their economic well-being. But what of the many firms which suffer temporary profitability difficulties, but in actuality do not become bankrupt. A bankruptcy

Table 3-7
Classification Results, Secondary Sample of Bankrupt Firms

			Predicted	
			Bankrupt	Nonbankrupt
		Bankrupt Group (Actual)	24	1
	Number Correct	Percent Correct	Percent Error	n
Type I (Total)	24	96	4	25

classification of a firm from this group is an example of a *Type II error*. An exceptionally rigorous test of the discriminant model's effectiveness would be to search out a large sample of firms that have encountered earnings problems and then to observe the MDA's classification results.

In order to perform the above test, a sample of sixty-six firms is selected on the basis of net income (deficit) reports in the years 1958 and 1961, with thirty-three from each year. Over 65 percent of these firms had suffered two or three years of negative profits in the previous three years. The firms are selected regardless of their asset size, with the only two criteria being that they were manufacturing firms which suffered losses in the year 1958 or 1961. (They were taken at random from all the firms listed in *Standard and Poor's Stock Guide*, January 1959, 1962, that reported negative earnings.) The two base years are chosen due to their relatively poor economic performances in terms of GNP growth. The companies are then evaluated by the discriminant model to determine their predictive bankruptcy potential.

The results, illustrated in Table 3-8, show that fifteen of the sixty-six firms are classified as bankrupt, with the remaining fifty-one correctly classified. The number of misclassifications is actually fourteen, as one of the firms went bankrupt within two years after the data period.

Therefore, the discriminant model correctly classified 79 percent of the sample firms. This percentage is all the more impressive when one considers that these firms constitute a *secondary* sample of admittedly *below average* performance. The·t-test for the significance of this result is $t = 4.8$; significant at the .001 level.

Another interesting facet of this test is the relationship of these "temporarily" sick firms' Z scores, and the "zone of ignorance." The zone of ignorance is that range of Z scores (see Figure 3-1) where misclassification can be

Table 3-8
Classification Results Secondary Sample of Nonbankrupt Firms

			Predicted	
			Bankrupt	Nonbankrupt
		Nonbankrupt Group Actual	14	52
	Number Correct	Percent Correct	Percent Error	n
Type II (Total)	52	79	21	66

observed. Figure 3-1 illustrates some of the individual firm Z scores (initial sample) and the group centroids. These points are plotted in one dimensional space and, therefore, are easily visualized.

Of the fourteen misclassified firms in this secondary sample, ten have Z scores between 1.81 and 2.67, which indicates that although they are classified as bankrupt, the prediction of their bankruptcy is not as definite as it is for the vast majority in the initial sample of bankrupt firms. In fact, just under one-third of the sixty-six firms in this last sample have Z scores within the entire overlap area, which emphasizes that the selection process is successful in choosing firms which showed signs (profitability) of deterioration.

(6) Long-Range Predictive Accuracy

The previous results give important evidence of the reliability of the conclusions derived from the initial sample of firms. An appropriate extension, therefore, would be to examine the firms to determine the overall effectiveness of the discriminant model for a longer period of time prior to bankruptcy. Several studies, e.g., Beaver and Merwin, indicated that their analyses showed firms exhibiting failure tendencies as much as five years prior to the actual failure. Little is mentioned, however, of the true significance of these earlier results. Is it enough to show that a firm's position is deteriorating or is it more important to examine when in the life of a firm does its eventual failure, if any, become an acute possibility? Thus far, we have seen that bankruptcy can be predicted accurately for two years prior to failure. What about the more remote years?

To answer this question, data are gathered for the thirty-three original firms from the third, fourth, and fifth year prior to bankruptcy. The reduced sample is due to the fact that several of the firms were in existence for less than five years. In two cases, data were unavailable for the more remote years. One would expect on an *a priori* basis that, as the lead time increases, the relative predictive ability of any model would decrease. This was true in the univariate studies cited earlier, and it is also quite true for the multiple discriminant model. Table 3-9 summarizes the predictive accuracy for the total five-year period.

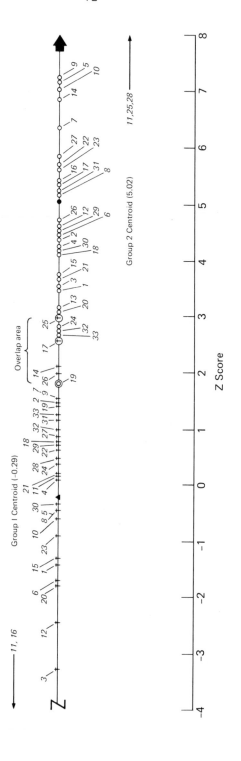

Figure 3-1. Individual Firm Discriminant Scores and Group Centroids, One Year Prior to Bankruptcy.

$$(Z = .012\,X_1 + .014\,X_2 + .033\,X_3 + .006\,X_4 + .999\,X_5)$$

Table 3-9
Five-Year Predictive Accuracy of the MDA Model (Initial Sample)

Year prior to Bankruptcy	Hits	Misses	Percent Correct
1st $n = 33$	31	2	95
2nd $n = 32$	23	9	72
3rd $n = 29$	14	15	48
4th $n = 28$	8	20	29
5th $n = 25$	9	16	36

It is obvious that the accuracy of the model falls off consistently with the one exception of the fourth and fifth years, when the results are reversed from what would be expected. The most logical reason for this occurrence is that after the second year, the discriminant model becomes unreliable in its predictive ability, and, also, that the change from year to year has little or no meaning.

Implications

Based on the above results, it is suggested that the bankruptcy prediction model is an accurate forecaster of failure up to two years prior to bankruptcy and that the accuracy diminishes substantially as the lead time increases. In order to investigate the possible reasons underlying these findings, the trend in the five predictive variables is traced on a univariate basis for five years preceding bankruptcy. The ratios of four other important but less significant ratios are also listed in Table 3-10.

The two most important conclusions of this trend analysis are (1) that all of the observed ratios show a deteriorating trend as bankruptcy approaches (Figures 3-2—3-4 show the deterioration of the selected ratios as bankruptcy approaches); and (2) that the most serious change in the majority of these ratios occurred between the third and the second years prior to bankruptcy. The degree of seriousness is measured by the yearly change in the ratio values. The latter observation is extremely significant as it provides evidence consistent with conclusions derived from the discriminant model. Therefore, the important information inherent in the individual ratio measurement trends takes on deserved significance only when integrated with the more analytical discriminant analysis findings.

Establishing a Practical Cut-off Point

The use of a multiple discriminant model for predicting bankruptcy has displayed several advantages, but bankers, credit managers, executives, and

Table 3-10
Average Ratios of Bankrupt Group prior to Failure—Original Sample

Ratio	Fifth Year Ratio	Fifth Year Change[a]	Fourth Year Ratio	Fourth Year Change[a]	Third Year Ratio	Third Year Change[a]	Second Year Ratio	Second Year Change[a]	First Year Ratio	First Year Change[a]
Working Capital/Total Assets (%) (X_1)	19.5		23.2	+ 3.6	17.6	− 5.6	1.6	−16.0[b]	(6.1)	− 7.7
Retained Earnings/Total Assets (%) (X_2)	4.0		(0.8)	− 4.8	(7.0)	− 6.2	(30.1)	−23.1	(62.6)	−32.5[b]
EBIT/Total Assets (%) (X_3)	7.2		4.0	− 3.2	(5.8)	− 9.8	(20.7)	−14.9[b]	(31.8)	−11.1
Market Value Equity/Total Debt (%) (X_4)	180.0		147.6	−32.4	143.2	− 4.4	74.2	−69.0[b]	40.1	−34.1
Sales/Total Assets (%) (X_5)	200.0		200.0	0.0	166.0	−34.0[b]	150.0	−16.0	150.0	0.0
Current Ratio (%)	180.0		187.0	+ 7.0	162.0	−25.0	131.0	−31.0[b]	133.0	+ 2.0
Years of Negative Profits (yrs.)	0.8		0.9	+ 0.1	1.2	+ 0.3	2.0	+ 0.8[b]	2.5	+ 0.5
Total Debt/Total Assets (%)	54.2		60.9	+ 6.7	61.2	+ 0.3	77.0	+15.8	96.4	+19.4[b]
Net Worth/Total Debt (%)	123.2		75.2	−28.0	112.6	+17.4	70.5	−42.1[b]	49.4	−21.1

[a]Change from previous year.
[b]Largest yearly change in the ratio.

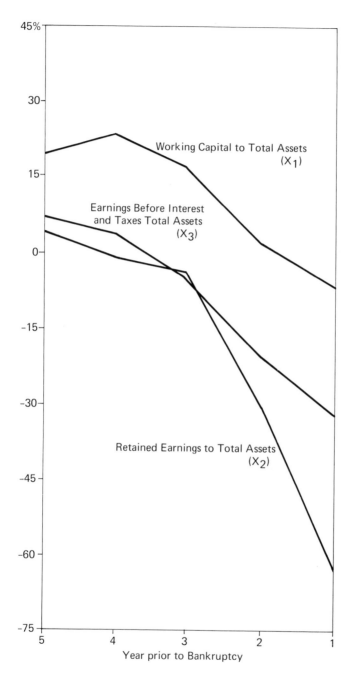

Figure 3-2. Trend of Three Discriminant Financial Ratios Prior to Bankruptcy.

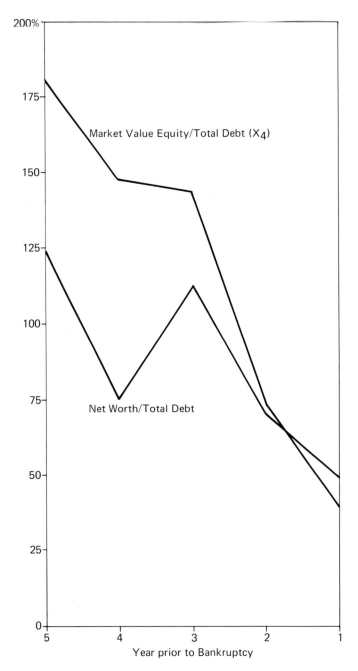

Figure 3–3. Trend of Solvency Ratios Prior to Bankruptcy.

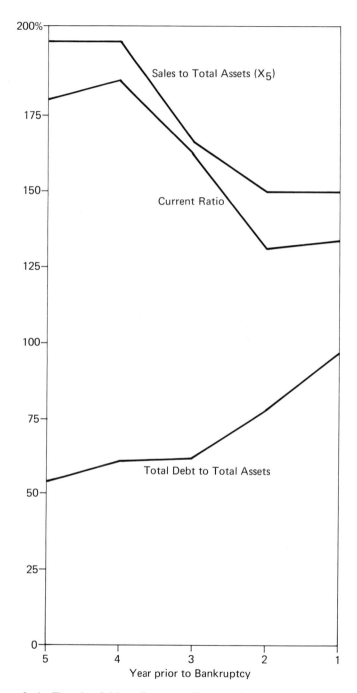

Figure 3-4. Trend of Miscellaneous Financial Ratios Prior to Bankruptcy.

78

investors will typically not have access to computer procedures such as the Cooley Lohnes MDA program. Therefore, it will be necessary to investigate our results and to attempt to extend our model for more general application. The procedure described below may be utilized to select a cut-off point, or optimum Z value, which enables predictions without computer support.[22]

By observing those firms which have been misclassified by the discriminant model in the initial sample, it is concluded that all firms having a Z score of greater than 2.99 clearly fall into the nonbankrupt sector, while those firms having a Z below 1.81 are all bankrupt. The area between 1.81 and 2.99 will be defined as the zone of ignorance or gray area because of the susceptibility to error classification (see Figure 3-1). Since errors are observed in this range of values, we will be uncertain about a *new* firm whose Z value falls within the zone of ignorance. Hence, it is desirable to establish a guideline for classifying firms in the gray area.

The process begins by identifying sample observations which fall within the overlapping range. These appear as in Table 3-11. The first digit of the firm number identifies the group, with the last two digits locating the firm within the group.

Next, the range of values of Z that results in *the minimum number of misclassifications* is found. In the analysis, Zs between (but not including) the indicated values produce the misclassifications shown in Table 3-12.

Table 3-11
Firm Whose Z Score Falls within Gray Area

Firm Number Nonbankrupt	Z Score	Firm Number Bankrupt
2019*	1.81	
	1.98	1026
	2.10	1014
	2.67	1017*
2033	2.68	
2032	2.78	
	2.99	1025*

*Misclassified by the MDA model; for example, firm 19 in Group 2.

Table 3-12
Number of Misclassifications Using Various Z-Score Criteria

Range of Z	Number Misclassified	Firms
1.81-1.98	5	2019, 1026, 1014, 1017, 1025
1.98-2.10	4	2019, 1014, 1017, 1025
2.10-2.67	3	2019, 1017, 1025
2.67-2.68	2	2019, 1025
2.68-2.78	3	2019, 2033, 1025
2.78-2.99	4	2019, 2033, 2032, 1025

The best critical value conveniently falls between 2.67—2.68 and therefore 2.675, the midpoint of the interval, is chosen as the Z value that discriminates best between the bankrupt and nonbankrupt firms.

Bankruptcy Price Behavior

An interesting aspect of the bankruptcy-prediction model is that one of the variables, X_4, contains a market value element which partly reflects stock market opinion about the firm. Associated with this aspect is this writer's contention that investors, in general, tend to underestimate the financial plight of those firms that eventually go bankrupt. We have seen that the X_4 variable tends to drop as bankruptcy approaches (Figure 3-3) and this phenomenon tells us a little about investor expectations. Two other studies were strictly concerned with the market price performance of bankrupt firms prior to the failure date and we will now review their findings. The final chapter of this book will consider the *postbankruptcy* price behavior.

Beaver Study

The first of the two aforementioned studies, performed by Professor William Beaver,[23] considered the annual prebankruptcy rates of return of up to 79 failed companies. Beaver calculated the unadjusted annual rates of return of failed firms (and also the market adjusted annual rates) up to five years prior to bankruptcy. The unadjusted annual rate is simply the summation of dividends and capital gains (or losses) divided by the base date price. The adjusted rate takes the annual rate on the particular stock and subtracts the comparable "Fisher Link Relative" return, which is an average of the rates of return on all firms listed on the New York Stock Exchange.[24] The resulting residual rate (difference of the two rates) was then compared between one group of failed and another group of nonfailed firms.

The results were that the median rates of the failed firms were poorer than those of the nonfailed firms for five years prior to failure and the difference between the median values increased as failure approached. This was true for both the unadjusted and adjusted return measures, with the differentials slightly greater when using the adjusted data. The nonfailed firms showed no discernible trend as failure approached, while the failed firms' prices deteriorated consistently. Beaver also devised tests to assess the failure predictive power of the rates of return measures and several financial ratios from his 1966 study (e.g., the cash flow/total liabilities; net income/total assets; total debt/total assets; and working capital/total assets). These univariate tests showed that investors forecast failure sooner than any of the ratios did, with the *average* length of time from the year of the failure forecast to the date of failure being 2.45 years for the rate of return measure. Two of the ratios, however, had only slightly shorter lead times.

Beaver concluded that his findings of investor proficiency in forecasting failure earlier than ratios is consistent with the contention that investors utilize the informational content of ratios in assessing solvency expectations. He further contends, however, that the lack of perfect association between ratio forecasts and market movements implies that investors also respond to nonratio sources of information. Still, this author and Beaver stand firm on the conviction that ratios are efficient predictors of bankruptcy, especially when used effectively. This contention, however, is not shared by everyone and other writers have voiced concern about the validity of financial ratio predictors.[25]

Although Beaver asserts that investors continuously make failure assessments and adjust market prices accordingly, he still finds that the largest drop in failing companies' stock price occurs in the year immediately preceding bankruptcy. This finding tends to confirm our assertion that investors underestimate the failing firm's stock declines, and perhaps bodes well for some model to aid in a short-sale investment strategy. Further reference to this type of model will be made in Chapter 6.

Westerfield Study.

A more recent study investigated the market price movement of twenty bankrupt firms for ten years prior to bankruptcy declaration.[26] This study differed from the Beaver analysis in that Westerfield utilized monthly price and dividend data over a longer time period and introduced a new type of performance measure. Utilizing the now famous market-model developed by Sharpe[27] and others, he first ran the following equation,

$$(1) \quad R_{i,t} = a_{i,t} + \beta_i R_{m,t}$$

for the initial four-year period (months 120–72 prior to bankruptcy) in order to estimate the parameters a_i and β_i for each of the twenty firms. The β_i parameter measures the individual stock's relationship with that of the general market. A β_i of 1.0 indicates that the stock tends to move in perfect correlation with the overall market.

$R_{i,t}$ = Monthly Return Relative in Stock i in Period t.

$R_{m,t}$ = Monthly Return Relative in the Market in the Period t.
Fisher's Link Relative Index is Utilized Here also.

Parameter constants unique to security i.

After the parameter estimates are derived, the performance relatives for the twenty securities are estimated for the remaining six-year period (months 71–0 prior to bankruptcy), utilizing the *actual market* performance and the unique firm parameter estimates. A new disturbance term is then derived by comparing the actual performance of the *security* in this period with the estimated performance:

$$(2) \; \mu_{i,t} = R_{i,t} - (a_i + \beta_i R_{m,t})$$

where,

$\mu_{i,t}$	=	Disturbance Term
$R_{i,t}$	=	Actual Relative Performance of Security i in Period t
$R_{m,t}$	=	Actual Relative Performance of the Market in Period t
a, β	=	Estimates of parameters derived from equation (1)

Finally, Westerfield utilized an index of performance which is developed especially to measure the performance of his bankrupt firm sample.

$$(3) \; PAVG = \prod_{t=1}^{T} (1 + 1/N \sum_{i=1}^{N} \mu_{i,t})$$

where:

$PAVG$	=	Monthly Performance Average
$\mu_{i,t}$	=	Disturbance Term as Described before
N	=	Number of Firms = 20
T	=	Number of Monthly Periods = 71

The index assumes equal weights in each of the T periods over the N securities. For instance, if all securities have disturbance terms equal to zero, then the performance average equals 1.0. If the disturbance terms tend to be negative—that is, the performance of the bankrupt firms is lower in the second six-year period than in the first four-year period—then the $PAVG$ will cumulate to some amount below 1.0. The reverse, of course, is true if the stocks' disturbance terms are mostly positive in the second period and the $PAVG$ will cumulate to above 1.0. This assumes no extreme values.

The results of this study were quite emphatic. The $PAVG$ started out around 1.0 for the first 13 months or so (months 71–59) and then began to drop noticeably. The decline was fairly consistent, with only several minor upticks, and the final $PAVG$ in month #0 (bankruptcy declaration) was 0.277. Therefore, it appears that the market began bidding down the prices of the future bankrupt stocks as much as five years prior to bankruptcy. The fact that the market performance continued downward, especially in the year immediately prior to bankruptcy (the overall $PAVG$ had only one small uptick in the final 14 months), means that although investors were aware of the firm's deteriorating condition for a long time prior to failure, the situation's seriousness was consistently underestimated. We conclude again, therefore, that a model or technique which is capable of predicting impending failure might be of considerable assistance in a short selling context.

Concluding Remarks.

The purpose of this chapter has been to examine the characteristics of a sample of bankrupt manufacturing companies. The analysis was extended to several years prior to the actual bankruptcy date in order to determine the bankruptcy-prediction merits of a multiple discriminant statistical model. At the same time, we are seeking to assess the analytical quality of financial ratio analysis; several of these ratio types were the primary ingredients of the model. The results of our analysis showed impressive evidence that bankruptcy could be predicted as much as two reporting periods prior to the event and that the correct classifications were evident for holdout-secondary samples of firms as well as for the original groups of companies.

Whether or not such a general bankruptcy model is practically suitable for all manufacturing firms is debatable. The model did not scrutinize very large or very small entities, the latter classification comprising by far the largest number of business failures. Also, the period covered was quite long (almost two decades) and the analysis covered all manufacturing firms. Ideally, we would like to develop a bankruptcy prediction model utilizing a homogeneous group of bankrupt companies and data as near to the present as possible. For instance, if we are interested in a particular industry grouping, or perhaps a group of related industries, we should first gather data from healthy and failing firms in these groupings for the last couple of years. In this manner, the results are more closely representative of the type of firm and of the business environment. Unfortunately, this is not an easy task due to data unavailability. The analyst interested in practical utilization of a model is therefore cautioned to be careful in the utilization of the aforementioned bankruptcy model developed earlier in the chapter.

The practical and theoretical applications of such a bankruptcy-prediction model are many and varied. Perhaps the most likely application is credit evaluation. A commercial bank or finance company might utilize such a model in its commercial and industrial loan department. While there is some obvious resistance to this nonpersonal type of analysis, present trends suggest that this technique will be an aide, not a replacement, for the loan officer. Another area of potential application concerns investment and valuation analysis. What are the implications to present and/or prospective investors in the potential bankrupt entity? Finally, the analysis of bankrupt characteristics has obvious relevance for the management of those firms whose future is tenuous and for those aggressive firms interested in pumping life into a business which may otherwise fail.

4

Business Failure Prediction: Implications and Applications

The model developed in the prior chapter utilized data from manufacturing corporations and was concerned with bankruptcy prediction. In view of the current rash of corporate bankruptcies, even among the nation's largest firms, we might be content with the model's implications solely for bankruptcy. This relatively narrow assessment, however, is extremely limiting and falsely obviates several potentially useful extensions of this type of model. The purpose of this chapter is to explore several new areas where a failure prediction technique could make a significant contribution. Essentially, the proposed sectors for further analysis encompass (a) credit evaluation—both business loan and accounts receivable management; and (b) internal management control implications.

Business Loan Evaluation

The first area of extension directly concerns those financial institutions, predominantly commercial banks, which consistently make loanable funds available to business firms. We suggest that techniques similar to the one developed in the prior chapter be adopted and utilized by loan officers of our nation's lending institutions. Electronic data processing techniques have already made a significant impact on these institutions and will no doubt continue to do so. In making this proposal, we should make one aspect perfectly clear at the outset; the suggestion does *not* imply the *substitution* of mechanical, quantitative techniques for the present loan officers' more qualitative, intuitive type of analysis. Rather, the loan officer can be *aided* considerably by the inclusion of a mechanical credit-scoring device which should be introduced at the earliest possible time in the lending process. As long as commercial loan applications and needs for assistance remain so different from one another, the job of the competent loan officer is secure.

Consumer Loans

The adaptation of numerical scoring techniques to the area of credit management is certainly not a revolutionary idea. Important precedents have been set in the *consumer* loan evaluation sector. As early as 1941, the National Bureau of Economic Research commissioned a study to analyze and weigh those characteristics which best discriminate between acceptable and poor consumer credit risks in the installment loan market.[1] Other studies in the consumer loan market confirmed the accuracy and potential profitable use of discrimination techniques.[2] The reliability of any credit-scoring model depends upon its accuracy in isolating those characteristics related to the lender's ability to repay the loan. This same objective is true for commercial loans as well as consumer loans. In the latter area, such individual characteristics as: (1) age; (2) occupation; (3) income; (4) marital status; (5) home or renting residency; (6) credit record and references; (7) terms of loan itself; etc. were found to be effective indicators of the applicant's repayment ability.

The business pioneers in consumer loan credit-scoring techniques were the consumer finance companies and not the commercial banks. Banks did not institute such evaluation techniques until the early 1960s and then it was usually a finance company man recruited to the banking industry who introduced the technique to the installment loan department.[3] This is not surprising since only a small proportion of a commercial bank's total operating revenues comes from the consumer loan sector. Business loans, on the other hand, account for well over 50 percent of the total operating revenue of the nation's commercial banks.[4]

It should also be noted that the use of numerical credit-scoring techniques in the consumer area is not limited to formal loan applications. Other related areas include credit card applications, down payment on public utility equipment usage, and in a crude sense, general reference and credit quality. The essential point is that computerized credit-scoring models have been developed successfully to aid officers in charge of making loans and other types of credit decisions. Although there may be complex underlying mathematical operations involved, the actual day-to-day usage is extremely simple. If utilized properly, new credit applications can be screened in a matter of minutes and can be categorized in some predetermined manner to indicate the applicants' credit worthiness. Since the population of applicants is extremely homogeneous, the problems involved are not nearly as great as they are in the commercial loan sector.

Commercial Loans

Two recent papers in the *Journal of Commercial Bank Lending* advocate the adoption of computerized credit-scoring techniques to aid the commercial bank loan officer in his efforts to evaluate commercial loan applications.[5] The convincing thesis of these articles and the evidence discussed in Chapter 3 imply that there will eventually be accurate analytical and objective techniques integrated into the commercial loan officer function.

The suggested process is fairly simple. Individual banks, or perhaps a group of associated banking institutions, will first analyze the characteristics of their prior loans which have (1) proved unsuccessful (default and/or delinquency); and

(2) proved successful in the repayment of principal and interest on schedule. Since the successful loans far outnumber the unsuccessful ones, the problem no doubt will be to derive a large enough number of the latter group. The statistical technique advocated here—multiple discriminant analysis—is similar to that used for consumer loans. The main difference lies in the nature of the data. Current financial statements and the most recent past statements are the primary data sources. These primary data will then be transformed into more meaningful financial ratios which no doubt will be similar to the ones analyzed in Chapter 3. The purpose of predicting the loan repayment potential of a commercial loan applicant is intimately related to a firm's bankruptcy potential. Other variables which should be considered are related to the qualitative nature of the applicant and the particular loan characteristics. These latter variables may include credit status and references, loan purpose, past performance of the loan (in the case of a loan review rather than an initial loan request), etc. Since the proposed analysis is quantitative, the last group of variables presents specification problems which can be overcome by the use of statistical dummy variables or proxy measures.[a]

The next step is to analyze the relevant data in order to assign differential weightings to the various important indicators. This process was described in detail in Chapter 3. After a weight is given for each selected factor, a final credit score is assigned to each of the applicants being assessed. A cut-off score is established according to the objectives of the lending institution and loans are then classified as acceptable or not based on their scores. The derived classifications are then compared with their actual loan repayment performance in order to assess the accuracy of the model. If data availability permits, the model should then be tested by a completely new sample of loans whose actual performance is also known but which did not figure in the development of the initial model. This is what we referred to earlier as the hold-out sample. The results of this second test are a more rigorous barometer of the model's accuracy. Finally, management must decide whether or not to apply the model to *new* loan applicants and to formally integrate the system into the loan officer function.

Costs of Errors Associated with Computerized
Loan Evaluation

The previous discussion illustrates the potential and mechanics involved in the development of a discriminant model for commercial loan evaluation. Inherent in the analysis, however, is the chance of error or misclassification. Assuming the lending institution had fully automated the process, errors in the model's classification are of two types. A Type I error is made when a firm which eventually defaults on its loan is originally classified as a good credit risk; a Type

[a]Statistical dummy variables represent methods to quantify those measures which are generically qualitative. For instance, a good credit reference might be assigned a value of one, while a poor rating would receive a value of zero.

II error is made when a successful loan is assigned to the rejection group. In the latter case, the loan applicant is denied his request when, in fact, the firm would have been able to meet its obligation successfully.

What are the costs associated with the Type I error? The primary cost, of course, is the loss of interest and/or principal on the defaulted loan. The result may be complete loss of the principal, or partial loss due to a composition of claim or reorganization arrangement. In the case of a secured loan, the value of the property used as collateral becomes crucial but, in many cases, the realizable value is below the amount of the loan and some loss is incurred by the lending institution.

How significant are losses on commercial and industrial loans to commercial banks? Unfortunately, nobody knows the precise answer. A recent survey of commercial loan charge-offs at fifteen western commercial banks revealed some interesting and helpful statistics.[6] The *median* figures for business loan charge-offs as a percentage of outstanding commercial loans in 1967 and 1968 were 0.21% and 0.12%, respectively, and indications are that 1969 losses will be quite high. The comparable 1969 figure was 0.28%, up substantially from prior years. If we assume these results are somewhat typical for the nation, we can attempt to ascertain the business loan charge-off contribution to bank profits. In the past five years, net operating income before related taxes has averaged about 1% of total assets for insured commercial banks.[7] At the same time, commercial and industrial loans have averaged about 20.0% of total bank assets. If we assume that 0.2% of these loans result in charge-offs, the resulting cost to commercial banks is approximately $.04 per $100 of total assets. If the losses were eliminated, net operating income before taxes would rise to $1.04 per $100 of assets (1.04%)—a small but not insignificant increase.

The same loan charge-off study and a recent update revealed that of those loans which were charged-off, as many as 66% of the total in both years, and as high as 80% in 1969, were marginal or should not have been made in the first place, i.e., they were the result of poor lending judgment. The entire breakdown of post charge-off loan reassessment is shown in Table 4-1. Figures are percentages of total loan charge-offs:

Table 4-1
Loan Charge-Off Evaluation, 1967-1969

Evaluation	1967	1968	1969
Loans would be made again	33%	42%	36%
Loans recognized as marginal when made	25	26	25
Loans should not have been made	41	31	55

These results occurred during relatively tight money conditions and we might expect greater loan charge-offs in liberal monetary periods when loans are solicited on a more aggressive basis. The study concludes that,

Obviously, the cure must be more experienced credit personnel, not only to evaluate each loan, but also to use sound judgment in closely supervising loans that are marginal when made or those that become so later.[8]

We agree that closer supervision is beneficial but doubt that it will have a significant effect. There is no guarantee that human failings can be eliminated by increased diligence alone. Rather, the situation can be improved by giving these very same loan officers better tools to work with—namely, ones which can help spotlight quickly and cheaply those marginal or submarginal loan applicants and trigger an immediate and more thorough investigation.

In addition to the dollar cost associated with a loan default, there are intangible costs of considerable magnitude. Even if 100% of a defaulted loan is recovered, the time spent by bank executives and credit managers in the collection phase is often considerable and is a terrible nuisance, not to mention any legal fees involved. From the branch or district manager's standpoint, the avoidance of faulty loans is especially desirable.

Misclassifying an unsuccessful loan also involves opportunity costs of lost income. The opportunity cost on the interest and principal not repaid is that return which could have been earned on other alternative loans or investments. During periods of tight money, this cost is especially evident. Another cost is the loss of a customer upon termination of the loan. Banks and other credit institutions would certainly rather deal with old, established customers rather than evaluate new applicants. If the old, defaulted customer cannot be replaced immediately by a new applicant, the financial institution will suffer the loss of that income which would have been earned if the initial firm had not defaulted. Conversely, the loss involved with a Type I error will be diminished if the bank can immediately turn around and replace the bad loan with a new, healthy one.

The costs of a Type II error are considerably less than those noted above. If a firm is denied a loan because the model has misclassified it as a potential default, the costs include the following items. First, the interest income on the loan is lost. This lost revenue, however, is not the total interest rate—only the differential between the rate that would have been charged and some riskless rate, e.g., the rate on a government bond of the same maturity. This loss of interest is essentially zero if the loan officer has other similar risk alternative uses for his funds which will return an income commensurate with the rate that would have been charged on the denied loan. As with the Type I error, a customer will be lost when a firm is mistakenly turned down. The costs are proportional to the Type I error in this case. Finally, the psychological cost of not making a loan to a deserving company is negligible compared to the possible benefit of denying a loan to a company which would have defaulted.

It should be noted that the losses caused by incorrect decisions on loan requests are identical regardless of the technique used to evaluate the loan. If a combination of loan officer experience, qualitative knowledge of the applicant, and some mechanical credit-scoring technique can reduce these losses (net of any incremental costs involved with the scoring technique), then the system would appear worthwhile. As mentioned, however, the real losses involved are much greater for a Type I error. With this knowledge, the analyst could adjust the cut-off score of the credit-scoring process such that the probability of this type of error is reduced at the expense of the increased probability of a Type II error. This can be accomplished simply by increasing the acceptable score. Of course, the bank's demand function for its loanable funds must be inspected to ensure that those rejected loans, which will be an increased number, can be replaced by other more acceptable applicants.

Integrative Suggestions

The first suggestion relates to the prior statement that this credit-scoring system should be looked upon as an important tool for the loan officer. Credit scores above some established cut-off point would imply superior financial resources for the applicant and could reduce substantially the normal time spent on analyzing loans of this type. At the same time, scores below some very poor credit score might trigger rejection unless extenuating circumstances exist. Applicants whose scores fall within some questionable area would then be further scrutinized by the loan officer in order to more precisely estimate the firm's repayment ability; that is, energies could be applied more effectively to borderline applicants. The essential feature here is the time-saving quality of the credit-scoring technique. It could be applied quickly and cheaply at the initial stages of negotiation and conceivably diminish follow-up investigation. The commercial lending officers of large banks are indeed an important resource and like most other valuable resources, they are scarce. These men and women are usually the premiere salesmen of the bank; expected to acquire, retain, and service account relationships. If a computerized scoring technique can reduce the time involved in any loan evaluation, the account executives can devote more time toward expanding the bank's business. This is more crucial in times of easy money and credit since the bank has the ability to expand during these more liberal times.

What about the small bank? They may not have the resources, both human and mechanical, to develop the requisite loan evaluation techniques. Yet, the small bank salesmen are usually also high-ranking administrative officers. Therefore, the time-saving ingredient is even more crucial to these men and women. One suggestion to help alleviate this burden is to make available to these small banks the commercial loan credit-scoring techniques via computerized time-sharing facilities or by the outright transfer of technology from the larger to the smaller institutions. Compensation to the large bank innovator can take various traditional banking forms.

A second suggestion concerns the periodic adjustment of the cut-off score between acceptable and possibly unacceptable applicants. This score could reflect changing money market conditions, volume and profit incentives, and the confidence top management has in its loan officers. In addition, the weights of the individual variables can be updated periodically according to the most recent experience of the bank's loan portfolio.

A final suggestion relates to a serious problem in the development of any *commercial* loan credit-scoring technique. This problem involves the basically heterogeneous nature of commercial loans and will be discussed in more detail in the following section. Suffice it to say that loan applicants are from vastly divergent lines of business and that some potential variable discriminators between successful and unsuccessful loans are sensitive themselves to various industry or product-line activity. For instance, acceptable financial leverage measures are higher in public utility companies than in business equipment manufacturers because of among other things, the reliable nature of the former's earnings stream. A credit-scoring model developed from all types of firms could not adjust completely for this potential bias. What can be done?

The solution to this perplexing problem is dependent upon the availability of past data on both successful and unsuccessful loans for a large number of companies in each of the primary industry or product-line classifications. How many companies in each industry? Based on our experience, a reliable model could be obtained from a sample of fifteen to twenty firms in both the successful and unsuccessful categories. If more than this number exist, the remainder should be used for hold-out sample tests. Obviously, the problem lies in the number of statistically viable observations available in the unsuccessful category. If one bank does not have sufficient data bank files, then a joint effort involving several of the largest commercial banks is advisable. The more homogeneous are the firms which make up the model's sample and the more recent the timing of the data, the better the chance for accurate credit-scoring results. The time element is also important since selected financial ratios themselves tend to change over time. Liquidity and leverage norms in the early 1950s were indeed different from the norms in 1970.

In summary, the answer to the problem of industrial heterogeneity among loan applicants is to develop credit-scoring models in each of the major customer product-line or industry classifications. Since one bank may specialize in a particular type of industrial loan, e.g., chemicals, and another bank in a second type, e.g., steels, there certainly could be a diversification of effort based on peculiar data-availability resources.

Problems Involved

Despite the aforementioned discussion on numerical credit-scoring techniques for commercial loans, at the present time none of these systems is formally installed in commercial banks or other business lending institutions. This is surprising in that the magnitude of commercial and industrial loans reached an average of over 100 billion dollars for the year 1969. Unlike consumer loans, the risks involved in business loans are significantly greater since the average dollar amount is much larger. The commercial loans, however, are treated differently by banks, mainly because of the feeling on the part of bank officials that each commercial loan is different from the past ones and the acceptance or rejection of the loan should not be left up to some mechanical technique. While many of the larger banks are already using sophisticated techniques for detecting slow and delinquent loans and for determining optimum costs and durations for pursuing defaulted loans,[9] little has been done to eliminate the source of trouble at the initial screening stage. The following arguments are presented as possible reasons for this reluctance to develop credit-scoring techniques for commerical loans.[b]

Heterogeneous Loan Applicants

This problem was mentioned earlier in the section on suggestions. Unlike customers for consumer goods, the commercial loan applicants are drawn from a vast myriad of different lines of business. Variable values are often as much a function of the line of business and size of the enterprise as is the basic underlying economic condition of the firm. Because of this realization, bank personnel are reluctant to investigate the potential of the seemingly inflexible credit-scoring systems. At the same time, these dissimilarities make it quite difficult to specify those variables which will yield significant relationships about *all* firms. Where the lack of homogeneity is a serious problem, the bank has little alternative but to develop specific credit evaluation models to obviate this problem. If the latter approach is adopted, a second problem, always present, becomes even more acute.

Lack of Adequate Data

The lack of data primarily for unsuccessful past loans in all firm classifications, as well as for the specific industries which make up the whole, is a serious stumbling block. There is a chronic lack of financial data on past and prospective loans and this is especially the case for small business loans. Without accurate and comprehensive data, the prospect of successfully developing credit-scoring techniques is dim. Because of this data problem, the responsibility for model development lies with the large banks. Not only must this responsibility be accepted *within* the systems and loan departments of the large banks, but interbank cooperation might also be needed. The transmission of technology can then take place such that all the interested banks, regardless of size, can share in the results.

---

[b]Hammer and Orgler, also present several arguments on the difficulties involved in setting up commercial loan credit-scoring techniques.

Loan Purpose and Repayment Differences

Another problem is the differences in the loans themselves. Although there are standard classifications for loans, e.g., equipment purchase, line of credit, financial repayment, working capital, etc., the list is long and therefore the differential problems are magnified. Not only are the loan purposes diverse, but the manner of payment, e.g., interest rates, compensation balances, collection rights, etc., are also different from loan to loan and from bank to bank.

Human Reluctance to Change and Innovation

Finally, a source of resistance in the area of computerized loan evaluation is the lack of faith in some mechanical monster and the feeling that the traditional function of the loan officer will be permanently altered and possibly eliminated. This is simply not true. To repeat, advocates of computerized evaluation methods, like this writer, do not preach the elimination of the loan officer nor is this notion felt to be advisable. The analysis of financial statements is a single, but important, step in the analysis of loan applications. Often, the particular *bank* characteristics are equally important to the decision-making process. The credit evaluation process has been specified as but one procedure out of a total of eight in a comprehensive investigation of the entire process of commercial bank loan application procedures.[10] In the article by Cohen et al., a simulation model is developed and the computer is programmed to perform judgments analogous to those made by experienced analysts. In other words, the computer is utilized to investigate how decisions are made and not to attempt improvement of the system. If any improvement is to be made, it is in the attainment of documented information on the decision-making process in order to make it easier to train new analysts. Also, the authors point out that the only process which is presently amenable to computerized simulation is the one involving analysis of financial statements.

Despite the problems involved in the development of credit-scoring procedures for business loans, progress is being made and we predict that systems of the type outlined above will become realities in the next decade. Whether the breakthrough will take place in the commercial bank area or other lending institutions, like commerical factors, will be a function of the progressive attitude on the part of the respective managements. More than likely, bankers will not be inspired to make inroads in the credit-scoring system area until money market conditions and loss ratios make it more profitable to do so. As long as money is relatively tight and only the best blue-chip companies are acceptable to the lending institutions, the need for more sophisticated techniques of credit evaluation is not going to be very great. But as loss ratios increase, the pressure for developing efficient loan evaluators will probably also increase.

Accounts Receivable Management

The utilization of analytical credit evaluation procedures is not limited to financial institutions. Within the individual corporation, the accounts receivable sector appears to be particularly amenable to a similar type of statistical scrutiny. In fact, the determination of acceptable customers for corporations is perhaps even more feasible due to the likelihood that the firm's customers will be homogeneous, whether the receivables themselves are individuals or other companies. In most cases, the customers will have one important characteristic in common—demand for a particular type of product—as opposed to the more general demand for money in the case of business loan evaluation. As noted earlier, the greater the basic homogeneity of the statistical sample used in credit evaluation, the greater the probability for valid discrimination. The analyst can more easily concentrate on those characteristics of the receivables which indicate their ability or inability to meet the obligation. In addition, many of the aforementioned indicators of corporate bankruptcy and insolvency are relevant in the assessment of accounts receivable quality.

The determination of acceptable customers is but one aspect in the entire receivable management function. Other important factors include the credit period extended, the cash discount given (if any), special terms such as seasonal dating, and the amount of time and money spent on the collection of receivables. In each of these policy areas, the decision depends on a trade-off between the cost of changing that particular element and the resulting profitability. For instance, a firm may liberalize its credit period or lower its standards on acceptable customers in order to increase its revenues. By doing so, however, it must realize that it now will be carrying customers for a longer period of time and, in the case of lowering standards, increasing the probability of bad debts.

Credit applicant evaluation is present in almost all firms regardless of the product or type of customer. It usually entails obtaining financial and other information about the applicant, analyzing these data, and reaching a decision on whether or not to sell to him. In the case of a continuing customer, the most important quantitative factor is his record of payment. If the account is new, the credit analyst would normally attempt to learn of the applicant's past payment record with other firms. Sources of information usually are Dun & Bradstreet ratings, bank references, exchange of information with other companies, and finally, the firm's own past experience with similar individuals. Other potentially relevant variables in a trade credit situation are liquidity, leverage, and income measures. This is true even if the applicant is an individual rather than another company.

One important difference between accounts receivable quality assessment and business loan evaluation should be kept in mind. The time duration in the field of trade credit is generally quite short and therefore the liquidity measures are probably more relevant. Under normal circumstances, the account is expected to be continued and therefore, assets and liabilities generating cash and falling due within a slightly longer period, e.g., one year, would also be relevant.

Although usually less crucial than liquidity measures, financial leverage data are still important. The probability of successfully discharging debts, i.e., solvency, decreases with increases in leverage. We also know that the ability to meet debts is partly a function of the amount of fixed interest and principal repayments and the random fluctuation in gross cash flows. The latter serves as the primary source of funds to meet financial commitments. Since this factor is itself dependent upon the revenue-generating ability of the firm, we can see clearly that many factors are relevant in the determination of acceptable customers.

It is precisely the above reasoning which leads this writer and several others[11] to suggest the adoption of a multiple discriminant procedure for accounts receivable management. As noted in Chapter 3, more satisfactory results are likely if several debtor characteristics are considered and objective weights assigned to each relevant variable. The process may be initiated in two ways. First, and sometimes more preferable, is to be able to analyze past data on those customers who have successfully paid their obligations and then to do the same for those delinquent and/or bad debt cases. If significant differences exist between the good and bad groups, then statistical discrimination may be feasible. After a model is developed, its accuracy tested and the results found satisfactory, it is applied to *new* credit applicants.

The above suggestion assumes that comprehensive data on past customers are already available. Usually, this will not be the case and to attempt to develop a model based on insufficient data is foolhardy. A more advisable, more time-consuming alternative is to develop the model from scratch. Credit analysts should first determine those measures which have some potential discriminating power between successful and unsuccessful receivables and require its customers to supply these data. During this period, decisions should be made based on the same standards that the firm has always been using. After a sufficient receivable turnover period, the good and delinquent accounts should be separated and scrutinized in order to determine the critical discriminating variables. If possible, a hold-out sample of good and bad accounts should also be utilized.

Cutoff Scores

One possible goal of the credit department is to minimize the number of total misclassifications. In this case, the critical discriminant score should be chosen in a manner similar to the procedure detailed in Chapter 3. This minimizing goal, however, may not be in the best interests of the firm because it may detract from overall profitability. Called suboptimization, it is a real danger in firms especially where interdepartmental coordination is poor. While the credit manager is pleased that bad debts are low, the sales manager may object because many of his customers are being turned down. Therefore, a cut-off value should be determined whereby the expected marginal revenue generated from one new customer equals the expected loss of adding one more potential bad debt.[12] The optimal cut-off score, however, is not a permanent value. It should be treated as a variable dependent upon such other factors as competition, product price changes, capital market conditions, and perhaps even management changes which lead to different risk tolerances. One other factor not mentioned thus far is the resources spent on collections. An optimal procedure for pursuing delinquent accounts could reduce the expected cost of bad debts and decrease the optimal cut-off score.

Automation

Although the loan officer will not be replaced by mechanical procedures because of the various complexities of business loans, it is possible that some firms could virtually eliminate their credit department by instituting mechanical credit evaluation techniques if the customer population is extremely homogeneous. In most cases, this will mean individuals as opposed to business customers. The criteria for assessing credit card applicants are perfect examples. Computerized techniques are already involved in collection procedures and in some firms credit evaluation is becoming almost completely automated.

Internal Management Control Implications

Analytical techniques for assessing failure potential have practical benefits in areas other than credit evaluation. Admittedly, the management of accounts receivable is quite important to the growth and prosperity of companies, but even of a more crucial nature is the control of overall operations. Financial and economic flexibility has always been considered in the total realm of management functions, but perhaps never has the need for its scrutiny been greater than during the most recent recession (1969-70). The purpose of this section is to discuss those relevant alternatives which should be considered seriously by management immediately upon detection of possible future problems. Again, we advocate the use of an analytical technique, such as the discriminant analysis model—this time as a type of early warning device.

Business managers, financial analysts, and general students of management agree that in order for a firm to plan and grow successfully, it must from time to time be able to assess honestly its present condition. By so doing, important strengths and weaknesses may be recognized and, in the latter case, changes in policies and actions will usually be in order. Unfortunately, the attainment of an honest and objective evaluation is often difficult to implement within a firm until some catastrophe strikes. This phenomenon, sometimes referred to as the crisis principle, is common in growing and healthy firms,[13] as well as in those companies facing problems or even failure. In the healthy firm situation, the solution to the problem is often some type of organizational change, for example, decentralization of authority. Although changes in policy and operations are important in the expanding enterprise, the need for periodic evaluation and management flexibility is crucial to the potential bankrupt firms. The essence, once again, is to know what to look for, to be able to interpret correctly any findings, and, finally, to use this information for corrective measures if needed.

The suggestion here is that the discriminant model, if used correctly and periodically, has the ability to predict corporate problems early enough to enable management to realize the gravity of the situation in time to avoid failure. This is not typically the case, however, as Dewing has noted:

Finally, when the load of accumulated obligations becomes so great that it cannot be relieved even by extensions and renewals, the corporation confesses its insolvency, but ascribes the impending crisis to lack of current capital. A corporate management does not confess to failure with money in the till.[14]

Dewing observed firms following the pattern of getting further and further into debt until failure becomes the only alternative. The problem, therefore, is twofold: one, to convince management of the gravity of the situation and, two, to do something about it.

It should be noted that a financial ratio bankruptcy model will not under normal circumstances be the physician and panacea to the sick patient. It merely serves as objective quantification of the patient's illness but it cannot point directly toward the area(s) of most pressing need. Once management is convinced of the immediate need for change, then it is its responsibility to implement those new business policies which will either save the firm, or hasten its death. The latter choice can be extremely important to the present creditors and even the owners.

Since the specific problems which beset firms are in some way unique to that firm, we will accomplish little by trying to deal with specifics. Instead, we will list and evaluate general alternatives facing management. These alternatives include: (1) changes in product line and/or management personnel; (2) sale of unprofitable equipment and/or entire unprofitable divisions; (3) active solicitation of a merger agreement; (4) financial arrangements—debt changes and equity adjustments (quasireorganization); (5) bankruptcy-reorganization; and (6) liquidation. The first three actions are recommended when the threat of failure is clear but not necessarily imminent. The fourth is advisable when the danger of failure is extremely imminent but expected to be temporary. Finally, the fifth and sixth actions are the most drastic and difficult steps that can be taken, but these decisions, if made early enough, can be extremely beneficial to all involved.

Product Line and Management Changes and/or Sale of Property

These actions involve operating policy decisions and one or the other is often implemented when problems are perceived regardless of their severity. Often, a firm's growth has diminished drastically due to an obsolete product line and it behooves management to get back on the high-growth path of a new product(s). This decision usually entails new divisions and management if the change is done internally and always involves them if a new firm is bought outright. If the inherent problems are not serious, then measures such as these can prove effective. Our experience has been, however, that an accurate failure-prediction model will usually signal more drastic action.

The outright sale of unprofitable equipment and possibly whole divisions along with a thorough management shake-up are many times effective policy changes. Time after time, we have observed such changes *after* bankruptcy has been declared and even then, the decision does not emanate from the top management, but is the result of changes made by an impartial, objective bankruptcy trustee. If the requisite management change is at the very top, then only rarely do we see boards of directors implementing such policies while the firm is still existing normally. The sale of unprofitable property is, unfortunately, usually done at such a late date that significant losses have already been incurred. Since time is of the essence here, a model which can point toward savings earlier than is normally the case has clear advantages. This is especially the case when delays of property sales and management changes mean that the only remaining changes are the more extreme ones.

Merger Solicitation

Often, the most simple and effective means to overcome serious financial problems is through a merger with a financially sound and/or management enriched company. Although mergers have become quite a commonplace occurrence, they still represent a rather drastic change. The type of merger advocated here involves a firm which realizes its own shortcomings early enough to still be a relatively vibrant enterprise, thereby able to command a respectable price from the buyer. This takes a considerable amount of management skill—all of which is impossible unless management is shown convincingly that continuation of present conditions can only worsen the situation.

At this point, only a few statements regarding mergers will be made (see Chapter 5). The importance of timely mergers is perhaps most evident in regulated or quasiregulated industries such as railroads, savings and loan associations, commercial banks, and insurance companies. In these industries, bankruptcy in its traditional form is highly objectionable since there is usually significant public interest involved. Therefore, when failure is imminent, the regulatory or supervisory body steps in and either initiates or specifies a merger between the embarrassed company and another company in the same industry. The savings and loan industry, especially on the West Coast, has witnessed this phenomenon on several occasions. A currently beseiged industry which is regulated and which represents a significant public interest is the financial securities brokerage group centered around Wall Street. The year 1970 saw the combination of several of the largest brokerage concerns. What is unique is that in many cases the firm which would have failed (and may still do so) if not for the merger was the larger enterprise of the two. We no doubt can look forward to a greater number of mergers of this type.

The essential point to be made is that the decision to actively seek a merger is a crucial one and the earlier it is made, the better. The McDonnell-Douglas merger in 1967 is a prime example of relatively early assessment of future doom and the savings accomplished through a well-planned and executed merger.

Financial Arrangements

Economic and financial problems which lie between the need for changes in business policies and the necessity to declare bankruptcy call for several alternative financial measures. These measures are specific in a technical sense, but they are by no means uncommon. One set of financial arrangements solely involves the creditors of the embarrassed company. Often, a firm will be able to remain in existence if the claims of creditors are either reduced in amount or postponed for a period of time beyond the due date. These arrangements are referred to as creditor composition and extension, respectively. The theory behind the voluntary acceptance of these measures by the creditors is that, although they absorb a temporary loss, the total amount received will be greater than it would be if the firm defaulted on its obligations and was forced into a costly bankruptcy.

A second type of financial arrangement only involves the equity portion of the firm's capital structure and, as long as accepted accounting standards are met, does not require formal endorsement by any of the security holders. Essentially, this process involves a redesign of the retained earnings to eliminate a deficit in this account. Recall, we found that one of the important predictors of corporate bankruptcy was the Retained Earnings to Total Assets ratio. Therefore, readjustments must be made for forecasting purposes. A long string of negative profits will result in negative retained earnings and possibly even negative net worth. Quasireorganization implicitly accounts for this condition and seeks to artificially eliminate the accumulated losses by charging the deficit against the capital surplus account. Downward revaluation in assets so that returns on total assets or total equity will appear more favorable is also a tactic of quasireorganizations. In this process, retained earnings deficits are also eliminated.[15] The firm, therefore, cleans up a bit and prepares itself for a more prosperous future. It should be realized, however, that nothing really has changed, except perhaps the firm's ability to raise new capital. Even this is questionable and unless the future actually is profitable, the entire quasireorganization is worthless and, in fact, is potentially harmful.

The essential ingredient about these rather extreme measures is that the current problems faced by the firm are temporary and the future looks well for positive earnings and cash flow performance. We cannot emphasize this too strongly. Unless the future is encouraging, the reduction or postponement of claims will prolong the firm's agony and ultimately reduce the total flows to the very creditors who voluntarily have approved the financial arrangement. Likewise, a quasireorganization in a situation that continues to deteriorate serves no purpose (except it may cover up management incompetence—but only for a short time). The astute analyst, however, will probably become aware of the true nature of events in a short time. Management, therefore, has the responsibility to resort to such measures as creditor arrangements or quasireorganization only if it will eliminate costly interruptions of normal business operations and expensive court costs and enable the firm to get back on the right track. The corporate decisionmakers must be honest and as objective as possible in their choice of action. The tendency to avoid formal bankruptcy proceedings is pervasive, but unless the immediate future of the present operating and financial situation is encouraging, the stop-gap measures will fail. It would have been more beneficial to bypass these arrangements and go directly to bankruptcy.

Bankruptcy Reorganization

If the company's situation is so drastic that creditors can wait no longer for payments on their claims, and expected operating conditions are not expected to improve, the decision to petition the courts for bankruptcy will often be the only wise decision. The essential factor is *timing*. A firm should not throw in the towel if it can possibly avoid it, but at the same time, to delay this most difficult decision is, in the opinion of this writer, tantamount to fraud. Fraud is used here in the broad sense of the word and it refers to management's having the necessary knowledge of its precarious situation but refusing to admit failure.

Rather than repeat many of the institutional factors discussed in Chapter 1, we present a case study of one bankruptcy reorganization which will highlight the benefits of this financial-legal process.

Muntz-TV

The company was incorporated in 1950 and took over the operations of a California company of the same name. Through its two wholly owned subsidiaries, Muntz manufactured, assembled and sold television sets directly to the consumer via nationwide distribution outlets. The company grew rapidly in the first few years and by March 1954, it had a total of 78 branches. Annual earnings after taxes averaged over $800,000 for the period 1951-1953. During the first five months ending August 1953, Muntz and its subsidiaries lost almost $1.5 million and the operating loss soared to $3.3 million for fiscal (April) 1954. An additional nonrecurring loss of $3.5 million was recorded due to liabilities of claimants in excess of recorded liabilities. The firm's two manufacturing plants were operating at much below capacity and *sales* at most distribution outlets did not cover operating expenses.

Factors contributing to Muntz' rapid decline included a softening in the TV market, decentralization of the assembly operation, depletion of working capital caused by too rapid expansion, and inflexible cost structures, especially at its distribution outlets. Management had made a key mistake in business policy since there was no way to reduce personnel at branches and still maintain sales and services on those sets already sold.

On March 2, 1954, an involuntary petition for bankruptcy reorganization was filed under Chapter X of the National Bankruptcy Act. Just one year earlier, the firm appeared to be a solvent growing concern. When it became apparent that Muntz was heading for disaster, the bankruptcy course was taken—although admittedly the firm's creditors were instrumental in this relatively early decision. The petition was approved and two trustees were appointed to continue the operations and management of the business. At this point, total liabilities exceeded the book value of assets by almost $4 million—therefore, this figure totalled Muntz' negative net worth. There was little doubt the firm was insolvent in a bankruptcy sense and if the balance sheet truly reflected the asset's valuation, the real net worth was also negative. Subsequent developments, however, showed that a cursory examination of the firm's condition at this critical moment would have been grossly misleading and, in fact, Muntz TV was not insolvent and was saved from extinction by the bankruptcy process.

The reorganization set up under the able guidance of the two trustees brought on important changes. Muntz liquidated all of its assets which were unrelated to the manufacturing operation; distribution outlets were sold as rapidly as possible and replaced by independent retailers. The firm also ceased to sell customer warranty contracts or handle time payment papers of buyers. Proceeds from this partial asset liquidation went to modernization of plant facilities and the actual manufacture of sets was suspended for six months. As in the case of all Chapter X proceedings, the major liabilities were frozen until a satisfactory reorganization plan was approved.

Liabilities and capital to be dealt with under the plan of reorganization as of March 1955 are listed in Table 4-2.[16]

The large tax liability was reviewed by a tax expert and the revised tax liability was set at a maximum of $1.45 million. The state taxes were also reduced by over $100,000. The general creditor claim carried on the balance sheet was at a maximum of what Muntz could possibly be liable for and was

Table 4-2
Liabilities and Capital, Muntz-TV, 1955

Liabilities		Capital	
Federal taxes	$2,758,000	Common stk. ($1 Per)	$1,115,000
State taxes	433,000	Capital surplus	916,000
Gen'l creditors	4,615,000	Earned deficit	(5,618,000)
	$7,806,000		($3,617,000)

reduced to $4.2 million. These conservative balance sheet figures are evidence against the contention, held by some, that firms in a bankrupt position tend to inflate their assets and conceal their real liabilities.

SEC Participation and the Reorganization Plan

Under Chapter X, the Security and Exchange Commission (SEC) is obligated to investigate and submit an Advisory Report on the reorganization plan if the total liabilities of the debtor exceed $3 million. The SEC did submit a report on the Muntz TV case in June 1955, and reported on the reduction in liabilities.

The trustees reorganization plan was a joint project involving the consolidation of Muntz TV and its two subsidiaries. The plan was predicated upon the assumption that the debtors were solvent on a consolidated basis. The decision regarding a firm's solvency is based on a comprehensive valuation of the firm's assets. If it is found that the real value of the assets exceeds that of the liabilities, an equity for the old stockholders exists and they *can* participate in the reorganized company. Muntz operated profitably in 1955 and because the mode of the firm's operations was significantly different than in the past, it was felt that the past operating results were unacceptable as a basis for determining the future earning power of the company.

The trustees hired two independent analysts to work out a valuation scheme and to testify as to the fairness and feasibility of the reorganization plan. The Bankruptcy Act specifies that the disinterested trustee is allowed, even encouraged, to solicit the advice of experts as to the value of the firm and the plan's feasibility. The technique generally used for valuation purposes is the *capitalization of income* method whereby some estimate of future average earnings is capitalized at an appropriate rate to arrive at a going concern value. It is this value that is compared with the firm's liabilities in order to aid in the formulation of the plan.

The reorganization plan utilized the capitalization of income method and was based on an annual sales volume of $16 million. This figure was substantially greater than 1955 sales but still some $4 million below that of the crisis year, 1954. A before-tax profit margin on sales of 6.35% resulted in an earnings estimate of just over $1 million. This profit margin was slightly above the industry average of 6%. The trustees then applied a 12.5% (8 times earnings) rate to the estimated earnings. It was their opinion that the management and productive assets of the company in 1955 compared favorably with those of other companies of similar size in the television industry and, therefore, the capitalization rate was based, to a large extent, on the market capitalization rates of other TV makers. The firm's huge $5 million loss-carry-forward was considered ample to eliminate income taxes for the next five years. The final valuation is described below.

Trustee Valuation Estimate

Going Concern Value	$ 8,130,000
Excess of Current Assets over Current Liabilities	2,135,000
	$10,265,000
Less: Working Capital Needs	950,000
Total Value	$ 9,315,000

The SEC disagreed with the reorganization plan on the basis that the trustee's report handled the tax loss benefit mistakenly. While it appeared that the firm would be free from taxation over the next four years (1956-1959), the subsequent income would become taxable again. However, if you consider this benefit for only four years on a discounted present value basis, the results will be quite different than they would be if you just ignore taxes and capitalize before-tax income. I interpret this to mean that the four-year tax benefit should be added to the *capitalized after-tax expected earnings* in order to arrive at a true capitalized earnings estimate. If this method is utilized with the SEC's earnings estimate of $840,000 (slightly below the $1 million trustee estimate), the results are quite different.

Going Concern Value $420,000/.12	$3,500,000
Present Value of Tax Loss benefit, $420,000 for 4 years (12%)	1,275,000
Excess Working Capital (Net)	1,500,000
	6,275,000

Comparing this $6.275 million estimate to the liabilities of $5.650 million, the SEC concluded that there would be an equity for the common stockholders and that any plan that included them would be *fair*. However, the high debt ratio (88%) made it essential that the debt be reduced substantially in order for the plan to be *feasible*. This was eventually accomplished by reducing the debt liability further by issuing stock and by extending the terms of payment.

This experience highlights the importance of the assumptions within the general format of valuation and bodes for a more formalized procedure to prevent incorrect techniques and unfortunate results. Muntz TV was very fortunate to have this high debt ratio made explicit and to have the time to revise the trustee plan to rectify this situation.

In January 1956, the U.S. District Court approved the revised trustee plan for reorganization of Muntz TV. The big change occurred when the claims of the unsecured creditors were reduced again substantially and made payable over an 8-year period, 75% in noninterest bearing promissory notes and 25% in preferred stock. Holders of the outstanding common stock received new stock on a share-for-share basis. No dividends on the common could be paid until the notes were completely paid off. Actually, the approved plan had elements of creditor extension and composition and a type of quasireorganization. The latter was evident as the negative net worth was reduced to $2.2 million as of August 1956.

Comment

Chapter X of the Bankruptcy Act requires that a plan of reorganization be fair and equitable. The absolute priority doctrine is generally used as a measure of fairness. In its strictest sense, this doctrine says:

... In the distribution of values of a corporate successor to the debtor undergoing reorganization all claims must be satisfied fully in order of their legal priorities in accordance with the laws of bankruptcy.[17]

What this means is that junior creditors with unsecured claims are satisfied in full only after prior parties; and only after all creditors are paid in full for their claims, can holders of common equities receive recognition of their interests. In the Muntz case, the government and unsecured creditors should have received full payment in some form. The reorganization plan, however, provided for a further reduction of the unsecured creditors' claims and present payables were converted into long-term payables without interest payment provisions. The common equity interests sacrificed nothing and retained their interest without contributing at all. Their only sacrifice was the loss of the right to vote for five of the seven directors. The question of fairness under the absolute priority doctrine is partly determined by the allocation of risk and there is little doubt that the risk is greatest in the common equity sector. Should this risk-taking, in the normal sense, be rewarded by preferential treatment?

The entire tone of this case seems to be contrary to the conclusions reached by Francis Calkins in his 1940s work. He concluded that the absolute priority doctrine discriminates in favor of the creditors of the firm and against junior creditors or equity interests.[18] We must admit that this appears to be the usual occurrence, but as the postreorganization experience in the Muntz case will show, the stockholders did extremely well.

Postreorganization Analysis

In order to fully assess the bankruptcy-reorganization process, we must evaluate the new firm's experience with respect to general operations and the various vested interests involved. Through the joint efforts of the trustee, the court, the SEC, and Muntz' remaining personnel, the following major changes were made during and slightly after reorganization: (1) A complete changeover in top management. None of the ten top ranking officers in the company held comparable positions after reorganization. (2) The firm became a one-product manufacturer. (3) The distribution process was altered radically. (4) The firm's capital structure was remodeled.

These changes provided the proper medicine for Muntz TV as testified by the company's subsequent performance. After reorganization, Muntz' sales dropped significantly, as the scope of operations was reduced, but in the six-year period (1956-61), operating earnings improved greatly over the prebankruptcy period (with the exception of 1957). Sales in this six-year period averaged about $8 million—much below the trustee and SEC estimates, but earnings after taxes jumped to about $850,000 in 1960 and 1961. The earnings results were significantly higher than both earlier estimates and showed a tremendous increase in profit margins. In 1961, the stockholders equity became positive for the first time since 1953. Muntz was able to catch its breath and then regain its momentum during and after the critical years of bankruptcy. Without the reorganization alternative, the firm would have had to liquidate or face a merger—the terms of which would have probably been extremely unfavorable.

The various security holders and creditors realized generally favorable returns in the period after reorganization. A five-year period is chosen arbitrarily for analysis. The plan provided for the issuance of promissory notes and preferred stock in lieu of the firm's unsecured liability. The notes remained unpaid until 1961 when Muntz offered to exchange them on the basis of one share of stock for every $6 of notes outstanding. In essence, therefore, these creditors received 75% of their claims in the form of common stock and 25% in preferred stock. The common stock sold at a high of $7 and a low of $4 per share in 1961 (average of $5.50). On a present value basis, explicitly considering creditor opportunity costs,[c] we can observe how well the unsecured creditors fared. This can be shown as:

$$\text{Creditor Claim (1956)} \quad \text{vs.} \quad \frac{\text{Common Stock Value (1961)}}{(1 + r)}$$

$$\underline{\$6} \quad \text{vs.} \quad \frac{\$5.50}{(1 + .11)^5} = \underline{\$3.22}$$

[c]The choice of an appropriate discount rate reflecting opportunity costs for the creditors (and later for the stockholders) is certainly not obvious. Since the original plan specified the major payment in the form of a promissory note, one rate which might have been utilized was the average rate for the 5-year period on debt instruments. The fact that the eventual payment was in the form of common stock seems to shift the opportunity cost concept to the equity market. Regardless of the appropriate payment instrument, the risk situation in 1956 was undeniably greater for Muntz than for most other companies' debt or equity securities.

After considering the above arguments, the opportunity cost chosen was the rate of return realized on a portfolio of common stocks listed on the New York Stock Exchange and reported comprehensively by L. Fisher and J. Lorie "Rates of Return on Investments in Common Stock: The Year-By-Year Record, 1926-65," *The Journal of Business*, Vol. xxxx, No. 3, July 1968, Table 2, Part F. This rate was chosen as a compromise and because of its availability. The relevant rate for the 1956-61 period is 11%.

Unquestionably, the creditors would have been better off had they received their claim in the form of cash in 1956 rather than the note-stock arrangement realized in 1961. It is doubtful, however, that Muntz could have made this payment and most certainly, it would have had to raise further funds in 1956 or else be forced to liquidate. The Court's decision was to avoid the attempt to obtain external financing and, therefore, possibly sacrifice some of the creditors' claim. The chance of success in raising and servicing the required financing was probably not very good anyway. Still, on an *ex-post* basis, it appears that the unsecured creditors did make sacrifices to the benefit of all others involved— common stockholders, future suppliers, employees, and even the government (through additional tax revenues).

The common stockholders, on the other hand, fared very well. The common was selling at a high of $2.625 and a low of $1 in 1956 ($1.81 average). (The average price just prior to bankruptcy was even lower—slightly less than $1 per share.) Using the same evaluation technique as was used in the creditor case, we observe that the old stockholders did indeed do well as of the year 1961:

$$\text{Shareholder Value (per share)} \quad \text{vs.} \quad \frac{\text{Value (1961)}}{(1+r)}$$

$$\$1.81 \quad \text{vs.} \quad \frac{\$5.50}{(1+.11)^5} = \underline{\underline{3.22}}$$

The common stockholder experience in bankrupt firms is, on average, not nearly as good as it was with Muntz TV, but in a surprising number of bankruptcy-reorganizations, the old shareholders have done significantly better than most analysts and theoreticians would have expected.

Conclusion

On an overall basis, it appears that Muntz TV was truly rehabilitated in the postreorganization period. Standard financial ratio analysis shows that the firm improved in just about every major category, with the most impressive gains chalked up in the profitability and leverage sectors. Although such complete rehabilitation is not usually the case, the Muntz experience is impressive evidence of the inherent potential in bankruptcy-reorganization programs. This case study involved many of the important concepts and areas of business finance, including valuation theory, trusteeship functions, capital structure analysis, investor experience, and marketing strategy.

5 Bankruptcy and Mergers

It might seem a bit peculiar to include a chapter on mergers in a book devoted to the general subject of bankruptcy. For one thing, favorable economic conditions which are conducive to increased merger activity are, at the same time, negatively correlated with business failures (see Chapter 2). Yet, we can argue that in two interesting ways the bankruptcy and merger phenomena are intimately related. The first relationship is observable and concerns the not too infrequent occurrence of bankruptcy reorganizations resulting in a merger between the debtor and another enterprise. The second type of relationship is not usually obvious but entails the merger of a firm which may be on the road to failure with a second, more healthy enterprise. In this instance, the merger solicitation may be initiated by the financially troubled firm itself or by the aggressive management of the purchaser seeking to obtain sick companies at a nominal cost.

The major theme of this chapter is to emphasize that management should develop the ability to forecast impending problems early enough in order to effect a merger before bankruptcy and/or liquidation becomes their only alternative. It will be argued that the debtor in a bankruptcy reorganization is placed in the unfortunate position of little or no bargaining power should the merger solution become mandatory. At this stage, it is usually too late for an equitable arrangement and the predominant factor in the merger is expediency. A merger between the same two companies if consummated prior to bankruptcy, will almost always result in more favorable treatment for the debtor. Although we cannot prove this contention, the reasoning seems logical and evidence will be presented in its support.

The methodology employed in this chapter will consist of several in-depth case studies. The cases involve several mergers which resulted from bankruptcy reorganizations and one which is believed to have obviated the need for a bankruptcy reorganization. The discussion will serve another purpose as well. Up to this point, we have described and discussed the bankruptcy process but, with the exception of the Muntz TV case in Chapter 4, and the Appendix to Chapter 1, the actual reorganization mechanism has not been studied in depth. We will now attempt to examine the bankruptcy process through several descriptive case studies which should portray it more clearly.

Tax Considerations in Mergers

A crucial factor in the overall analysis of mergers is the tax implications involved. Actually, the term merger is but a subclassification of the generic term, reorganization. A business combination, whether it be classified as a merger, a consolidation, or an acquisition is nontaxable only if the transaction is of a certain type of reorganization as defined by the Internal Revenue Code.[a] In this case, a reorganization means a readjustment of corporate capital structure and takes three basic forms, A, B and C.[b] Type A reorganizations are statutory mergers or consolidations whereby two or more corporations are combined into one entity—if one of the old companies survives, it is called a statutory merger, but if a totally new entity is formed, it is referred to as a consolidation. This type of reorganization permits a wide variety of securities to be issued by the purchaser for the stock of the selling firm. Type B reorganizations occur when 80 percent or more of the seller is exchanged for the voting stock of the acquirer. Finally, in a Type C reorganization, the selling corporation transfers virtually all[1] of its assets solely in exchange for voting stock of the purchaser. The voting stock can be preferred as well as common.

In a tax free reorganization, the seller does not realize a gain or loss upon sale of the company.[2] This preferential treatment bestowed by Congress is partly the result of thinking that corporate reorganizations are beneficial to the economy. We have already made a case for the value of bankruptcy reorganizations. Technically, income tax theory does not endorse taxation of paper profits which is the situation in a merger where the exchanged securities are not as yet turned into cash. If an investor still has his original investment, although possibly composed of a different form, he has not closed out his transaction and therefore no tax should be forthcoming as yet.

While the tax-free-or-not ruling is important in all mergers, the most relevant tax feature for our concern is the operating-loss-carryover attribute. In general, this feature enables the acquiring firm to utilize the tax loss benefits of the selling company to offset its own future operating profits, thereby reducing its future tax liability. Since the selling corporation in a bankruptcy merger almost always has suffered severe losses just prior to bankruptcy, this feature is a prime—legally it cannot be *the* prime—motivation for the merger. The tax loss benefit transfer is not peculiar to bankrupt companies, however, and is often cited as critical in mergers involving two firms, one of which has had operating problems.

Statutory provisions for net operating loss carry forwards have been part of the federal tax system since 1918 and were first permitted for most reorganizations after 1954. The basic theory for carry-back and carry-forward of operating losses is to even-out profit fluctuations under our present accounting system. If the prior loss is sustained by the firm seeking to utilize the carry-over, the theory is sound. Where a corporation seeks to utilize some other firm's loss, as occurs in a merger, the question of continuity of the loss firm's business arises.[3] A

---

[a]Tax-free reorganizations are strictly limited by Section 368 (a)(1) of the Code, except in the case of an insolvency reorganization.

[b]Actually, there are three other types of reorganizations, (D, E, and F) which include liquidations, recapitalizations, and changes in identity, respectively. These three, however, are not relevant to the subsequent discussion.

provision of the loss carry-over statute states that where a loss corporation is purchased, the carry-over does not survive unless the business which generated the losses is continued. The merger must also be for a legitimate business purpose and not primarily for tax purposes. In order to preserve the full loss carry-over in a Type A or Type C tax-free reorganization, the stockholders of the loss corporation must receive at least 20 percent of the fair market value of the purchasing corporation. If they receive less than 20 percent, the tax loss feature is reduced by 5 percent for each 1 percent below the 20 percent criterion. For instance, if the old stockholders receive 15 percent, then only 75 percent of the loss carry-over is applicable. In a Type B reorganization, this 20 percent rule does not apply.

In the case of a bankruptcy reorganization merger, the Court may rule that the debtor's stockholders not be permitted to participate in the merged company because of insolvency. In order for the tax loss carry-over to remain applicable, the acquiring company must get special permission from the Internal Revenue authorities since obviously a continuity of interest is not evident and usually the reorganization plan includes a transfer of many types of securities. In a pre-1954 reorganization, profits of the surviving corporation could be reduced by a deficit of the predecessor corporation provided that the reorganization was voluntary. The 1954 statute was more liberal as the following cases will illustrate.

Northeastern Steel Corporation

Northeastern Steel was incorporated in December 1954 as a nonintegrated steel producer and was the result of continuous efforts to establish a steel producer in the New England area. The firm commenced operations in January 1955 and was unsuccessful in its efforts to earn a profit right until its bankruptcy petition in February 1957—just two years after inception. At that time, the company was in default on its long-term debentures and was threatened with damage suits from other creditors. How the firm failed to achieve its economic objectives during an expansionary business cycle is a classic example of inept management accompanied by some unfortunate operating difficulties. The resulting bankruptcy reorganization and merger with Carpenter Steel illustrate clearly an expedient, but not necessarily equitable, solution to a corporate failure.

The nonintegrated steel industry, unlike the basically oligopolistic integrated segment, is comprised of a large number of highly competitive firms. Northeastern entered this more specialized market which possesses natural barriers to entry in the form of large and complex plants requiring a large capital investment. Since prices have a tendency to be tacitly agreed upon by manufacturers, the less efficient firms find it difficult at times to compete on a favorable basis. The industry is marked by its cyclical nature, with the intensity of competition varying inversely with the amount of business in prospect.

The steel industry, at the time of Northeastern's entrance, had a great deal of excess capacity but a favorable outlook for the future. The short 1953-54 recession had just ended, contributing toward the aforementioned excess capacity—especially true for the nonintegrated steel manufacturers. The company's experience, however, was unfortunate from the outset. The initial financing necessary to purchase the old Stanley Works steel plant was increased substantially due to the conversion of standard steel production to a specialty steel arrangement. Total capital raised exceeded $17 million as described below.

	$ million
4½% first mortgage bonds	$ 6.0
6% subordinated debentures	6.8
Common stock (970,000 shares outstanding)	4.4
	$17.2

Despite the fact that the year 1955 was a particularly successful year for the steel industry, Northeastern struggled to survive. Its difficulties included: (1) greater than anticipated capital, construction and start-up expenditures; (2) equipment problems and supplier difficulties; (3) channels of distribution inadequacies; (4) increased costs of production without sales increases; and (5) excessively high financial interest and sinking fund charges as a result of a grossly overleveraged capital structure.

The firm was unable to conserve cash in its initial stages of operation—a crucial factor to a new firm. The only cash conserving feature undertaken was overdone—the use of borrowed funds. Improper assessment of the capability of the old Stanley Works plant necessitated the construction of a new mill which increased capital expenditures by 16%. The new construction also caused delays in production and so Northeastern was unable to tap the growing demand for specialty steel products. The company also used the most expensive source of fuel (scrap) in their electric furnaces. It became increasingly apparent that if the high costs of production and construction were forecasted accurately, the firm's promoters might not have decided to begin operations in the first place. In addition, the firm suffered further hardships early in 1956 when equipment malfunctions caused its mill to be closed down for several weeks and a labor strike at a company which supplied electrical equipment delayed completion of its new plant.

Another crucial error in business judgment made by Northeastern's management was the decision to establish its own sales force to develop markets for its products. This was instituted despite the fact that there existed numerous independent wholesalers who could have taken some of the initial burden off the inexperienced Northeastern management team in its early stages. The new sales force failed to develop markets—which may not have existed in the first place—and the firm's sales volume did not rise very much. Further, Northeastern suffered from its unfavorable location for inexpensive, skilled labor. As a result of these negative factors, the firm suffered losses of $1.25 million and $1.83 million in its first two years (1955, 1956). In the first six months of 1957, losses totalled over $2 million. The firm barely covered variable costs in 1955 and failed to do so completely in 1956. The handwriting of failure was on the wall.

Immediate Causes of Bankruptcy. The final cause of failure was, as is usually the case, the inability to meet current expenses. As early as August 1956, the first mortgage bondholders extended the time for meeting both the sinking fund requirements and a preestablished working capital requirement of $2 million. Some five months later, however, these same bondholders filed a damage suit to collect their loan when Northeastern's working capital went below $2 million. One day prior to this event, Northeastern filed a voluntary petition for reorganization under Chapter X. The petition was approved on February 5th, and the firm's liabilities were frozen for the duration of the reorganization proceedings. The firm's president was confident, however, that Northeastern could pull out of its troubles.

Northeastern's failure to meet its fixed charges should not have come as a surprise to anyone—except perhaps its own management. The company was formed with a capital structure more similar to the public utility industry than the steel sector. Somehow, the promoters were able to secure financing from creditors who were willing to invest in a firm whose debt to total assets ratio was 83% in 1955 and almost 75% at its outset. This is excessive for any industry and compared to a steel industry average of 34%, it is clear that Northeastern was far out of line. This is especially peculiar in light of the extreme cyclical nature of the steel industry.

While the direct causal factor of bankruptcy was financial, the events that precipitated the trouble were shared equally by economic, managerial, and financial conditions. It was clear (at least with hindsight), however, that financial readjustments could not rehabilitate the firm. This is a point which is often overlooked in the literature and by those involved in a bankruptcy petition. The reorganization process can only be successful if the malignant conditions, both economic and financial, can be cut out.

Reorganization Leads to a Merger. Economic principles might suggest that a firm unable to cover variable costs should discontinue operations, but this was not the case at Northeastern. The trustees assigned to the bankruptcy decided that maximum realization of values could only come by continued operation and in the event that reorganization would prove to be unfeasible, there still existed the possibility of a merger with a more established firm in the industry. In other words, a merger was considered as a policy of last resort—really a next-to-last resort since liquidation usually claims that ultimate distinction.

Despite these plans, operating losses continued to mount and for the first six months of 1957 exceeded $2 million with a cash flow deficit of roughly $900,000. It seemed apparent that the firm had little rehabilitory potential in its present form, although the steel industry, in general, continued to boom.

Finally, the trustees were convinced that reorganization was not feasible and its report in June 1957, stated that present management was inefficient and inexperienced in its operation of the company and that there was no hope for profitable continuance. The only remaining hope was to combine Northeastern with a financially and management enriched steel company—time was of the essence. Trustee solicitation of outside interest finally was instituted.

After an earlier proposal by H.K. Porter & Co., Carpenter Steel Corporation began to show interest which was considered genuine by the trustees. That is to say, their motives for a merger went beyond the obvious tax-loss benefits involved. Carpenter Steel was one of the oldest specialty steel producers and its most recent operations were very profitable. Like most of the nation's steel companies in 1957, Carpenter was considering increased capacity to take advantage of expanding markets. Therefore, along with the obvious tax benefits, Carpenter's motives included its desire to increase capacity substantially, its inclination to purchase rather than build modern facilities, and its ability to absorb a considerable amount of debt. The negative factors were prospects of losses from operations in the next few years and the necessity to provide capital and manpower for improvement of facilities and managerial training.

The trustees' plan of reorganization submitted to the Court was based upon Carpenter's offer in June 1957. A condition of the offer was that plant and personnel of the debtor were to be maintained. The plan was rushed through negotiations and court considerations because of the time factor and Carpenter's threat to withdraw the offer unless prompt action was taken. The plan's financial terms were based on the assumption of *insolvency* of the debtor, thereby eliminating the outstanding stock, warrants and options from the future of Northeastern. Investors, who less than three years earlier contributed capital, now realized a 100% loss on their investment. The new capitalization would leave outstanding the $6 million of first mortgage bonds with defaults and provided for the issuance of new common stock by Northeastern (which was to become a subsidiary of Carpenter). This new stock was to be exchanged for Carpenter shares based on a formula—not to be less than 40,000 shares. The number of shares actually issued would depend on the working capital position of the debtor. In actuality, conditions continued to deteriorate such that the eventual terms called for the minimum of 40,000 shares issued to the remaining creditors of the old company—bank notes, unsecured creditors, and debenture holders. The latter actually received less since they were subordinated to the bank note. Based on Carpenter's expected common stock selling price of $70, the 40,000 shares plus $6 million debt equalled a total package of $8.8 million in value.

SEC Opinion and Court Conclusion. The Court, after swift consideration of the trustees' plan and SEC opinion, approved the plan and ordered it submitted to a vote of the creditors involved. Although the judge did not think the creditors "were made whole," he commented that the plan was fair to all concerned. He cautioned that the trustees could only claim Northeastern's potential contribution to the earnings of the merged company and not the difference Carpenter's contribution might eventually make. As for the SEC opinion that the plan was unfair because the trustees' valuation (approximately $9 million) underestimated the real value by $2 million, the judge ruled that since the only real alternative to Carpenter's offer was liquidation, the offer would be acceptable.[c] In essence, expediency overruled the objections to valuation and fairness. Creditors were compensated with regard to their priorities and the old stockholders were rightfully eliminated. The SEC's position was one of objectively viewing the available facts and reaching an informed judgment. This case clearly illustrates the Commission's determined effort to remain an impartial and conscientious witness in bankruptcy proceedings.

Postreorganization Merger Results. In November 1957, Northeastern Steel Co. ceased to exist and Carpenter Steel Co. of New England was formed as a subsidiary of the parent company. Although some new management was brought into the floundering operation, a nucleus of the best plant employees was retained and about $5 million was invested in new facilities. Much of the older Northeastern property was sold off and output was restricted to the more profitable products. The narrower product mix was slowly integrated with Carpenter's existing line and resulted in some economies, especially in channel of distribution outlets. Very little was produced for shipment, however, in the first fifteen months during which time Carpenter suffered losses from these operations estimated at $3 million. It was not until early 1959 that Carpenter products from the Northeastern facilities were shipped on a profitable basis. Although the major cause of the reduced total sales for Carpenter was the nation's economic recession, the increased costs involved with the merger and earnings dilution caused by the additional 40,000 shares added to the reduced profit picture. Conditions improved measurably after 1958 when the new facilities and capacity began to be utilized. Also, Carpenter was in a position to take advantage of at least two very favorable situations as a result of the merger—tax considerations and financial leverage.

Before the merger, Carpenter was extremely vulnerable to federal income taxes, paying an average of 55% of earnings in taxes for the years 1955-57. As a result of the merger, the firm received a tax loss-carry-forward of over $6 million for the years 1958-61—adding $1.24, $.34, $2.24, and $2.64 to earnings per share in those four years. This tax benefit exceeded the trustee and SEC estimates. Before the Northeastern acquisition, Carpenter had no long-term debt outstanding and its total debt/asset ratio was under 24%, compared to an industry average of 30%. After 1958, Carpenter was in a much better position to take advantage of the leveraging effect without too great an increase in financial risk.

It should be noted, however, that Carpenter's record earnings per share in

---

[c]It is interesting to note that the SEC valuation in the Northeastern case was referred to as too high, whereas Calkins found a predominant conservative nature to the SEC's earnings estimates.[4]

1957 of $8.00 has never been approached again. Whether this can be traced to the effects of the merger is only conjecture. The firm's common stock price reached its historical high in 1958 (76 1/2), but showed a definite downward trend in the subsequent decade. Carpenter Steel is still an extremely solvent and prosperous enterprise, but there is little tangible evidence to show that the merger with Northeastern was a success. In 1968, the firm changed its name to Carpenter Technology Corporation.

Security Holders' Experience in the Bankruptcy Merger. As mentioned earlier, the old Northeastern stockholders were eliminated from participation in the merger due to insolvency (liabilities exceeded the valuation of assets). Only the first mortgage bondholders and the bank notes were paid off in full, but they, too, suffered due to the extension of time permitted to pay off their claims. The latter received common stock for its $250,000 claim and now faced the dilemma of whether to sell these shares or not. The unsecured creditors who split the remaining common stock did not fare very well, however. In order to evaluate just how these creditors did as a result of the bankruptcy merger, we can compare their possible future returns with their 1957 claim. Their returns are discounted for average stockholder opportunity costs for the five-year period 1958-1962.[5] Based on the number of shares remaining from the original 40,000 after the bank note was paid off, the unsecured creditors received approximately $320 worth of stock per $1000 in claims, while the debenture holders garnered slightly less than $300 worth per $1000 claim. Comparing their claims and receipts with the subsequent value of the securities received, we note that the creditors never came close to attaining their claims (see Table 5-1).

Since these creditors received only about 30 cents on the dollar (in stock) and Carpenter's stock subsequently fell, it comes as no surprise that the creditors did not fare very well. One advantage, however, for the subordinated debenture holders was the increased marketability of the common stock compared to the debt.

Several questions relating to the Northeastern-Carpenter experience come to

Table 5-1
Unsecured Creditor Experience, Northeastern Steel Corporation

| | 1957 | Discounted Value of Receipts | | | | |
		1958	1959	1960	1961	1962
Claim	$1,000	250	402	355	327	233
Receipt	$ 322					

| Debenture Holder Experience | | | | | | |
| Discounted Value of Receipts | | | | | | |
	1957	1958	1959	1960	1961	1962
Claim	$1,000	234	374	331	305	233
Receipt	$ 300					

mind. How would the old creditors have done if the debtor had liquidated upon bankruptcy? How would they have done if Carpenter's offer had not been accepted? Finally, would the entire bankruptcy reorganization have been averted if Northeastern's management had realized their fate *prior* to bankruptcy declaration and began merger solicitation at an earlier date?

Concluding Remarks. This case study presents a situation which is not typical of most bankruptcy reorganizations in that the bankrupt firm did not continue to exist as an independent operating entity after reorganization. The merger, however, did enable the assets to remain productive, workers to remain employed, and the creditors to realize full or partial compensation. The crux of this reorganization, however, is indicative of typical results. In the presence of adverse economic and financial conditions, important legal rights and expectations of security holders are sacrificed or even eliminated. As for the merger, it showed that in many cases, practical expediency supersedes economic values.

Perhaps the most important point to be derived from Northeastern's bankruptcy experience relates back to the implications of a model similar to the one developed in Chapter 3. In the case just described, the bankrupt firm's management and trustees realized that the only real alternative for the company was a merger. But this realization occurred after five months in bankruptcy. As a result, a merger did manifest itself, but at a time when creditor claims, employee security and further operating conditions had significantly deteriorated—common stockholders already had been eliminated. All of these various interests would have been better served if a merger had occurred before bankruptcy. No doubt, Northeastern's negotiating ability would have been superior to their almost impotent position in bankruptcy.[d] In fact, the trustee in the case argued for acceptance of the Carpenter merger in September 1957:

It would have been possible to realize 50¢ on the dollar *3 months ago* if the plan (merger) had been accepted but now it looks doubtful they (creditors) will receive in excess of 25¢ on the dollar.[6] To this quote we add the question: How much would have been received if a merger were consummated 12 months "ago"—6 months *prior* to bankruptcy declaration?

Green River Steel Corporation

This case study is very similar to the Northeastern Steel situation involving a bankruptcy reorganization followed by a merger of two steel companies. The primary differences lie in prebankruptcy profitability results and the fact that the *merger* was predicated upon the bankruptcy petition.

---

[d]In correspondence with Carpenter's present management, this writer was told that the Northeastern purchase and analysis was considered like all other investment possibilities and would have been similar even if the Chapter X situation had never occurred. In other words, the asset's value determined the merger offer. Whom do you believe?

Green River was incorporated in 1950 for the purpose of producing and selling semifinished steel products. Actual operations commenced in less than three years. Due to operating and financial difficulties, the firm reported a large net loss in 1954, followed by a smaller loss in the following year and finally achieved a net profit in 1956. This brightening profit picture, however, did not prevent Green River from declaring bankruptcy under Chapter X in September 1956. The interesting reasons and lessons to be learned from this seeming paradox—profitability and bankruptcy—follows.

Prebankruptcy Conditions. Without doubt, the single most important contribution to the eventual bankruptcy goes back to the initial financing of the firm's operations. Since a large capital investment is necessary for steel manufacturing, the Green River promoters had to raise over $12 million. This consisted of:

	$ Million
4½% First Mortgage Note	$ 3.56
4½% Second Mortgage Note	5.00
3½% Subordinated Debentures	4.00
Common Equity	.08
Total Capital	$12.64

The funds from the first and second mortgage notes were supplied by the federal government. The debt portion, therefore, was an almost unbelievable 99% of total capital with *fixed* interest and principal payments in 1954 (the first year of operation) totalling over $1 million and would rise to over $2 million in 1957. This financial handicap was indeed a severe problem at the outset.

Green River's operating problems started with their entry into the steel market during a short but sharp economic recession, 1953-54. Large steel inventories had been built up during the Korean War and were now being worn down slowly. Steel industry production dropped from a high of 87% to 40% of capacity in December 1953. Green River achieved only a 20% of capacity production in 1953 and early 1954. Despite low sales, working capital needs forced the firms to pledge accounts receivable with banks. Green River's problems were internal as well. The product mix at their semiintegrated plants was extremely diversified, ranging from very low priced carbon steel products to high-grade aircraft steel. The inexperienced sales force simply was not capable of handling this product line successfully.

Another more subtle problem involved the high management turnover in the firm's short existence. One of the important factors looked at by financial institutions and other sources of capital is the quality of management. Green River ran into severe financing problems after the 1954 operating problems. In hindsight, it appears that the unstable management conditions were instrumental in the early working capital shortage and the eventual failure.

Despite the early difficulties, Green River managed a steadily improving trend in both sales and profits. The figures for the first three full years are shown in

Table 5-2. Recall that the steel industry enjoyed unprecedented success during the 1955-57 period and the growth at Green River should not be construed as unqualified success. However, Northeastern Steel failed to achieve a profit during this same period.

The key to Green River's final demise was its inability to grow without strangling itself. The high financial leverage condition augmented by an excessive operating leverage asset structure proved fatal. In fact, due to the early operating losses, Green River's total debt to total asset ratio was 116% at the end of 1954 and 127% in 1956. The industry average for those two years was 25% and 34%, respectively. While the steel industry was producing at near capacity levels in 1955 and 1956, Green River only could manage a high of 60% of capacity in 1956. Fundamental financial theory tells us that a firm with extremely high financial and operating leverage can do very well if it increases sales beyond some breakeven point. Unfortunately, Green River did not capitalize on this opportunity.

Bankruptcy Reorganization and the Merger Offer. The final embarrassment to Green River was, as is usually the case, financial in nature. The entire first mortgage note held by the Reconstruction Finance Corporation was due on January 1, 1957, and it was obvious to management that its earnings and financial condition could not improve sufficiently by that date to make refinancing possible. Toward the end of 1956, Jessop Steel Corp. became interested in purchasing Green River and a take-over bid was made to the directors of the beleaguered debtor. One of the conditions of the Jessop proposal was that Green River effect a reorganization under Chapter X of the Bankruptcy Act. This was done on September 12, 1956. The situation must have been particularly frustrating to Green River's management and stockholders since 1956 was their first profitable year, and just two weeks later, the steel industry was reported to be producing at 100.2% of capacity. The Green River reorganization plan was based on the Jessop Steel offer just as the Northeastern plan was based on a proposal submitted by Carpenter Steel. It had been concluded that "the debtor could not successfully operate independently and must be affiliated with a firm which is willing to furnish additional capital, experienced management and a sales force."[7]

The trustee's evaluation of "successful operation" must be questioned by this writer. It seems that Green River had demonstrated an ability to operate

Table 5-2
Operating Experience, Green River Steel, 1954-1956

Year	Net Sales	Net Profits (Loss)
1954	$ 5,400,000	($2,185,000)
1955	$10,780,000	($ 574,000)
1956	$12,273,000	$ 204,000

profitably and meet its fixed interest payments. What the debtor could not meet successfully was the principal repayment on its obviously overleveraged debt structure. Therefore, it is our opinion that criticism of both financial and economic performance should not be lumped into a single generalization although the two are obviously related.

The plan was based on the assumption that Green River *was* solvent and therefore *all* security holders were to be affected by the reorganization. The original proposal by Jessop contained all the qualities of typical financial adjustments described earlier: extension, composition, and the alteration of financial commitments to a contingent basis. These were as follows:

(1) extension: The United States government as holder of the first and second mortgages would receive a new first mortgage note of the same combined principal amount bearing 3% interest for 3 years and 4½% thereafter. No provision was made for the accrued interest.

(2) extension, composition and contingency: The holders of the subordinated debentures were to receive a new similar debenture of the same principal maturing in 25 years, bearing annual interest payable only if earned. This interest would not be cumulative and paid at the rates of 2% from years 2-6, 3% during years 7-10, and 3½% thereafter. Again, no provision was made for the accrued interest amounting to $29 on each $1000 debenture.

(3) exchange: Common stockholders were to receive one new Jessop share, selling at $18 per share, for each 10 old Green River shares (selling at $1.75).

SEC Evaluation and Subsequent Plan Changes. The SEC agreed that a small equity portion remain in the Green River bankruptcy but objected to the treatment of the debenture holders. The other creditors, including the government, received less than their "claim" but still accepted partial payment. In this respect, it follows that a creditor's claim is not necessarily his contribution but merely what he is willing to accept. Regarding the debentures, however, the particular provisions attacked were the lack of compensation for accrued interest, the noncumulative interest feature, and the fact that no interest would be required on the new debentures for two years and would be reduced thereafter. The SEC felt that these sacrifices should be compensated or altered in some revised format which included a further contribution from the old stockholders. The key feature was that the *total* compensation depended upon the assessed value implicit in the Jessop offer; therefore, any increased compensation to one set of security holders must be balanced by reduced amounts to another.

Comment: This kind of thinking clearly highlights the lack of debtor power inherent in a bankruptcy reorganization merger. While we agree that the creditors were poorly provided for in the original plan, we also feel that any further compensation should not necessarily come from the common stockholders. The result should be a slightly added total compensation, which understandably, is rarely forthcoming in a case such as this one.

Due to the SEC and the court's objections, the original Jessop plan was revised to include a slightly higher interest rate on the new debentures and a cumulative nature to these payments. The added compensation was balanced when it was decided to change the common shareholder terms from the original one-for-ten share arrangement to a one-for-fifteen plan. The revised plan resulted in an increase of $360,000 to the debenture holders and a like figure decrease to the common holders.[e]

Valuation Procedures. Valuation was assessed on the basis of a capitalization of expected earnings procedure whereby Green River's assets were valued on their contribution within the superstructure of the new merged entity. Based on assumptions of a combined product mix and new contribution of capital, the new earnings after interest and taxes were valued (by an expert witness) at about $2 million. Estimates were that this level would not be achieved for several years. The SEC valuation differed in that estimated sales were higher than the trustee's witness valuation but its estimated profit margin was considerably less. The basic difference being that the SEC built into their estimates allowances for steel price changes in the future while the trustee estimates did not. The result was a slightly lower SEC estimate although the inputs were vastly different. Both the SEC and trustee estimated the appropriate capitalization rate based on those rates of similar firms in the industry. Earnings after taxes and before interest was divided by total capitalization (market value of equity plus book value of debt and preferred) and a rate of 12½%, or a multiplier of eight times, was applied.

The Northeastern Steel and Green River Steel cases provide ideal illustrations as to the procedures and assumptions utilized in the critical analysis of capitalization rates. This rate should reflect basic industry and product-line risks *and* the firm's unique risk characteristics. Since both cases are examples of firms in the same industry at approximately the same time, the only differences, if any, should result from different internal situations. The following are the capitalization rates applied by the SEC and the trustees in these two steel company cases.

	Trustee Estimate	SEC Estimate
Northeastern	14 2/7%	12 1/2%
Green River	12 1/2%	12 1/2%

Comment: The SEC based its estimate not so much on the individual firm's situation but more in line with competitor rates. The Northeastern situation was inherently riskier in light of its past record of unsuccessful operations and the

[e]It can be argued that Jessop actually benefited by this change due to the difference between costs of equity capital and debt capital. Since equity capital is generally considered the higher of the two, any decrease in equity and increase in debt will lower the overall cost of capital. Also, the increased interest payments of from ½% to 1½% would accrue over a ten-year period while the reduction in common stock was effective upon ratification of the plan.

necessity for a complete overhaul of operations after the merger. Green River had already established itself as a profit maker and, therefore, it is felt that the capitalization rates utilized by the trustees reflected the situation more realistically. The SEC seemed to consider only a portion of the factors influencing capitalization rates. In other bankruptcy reorganization cases, however, we have observed that the SEC did a more realistic analysis and therefore, to generalize about valuation procedures of the SEC is unjustified. Still, it bodes well for a thoughtful assessment of valuation procedures by present Commission personnel.

Jessop's Position. The Jessop Steel offer should be viewed as a special type of merger whereby the acquired firm was instructed to go through bankruptcy reorganization proceedings. The motives behind these instructions are not completely clear but it is possible to make some intelligent guesses. The merger became effective in May 1957.

Like most other successful steel producers, Jessop decided to expand operations during the boom of the middle 1950s. A quick and sometimes relatively inexpensive method of expanding is to acquire existing facilities. The Green River situation presented an opportunity to more than double Jessop's assets and it was felt that the new facilities complemented the existing ones, particularly in the integration from semifinished to finished steel production. Jessop's finishing capacity was about three times its melting capacity and the basic melting facilities of Green River seemed an ideal addition. The facilities at Green River, however, would be of little use if while the two firms were negotiating a merger, the principal on the first mortgage notes became due and unpaid. The creditors would then have recourse to Green River's property. The Chapter X proceedings automatically protect the assets until an agreement can be reached.

Another factor which entered the picture very strongly was Green River's tax loss carry-over. One of the provisions of the Jessop acquisition was that the tax loss benefit be preserved during the reorganization. The relevant figure in this case was a $2.1 million tax loss benefit. As in the Northeastern case, the tax benefit was simply added to the earnings valuation. Fortunately, Jessop received a favorable ruling on this tax feature.

One of the major factors in the merger was Jessop's automatic jump from an almost total equity permanent capital firm to one with a heavy debt structure. Since Jessop continued to file unconsolidated statements after the merger, it is difficult to measure how the new debt affected Jessop's financial conditions. If the two firms simply combined balance sheets, the total debt/total assets ratio would jump from a respectable 31% to over 75% after the merger. It should be recalled that $4 million (16%) of this new debt was in the form of securities equivalent to income bonds. There is little doubt, however, that Jessop's inherent riskiness increased substantially.

Postreorganization Results. Jessop continued to report operations on an unconsolidated basis for eight years after the merger(1958-1965). Some information and conclusions can be derived from these data. Green River's rehabilitated operations were not very impressive in 1958 as the United States economy, particularly the steel industry, was hit by a short recession. Operations were severely reduced at the Green River facilities and much of the lower priced steel was phased out. Sales dipped by almost two-thirds from the 1956 high. The net loss in 1958 after interest payments amounted to over $900,000.

The situation improved greatly in 1959, with sales more than doubling and the old Green River operation enjoying its highest profits in history. Net profits reached over $1.3 million after interest and $1.8 million before interest; 8.6% and 11.5% profit margins, respectively. These results far exceeded early post-reorganization estimates of the trustee and were only $500,000 less than estimates used for Green River as a going concern. Although Green River operations remained profitable (except in 1960), net income never reached the 1959 total again. It is difficult to measure how much of this improvement was attributable to the merger since it is conceivable that Green River might have achieved similar results on its own. The important point is that the assets continued to operate and contribute to the nation's output due, in large part, to the Bankruptcy Law's provisions.

Security Holder Experience. Some of the glow from this reorganization must be removed when the creditor position is investigated. As a result of the reorganization, the first mortgage holders were to receive between 3% and 4½% interest over the life of the security and the debenture holders expected a 3½% yield, if earned. Both commitments have not been fulfilled as yet. The accrued interest payments ($1.6 million) on the first mortgage notes from 1957 to June 1964 were subsequently deferred until maturity (1975), while the debenture holders had their interest deferred until 1982.[8] These obligations were subsequently assumed by Athlone Industries when it merged with Jessop Steel in May 1968.

While the creditors were experiencing extended and deferred payments, the stockholders were doing fairly well. Recall that the terms of the merger were one Jessop share for every 15 Green River shares. The Green River stock sold for $1.75 per share in January 1957, while the Jessop stock sold for $18 per share. Therefore, Green River shareholders gave up $26.75 worth of stock (assuming they could have sold them) and received more marketable but lower value ($18) securities. The following price data in Table 5-3 show how these stockholders did in subsequent years.

Table 5-3
Common Stockholder Experience, Green River Steel Company

	1957	58	59	60	61	62	63	64	65	66	67
Average Yearly Value	$21.2	16.0	26.7	26.0	21.7	16.2	13.9	17.0	19.2	19.2	35.5
Discounted Yearly Value	$23.6	13.0	19.0	18.8	12.9	10.8	8.1	9.2	9.6	7.4	12.5

These statistics show that the old Green River stockholders' wealth did not change very much after the merger reorganization; their new stock's value tended to fluctuate between the $18 of value received and the $26 given up. On a discounted basis, however, the shareholders would have faired more favorably had they sold their shares in 1957 and invested in other common stocks (opportunity cost). Still, the bankruptcy process probably enabled these stockholders to avoid total loss. It appears that the common shareholders again faired better than their senior partners, the creditors.

Conclusion. Although the evidence in the Green River case is less convincing than it was in the Northeastern case, it appears that a well-conceived merger executed *before* bankruptcy would have resulted in more favorable terms for the stockholders and certainly for the creditors. It must be noted, however, that this conclusion is subject to skepticism since Green River's most promising operating period and its bankruptcy petition occurred almost simultaneously. The discriminant bankruptcy prediction model of Chapter 3 predicted failure 21 months prior to the actual event. The terms of a merger consummated sometime during this period could have been conceivably *less* favorable. Nobody will ever know.

McDonnell–Douglas Corporation Merger

The three cases studied thus far were concerned with mergers but the joining of companies did not occur until the ailing firm had already exhausted all of its financial resources and was forced to declare bankruptcy. As outlined in the prior chapter, one potential implication of a failure prediction technique is to spotlight serious problems early enough so as to trigger corrective action—one such action being the solicitation of a merger partner. The McDonnell-Douglas case is an example of a situation where a merger quite probably headed off a financial disaster with the resulting arrangement proving, thus far, most satisfactory. The merger stimulus in this case actually was induced from external sources, but it is felt that honest assessment by incumbent management is also capable of similar action in situations which may otherwise result in bankruptcy.

Problems at Douglas. Douglas Aircraft Company had been a leader in the production and sales of commercial and military aircraft since the 1930s. The start of its critical problems occurred in the late 1950s when it was slow to recognize the need for the transition to jet powered aircraft. When it did, management jumped into the new market with the development of its DC-8 and DC-9 airplanes in the early 1960s. Its major competitor, Boeing Aircraft, had already captured the bulk of the long- and intermediate-range market and Douglas tried to compensate by signing more orders for its short-range DC-9 airplane than its cash flow and production facilities could handle. At the same time, the management situation was extremely unstable with financial control and personnel depth problems. In 1962, McDonnell made an attempt to entice Douglas to sell out, but these negotiations were squelched by Douglas top management.

The management and production problems finally manifested in observable financial setbacks in 1966. That year started out well with the first quarter showing over $4 million in profits. The following three quarters, however, were surprisingly bad, with net losses after taxes reaching over $27 million. The common stock dividend was suspended in October 1966 and sources of capital began to dry up. The situation was particularly distressing because Douglas' sales of aircraft had reached record levels—a factor which turned out to be one of the leading causes of its problems. The planning for its popular DC-9 was extremely poor. The firm took more orders than it could process and deliver. As a result, skilled labor shortages occurred with large increases in salaries to what personnel it had. Suppliers were also backed up, partly due to the Vietnam conflict. Costs continued to rise with little or no operations research and cost controls. Management seemed inept and, due to these poor controls, never saw the problems coming until their financial statements showed them in red and white.

As production problems developed, Douglas sought new lines of credit with its bank contacts and even tried to add new banks to its financing consortium. Several of the nation's largest commercial banks were involved without a single leader; therefore, the advice received was at first inadequate. Finally, in late 1966, the banks refused Douglas' request for a $200 million line of credit to be used for working capital and new management development and the *commercial banks suggested* Douglas merge with a management and financially healthy company before things got worse. It was at this point that the solicitation finally began.

Since profits in 1965 reached over $14 million and 1966 started out at record levels, an *outsider* could hardly have been expected to predict trouble. The bankruptcy prediction model developed in Chapter 3, however, would have pointed to possible future problems. The Z score for Douglas at the end of 1965 (available to external analysts during the first quarter of 1966) did not point definitely to bankruptcy, but it did register within the so-called zone of ignorance and below the cut-off value of 2.675.

$$Z = .012\,(X_1) + .014\,(X_2) + .033\,(X_3) + .006\,(X_4) + .999\,(X_5)$$
$$2.59 = .012\,(19.4) + .014(20.3) + .033(5.8) + .006(89.3) + .999(1.36)$$

By the end of 1966, the Z score had dropped to a very low 1.39 and the merger solicitation had already begun. If the bankers had not insisted upon a merger, a bankruptcy prediction model would have indicated that something should be done—and fast. Since Douglas did not have such a model, if it weren't for the external advice received, the company might have gone bankrupt or, at the very least, been forced to accept less favorable merger terms at a later date.

The Merger. In December 1966, Douglas sent out invitations to six large companies asking for their expressed interest in aiding the beleaguered company.

Two of those firms, Chrysler and Lockheed Aircraft, said no immediately. The committee negotiating the merger set out several criteria for the merger. These included providing at least $100 million of debt or equity capital, that Douglas shareholders get a "fair shake," that all levels of management be available to Douglas to help solve its problems, and that the partner have the facility to establish tight controls of operations.

The reported details of the merger negotiations are intriguing, with McDonnell finally emerging the victor because of its willingness to assume financial risk immediately as well as to provide capital. The McDonnell offer was accepted on January 13, 1967, and provided for the immediate purchase of 1.5 million Douglas shares at $45.80 per share—Douglas shares traded at $47 3/8 on that date but at $45 1/4 on the previous day. This purchase infused $68.7 million for working capital and immediate financing requirements. The terms of the merger provided for the purchase of over 8.7 million Douglas shares on the basis of 1.75 McDonnell shares for every one share of Douglas. Since McDonnell's common stock closed at $35 on this date (up more than 3 points from the previous day), this amounted to a value of over $61 per Douglas share. Based on the prior day's closing price of Douglas at 45 1/4, the merger terms provided a $16 (35%) premium. If, however, you base the estimate on the McDonnell share price of the previous day, the premium comes to slightly more than $10 or 21%. In either case, the offer was extremely generous. The merger became effective on April 28, 1968.

While it is true that Douglas Aircraft was barely a viable company with a large backlog of sales, it still remains that its shareholders were treated very well by the merger. If the financial problems continued to exist without the merger, Douglas could have gone into bankruptcy reorganization. The company may still have had excellent sales, yet finding itself in formal bankruptcy proceedings, it is likely that the terms of a merger consummated *then* would have resulted in much poorer treatment for the Douglas security holders.

Postmerger Results. The Douglas Merger gave McDonnell something it had desired for many years—entry into the commercial aircraft market. Prior to the merger, McDonnell's sales were 95 percent government contracts with the postmerger figure becoming 50-50, government-commercial sales. The McDonnell motivation was simple; sales diversification—not necessarily by product, but by customer.

The benefits of the merger to Douglas operations were phenomenal. Within eleven months, Douglas facilities were producing at a profit. After 18 months, $450 million of Douglas debt was repaid. The major programs instituted under the able guidance of McDonnell personnel were the streamlining of subcontract work, setting up manpower training programs, increasing the work force from 8,000 to 25,000 men to handle the backlog of aircraft orders, cutting the production time drastically and cutting delays of suppliers, particularly engines. McDonnell pumped almost $70 million in cash in those expanded operations and created a financial subsidiary to handle the financing of planes. The latter move relieved Douglas from this continuous type of burden. Organizationally, Mc-Donnell-Douglas was now divided into 4 divisions, each with its own corporate staff controls led by top management back in McDonnell headquarters.

The new resources gave the firm the potential to compete for any new major contract. Perhaps the most important factor in the company's postmerger success is the spectacular showing in the development and sales of its DC-10; the all purpose airbus. This plane is already being acclaimed as the industry's hottest product. It is smaller than the Boeing 747 and can fly both medium- and long-range flights. Actually, Lockheed Aircraft had a slight lead in the development of its own airbus (L-1011), but when McDonnell-Douglas decided to go all out for this new market in 1967, it soon overtook Lockheed and by mid-1970 had over 40 more orders for its plane than Lockheed had. The fact that the DC-10 is smaller than the Boeing 747 means it can make more money on fewer passengers. The nation's airlines are particularly attracted to this situation. At a time (1970) when both Boeing and Lockheed were experiencing fantastic problems, McDonnell-Douglas emerged as the nation's "most prosperous looking aerospace company." (Forbes, July 1, 1970, p. 34.)

Note — As of December 1969, Boeing had a Z score of 2.15 and Lockheed's score was 2.20. That is to say, the bankruptcy model, developed in Chapter 3, predicted failure for these two companies even before their Congressional crises were manifest. In fact, Congress vetoed continued appropriations for the development of Boeing's SST project resulting in significant unemployment and operating problems. In a subsequent vote, both houses of Congress barely passed a bill providing for massive loan guarantees for Lockheed. The latter action, although temporarily saving the company from bankruptcy was, and still is, very controversial.

The road to recovery for Douglas was not totally without negative effect on McDonnell. Although total sales of the merged company almost tripled in 1967 over McDonnell's $1.06 billion figure in 1966, earnings per share in 1967 fell drastically to $0.03 from $2.66 per share in the previous year and $4.91 in 1965. Aggregate sales rose impressively in 1968 and earnings rebounded to $3.30 per share and rose to $4.06 in 1969. The Douglas turnaround situation did not become evident to external analysts until its 1968 figures were reported.

Security Holder Experience. Due to the timely infusion of capital by Mc-Donnell, creditors of Douglas Aircraft did not experience any interruption in their interest and principal receipts. The common stockholders did extremely well until the 1970 market crash. Stock price data taken at approximately six-month intervals from the time of merger acceptance to June 1970, are shown in Table 5-4.

By virtue of the large premium paid by McDonnell and the subsequent favorable movement in the merged company's stock, the Douglas Aircraft stockholders did extremely well in the first few years following the merger. In

Table 5-4
Relevant Common Stock Price Data, McDonnell-Douglas Corporation

Date	Douglas Aircraft Share Price	McDonnell-Douglas Equivalent Price[a]	Growth in Value from Base Date[b]	Growth in Value of NYSE Index[b]
1/12/67	$45.25	$55.80	21.1%	
1/13/67	47.38	61.25	35.4	
(merger approved)				
6/30/67		78.53	73.7	9.2%
1/2/68		94.06	108.3	16.6
6/28/68		93.86	107.8	21.8
1/2/69		86.20	90.5	25.7
6/30/69		56.88	23.5	17.6
1/1/70		47.70	5.1	11.9
6/30/70		23.19	(48.7)	(11.2)

[a]Based on 1.75 McDonnell-Douglas shares for each old Douglas share.

[b]Base date is taken as 1/12/67, the day prior to the merger approval. Since cash dividends paid were negligible over the study period, they are not included.

fact, the price more than doubled in just one year, while the price index for all stocks traded on the New York Stock Exchange rose slightly more than 16 percent over the same one-year period. The 1970 stock market downtrend, however, was particularly brutal for the aerospace industry and all of the postmerger capital gains were wiped out and large losses recorded. The overall effects of the merger on the common stockholders will not be truly assessed for many years. Almost all indications are, however, that the McDonnell-Douglas merger was a huge success.

6

Invester Implications of Corporate Bankruptcy

Numerous references and descriptions have been made throughout the book to the various security holders of bankrupt corporations with respect to their behavior and experience. Since the objective of most privately held corporations should be the maximization of its common stockholders wealth position, it seems appropriate to focus on the stockholders' experiences in greater depth. Another reason for our emphasis on this particular group of persons, as opposed to the firm's employees, creditors and the public at large, is the fact that this writer has found adequate analytical methods and relevant data available for rigorous analysis. The purpose of this chapter, therefore, is to investigate the various implications that corporate bankruptcy has for the common stockholders.

The first part of this chapter is concerned with the effect of potential corporate bankruptcy on expected shareholder wealth over time and its effect on share valuation. The second part utilizes a model developed to assess common stockholder experience once bankruptcy has been declared. The latter sections of the chapter explore the market risk dimensions of bankruptcy and attempts to use the ability to predict bankruptcy in order to establish a short-sale investment strategy.

Bankruptcy Potential and Share Valuation

One of the underlying themes of this book has been that the bankruptcy phenomenon in the United States is treated by academicians as an institutional problem of limited importance and by almost everyone else as a specialized financial development of little general interest. On the few occasions when bankruptcy is considered within a theoretic context, the analysis generally follows the argument that high levels of financial leverage increase the probability of bankruptcy which in turn decreases the value of the firm. After discussing several of the prior works deemed relevant to this question, we will present a means to empirically test the validity of this statement.[1]

Prior Studies

In their seminal work on share valuation and leverage, Modigliani and Miller (M&M) conclude that leverage has no effect on the value of a firm. But the

126

treatment of debt is restricted by their assertion that "all bonds . . . are assumed to yield a constant income per unit of time and this income is regarded as certain by all traders regardless of the issuer."[2] M & M conclude that all debt yields the same rate of return and this yield is certain. Hence, bankruptcy is not included in their *formal* analysis. Few would argue, however, with the statement that firms do default on their obligations and that the federal courts are often crowded with bankruptcy cases. Criticism of the seemingly unrealistic assumptions found within the M & M framework is quite common (and relatively easy). But it is more challenging to show theoretically how these assumptions compromise their analysis, and even more difficult to illustrate this position empirically. Corporation bankruptcy potential is a prime example of a market imperfection, an economic reality, which may affect valuation properties, both theoretically and empirically.

A study by Fisher attempted to specify those characteristics of corporations which account for their debt instruments yielding rates above the riskless rate.[3] Several of the independent variables used in the Fisher study reflect a firm's default risk and clearly demonstrate bankruptcy potential. Whether the risk of default is real or imaginary is of vital importance to investors. Where the risk of default is real and the market perceives it as such, the price will adjust appropriately. If the market perceives such a risk but in fact the firm is quite solvent, a general underpriced situation will result. The reverse occurs when the risk is real but the market does not view it in that way.

One of Fisher's explanatory variables is a form of financial leverage measurement showing a positive relationship between financial leverage and the rate of interest on the debt. This finding is confirmed by results reported in Chapter 3 where it was shown that measures of financial leverage from a bankrupt group of firms were significantly different from a comparable group of nonbankrupt companies. The above results substantiate the plausible argument that *ceteris paribus*, the greater a firm's financial debts, the higher the probability that it will not be able to meet its compulsory obligations and fixed charges in times of operating difficulties, and therefore the greater its bankruptcy potential.

In another study, Robichek and Myers attacked the restrictive M & M assumptions and presented quite convincing arguments that there may be a difference between the rate of return that a firm promises on its debt instruments and the actual return received due to operating contingencies resulting in bankruptcy and/or reorganization.[4] The same line of reasoning is followed in their treatment of equity valuation. They go on to state that the basic M & M conclusions hold if, among other things, "there are no direct or indirect costs associated with bankruptcy." But further they comment: "However, bankruptcy and reorganization do not appear to be costless in fact. Aside from the direct costs and delays of the legal process of reorganization, the firm may incur operating inefficiencies and be forced to forego investments which would have been feasible and profitable if the firm had avoided bankruptcy by borrowing less."

A recent work, relevant to this subject, is Baxter's analysis concerning corporate bankruptcy and capital costs.[5] Essentially, his thesis is that increased leverage enhances a firm's bankruptcy potential and that the added administrative costs incurred during reorganization and reduced sales and earnings, which are manifest due to the bankruptcy condition, reduces the value of the firm and thereby increases its cost of capital.[6] This thesis, although oversimplified and potentially misleading, is important in that it highlights the bankruptcy variable and beckons more rigorous analysis. Baxter essentially attacked the problem of bankruptcy by analyzing the immediate effect of failure and reorganization on the earnings and sales of the entity. An analysis of this type, however, is a narrowly defined, short-run, profit-maximizing approach which does not consider the various security holders explicitly and can lead to inaccurate conclusions.[a] Certainly, the bankruptcy process itself is often costly, but these immediate outlays are not sufficient evidence to conclude that the firm's net worth necessarily falls.

Model to Assess the Problem

Perhaps the major shortcomings of the prior approaches are their lack of consideration and adjustment for time and risk dimensional variables. Given that the objective of the firm is to maximize the wealth position of the firm's stockholders, we find that wealth maximization is a concept in which time is a crucial variable. Another important variable concerning wealth is the capitalization rate, i.e., the discount rate. This rate is typically selected to reflect the opportunity costs of the relevant parties. A valuation analysis which does not consider these two variables, either explicitly or implicitly, is subject to suspicion.

The suggested theoretic framework for analyzing the effect of bankruptcy on shareholder wealth explicitly considers time and opportunity cost variables. Specification of this relatively simple model draws on the prior work of Francis Calkins in the area of corporate reorganizations.[7]

We suggest a model of the general form,

$$(1) \quad SPI = \frac{\sum_{t=0}^{n} \frac{R_t}{(1+k)^t}}{I}$$

---

[a]For an example of the possible inaccurate conclusions reached through this short-term approach, the reader is referred back to the Muntz TV case discussed in Chapter 4. Adherents to the theory presented by Baxter could point to the dramatic decline in sales and earnings suffered by Muntz in the immediate years subsequent to bankruptcy. But these statistics are at best circumstantial and do not reflect the important contribution made by the bankruptcy process. As the previous case description showed, the firm's operations improved considerably and the common stockholders did exceedingly well after bankruptcy reorganization, inclusive of discounting for their opportunity costs. Could one conclude in this case that bankruptcy reduced the value of the firm?

where
SPI = Stockholder Profitability Index
R = Returns from New (or Old) Securities
k = Stockholder Opportunity Cost
I = Investment

which also encompasses postreorganization experience, but it adjusts for timing of the cash flows involved. The analysis is restricted to common shareholder experience and therefore explicitly reflects *equity valuation implications only*. The structure of the model is essentially a modification of the discounted-cash-flow profitability index used in capital expenditure decision making.[b] Expression of the model in an index form enables the results to be standardized for the size of the investment and the return per dollar of investment measured.

The rationale for the above framework lies in the nature of the variables and their relation to stockholder wealth and valuation concepts. If V_t is the market value of a firm at the time t, with S_t and B_t the market value of its equity and debt, respectively, then

$$V_t = S_t + B_t.$$

Share market values reflect expected future returns, and the return to shareholders is typically measured as the time adjusted cash flows accruing to shareholders—namely, dividend income plus capital gains.

This quantity, $D + g$

where,
D = Dividend Income
g = Growth in Capital,

encompasses the returns stream (R_t) in the proposed model. Actually, the entire cash flow, not just the gain or loss, is included in R_t since the final result is expressed as an index with the investment serving as the base. Since the model is a postbankruptcy specification, the variable measuring the stockholders investment should be an amount that he could have received had he sold the security (assuming prior ownership) or would have invested had he bought the security (assuming new ownership) prior to the bankruptcy petition date.

---

[b]The decision to use a modified present value structure for analyzing the proposed subject is based on careful consideration of the nature of the problem. At first glance, the internal rate of return is an attractive alternative. Shareholder internal rates could be compared to average stockholder experience and conclusions as to the bankrupt firms' relative performance might be meaningful. This format also removes any question pertaining to the use of an arbitrary explicit discount rate which should exactly measure stockholder time preference for money, plus risk considerations. However, the internal rate argument is not necessarily superior to the present value structure and breaks down completely under closer scrutinization. The breakdown occurs in the event of 100 percent stockholder loss. It is obvious that there is no internal rate to equate zero returns to some positive investment.

The variable measuring the shareholder's opportunity cost is included to quantify the rate of return he could have realized had he invested in other common securities. Ideally, these other securities should be of similar risk characteristics, but this is probably impossible to specify in our study. Instead, the average experience of all securities on the New York Stock Exchange (NYSE) over the appropriate period will be utilized.

The interpretation of the bankrupt firm's stockholder's SPI is fairly straight-forward. A SPI of unity (1.0) indicates the investor has achieved returns exactly equal to his opportunities. For instance, a security with a prebankruptcy price of $10 that is sold for $20 after six years has done fairly well. However, if the investor could have realized an average return of 12 percent on other common securities during this same time span, his SPI for the six-year period is exactly 1.0.

Index scores below unity indicate below opportunity returns with complete loss of the investment reflected in an SPI of zero. In this manner, expectations as to shareholder experience are clearly illustrated and equity valuation implica-tions related to bankruptcy potential of corporations accurately assessed. To assume that bankruptcy potential automatically decreases a firm's equity value (and perhaps its total value) is tantamount to an SPI of below 1.0[c] Just how much below in an individual case is difficult to assess. For the purpose of rigorous analysis, however, the null hypothesis is that the net present worth of the firm's equity remains unchanged in bankruptcy when the shareholders' SPI is equal to 1.0, i.e., not significantly different from unity.

Empirical Test Outline

The initial step in the empirical examination of bankruptcy potential and its effect on shareholder experience is to compile an extensive list of those corporations that have petitioned the courts to reorganize under the rules of the National Bankruptcy Act between 1941 and 1965.[8] We will not investigate shareholder experience of firms which might have been financially insolvent but never actually declared bankruptcy. Therefore, conclusions will not be made concerning the valuation of firms in this amorphous state.

Data on the exact terms of the reorganizations are derived from the *Financial Daily Card Service* published in New York City. The final phase of data gathering is to record market values of the old securities from just prior to the bankruptcy petition date to the reorganization consummation date. If a continued equity interest is provided for, the market values of the new (or old) securities are traced for a period up to ten years after bankruptcy. A surprisingly large number (about 50 percent) of bankrupt firms that attempted reorganiza-

[c]To state that a firm's *total value* changes proportionately with changes in its equity segment assumes no change in its other capital components. This is obviously unrealistic in the event of bankruptcy and subsequent reorganization where a radical change in capital structure is the common occurrence.

tion and were listed in the previously cited sources were found to possess quoted publicly traded equity securities and thus we are able to use market value variables in this analysis. Total equity loss is recorded in the event of no available market data or the cessation of an equity interest.

From the original list of bankrupt corporations, a final group of seventy-six firms comprised the sample which was analyzed. The list includes all firms for which data on reorganization experience and quoted market values (including 100 percent common stockholder loss) are available. To restate the model in a more precise form, we have

$$(2) \quad SPI = \frac{\sum_{t=0}^{n} \frac{D_t}{(1+k')^t} + \frac{P_n}{(1+k)^n}}{P_{b-1}}$$

where,

SPI = Stockholder Profitability Index
D = Returns in the Form of Income
P_n = Price of New (or Old) Securities in nth Year
k,k' = Stockholder Opportunity Costs
P_{b-1} = Price of Old Common Stock One Month prior to Bankruptcy.

In all but four of the observations, the firm did not pay postbankruptcy dividends to its old stockholders and in two of these cases, the distribution was a liquidating dividend.[d] Therefore, we are essentially comparing the discounted value of the market price of the surviving security to the price one month prior to bankruptcy. This latter price, P_{b-1}, represents what the stockholder could have received and reinvested elsewhere at his opportunity cost, or alternatively, what a new investor would have paid for the shares of the soon-to-be bankrupt company.

The rates depicting shareholder opportunity costs are derived from the recent Fisher and Lorie study on common stock rates of return.[9] Their tables[e] appear to be particularly appropriate and enable a fairly exact means of comparing performance over various periods of time. For instance, from 1951-60, a

---

[d]The receipt, however, of an intermediate dividend necessitates using a different discount rate (k') than the one used to discount the price in the nth year. The time horizon to the terminal period, in the case of an intermediate payment, is shorter than that of the $t = 0 \rightarrow N$ period.

[e]It should be noted that the returns from *individual* bankrupt company shares are compared with these Fisher returns which are based on a *portfolio* of stocks. The practice of using overall market returns as a benchmark for individual stock price movements is well established in the literature. However, we might have considered returns on a random drawing of stocks from a population, e.g., NYSE, if we had access to a comprehensive periodic data source.

stockholder received an average after-tax return of 10.3 percent, while from 1953-60, he received 13.3 percent. This enables a year-by-year postbankruptcy analysis and reduces the possibility that the results will be sensitive to short-term stock market fluctuations. Year-by-year results enable average returns for various time durations, i.e., between one and ten years, to be analyzed.

Tax Implications

Prior to this point, we have restricted the model's framework to individual firm experience without including portfolio considerations. It is not unrealistic, however, to assume that our shareholders own and trade other securities and that the net result from these transactions determines income tax liabilities. Since tax loss benefits or capital gains on profits can be substantial, we adjust the structure, as proposed in equation (2), in order to more realistically specify the model. The final format and the one actually used in the empirical investigation is of the form,

$$(3) \quad SPI = \frac{\sum_{t=0}^{n} \dfrac{D_t (1 - .50)}{(1 + k')^t} + \dfrac{P_n - .25 (P_n - P_{b-1})}{(1 + k)^n}}{P_{b-1}}$$

Since the marginal tax rate of each shareholder is impossible to ascertain, a 25 percent capital gains rate is assumed in the model. To the extent that a particular individual's marginal tax rate is below 50 percent, we are overstating the tax-loss benefit or the tax liability.[10] This bias is not felt to be significant and the use of a single rate enables standardization of the investigation.

Reorganization Time and Terms — Empirical Findings

One of the important costs in the bankruptcy reorganization process is the additional administrative expense involved. These outlays relate to, among other aspects, trustee salaries, legal fees, creditor and stockholder meetings costs and the unquantifiable cost of the productive energies foregone by some of the firms' employees. These energies are necessarily diverted in order to concentrate on the task of reorganization. Although aggregate totals of these expenses for a large number of bankrupt firms are not available, the magnitude has prompted theorists to conclude that the reorganization process itself reduces firm value. Criticism of this general line of reasoning was expressed earlier. Nevertheless, it seems worthwhile to pursue one aspect of this subject a little further.

The one variable which is directly related to every cost cited above is time: time in reorganization. Obviously, the relationship between expense and time is positive. In order to estimate the average time spent in reorganization, the actual experience of 90 bankrupt firms is examined. Reorganization time is defined as that period between the month the reorganization petition is granted to the month the reorganization plan is consummated. The breakdown of this duration for the 90 firms is shown in Table 6-1.

The average time spent in reorganization of the 90-firm sample was 2 1/4 years, with the median time being 1 2/3 years. The range of values is between two months and 9 1/2 years. It is possible that the sample mean is below the population mean of all bankrupt reorganizations since bankruptcies before 1941 are not included. Several large railroad bankruptcies occurred in the 1930s and lasted over ten years before being settled. The 2 1/4-year period, however, appears to be a realistic estimate for contemporary manufacturing company bankruptcy reorganizations.

It is interesting to note that over 90 percent of the firms had reorganization plans consummated in less than five years. Although it is impossible to know for certain, it may be that the tax laws regarding operating losses have had some influence on this five-year total.[f] The majority of firms actually settled in under two years. The latter figure, however, includes a large number of firms whose stockholders suffered 100 percent losses. Approximately 65 percent (34 of 52)

Table 6-1
Bankruptcy Reorganization Time Experience

Months	Number of Firms	Percent of Total	Cumulative Percent
0-6	9	10%	10%
7-12	18	20	30
13-18	14	16	46
19-24	11	12	58
25-30	9	10	68
31-36	7	8	76
37-42	5	6	82
43-48	2	2	84
49-54	4	4	88
55-60	3	3	91
> 60	8	9	100%
Total	90	100%	

Average Time in Reorganization = 27 Months
Median Time   = 20 Months

[f]Current tax provisions provide for a three-year carry-back or five-year carry-forward on any ordinary operating losses. These provisions have been in effect over the entire sample period, except for the period between 1945-49 when the carry-forward varied between two and three years. The carry-back is not particularly relevant since bankrupt firms typically have several years of operating losses before bankruptcy itself.

of all those firms which consummated reorganization plans in two years or less saw their stockholders suffer a total loss. This percentage is slightly above the 56 percent figure for all firms in the study (see Table 6-2), but substantially greater than the 33 percent figure for firms whose reorganization was consummated after two years.

These statistics, and others to be presented shortly, indicate that the longer a firm remains in bankruptcy reorganization, the better the stockholder's chance for remuneration of some type. This appears to be the case because a firm's insolvency, or solvency, can usually be determined in a short time, but once solvency is established, the exact details of a fair and feasible plan often require a long period of time.

It remains for us to investigate just how shareholders of bankrupt firms have fared over the years. Two measures will be analyzed in light of this objective. The first, and the most relevant one, is the Stockholder Profitability Index (SPI). The SPI experience on a postbankruptcy year-by-year basis is illustrated in Table 6-3. This table relates to the number and percent of firms whose stockholders achieved an SPI $\geqslant 1.0$, indicating greater than average opportunity returns.[g]

It is clear that the majority of these firms did not achieve stockholder returns comparable to the average share performance (k). This was the case in every one of the ten postbankruptcy years analyzed. Those stockholders whose equity was intact in later years showed better results than they did for the earlier postbankruptcy years. This result is illustrated by the fact that in the last five years of the ten-year study period, the percent of firms achieving an SPI $\geqslant 1.0$ was 26 percent compared to 15 percent for the first five years. Statistical tests of mean SPI returns compared to the standard of unity are displayed shortly.

Conclusions as to relative stockholder performance in firms that reorganize in bankruptcy take on slightly different proportions if we only consider whether or not the initial investment, P_{b-1}, is recovered in years subsequent to this investment base date. In fact, Table 6-3 illustrates that in years 6-10, a majority of the observations (64 percent) achieved returns equal to or greater than the original investment. The payback of one's investment as an investment criterion,

Table 6-2
Common Stockholder Experience in Bankruptcy Reorganization

	Number	Percent
Old-Stockholder Participation	40	44%
100 Percent Loss	50	56
	90	100%

---

[g]The model includes several proxy variables for specific ingredients thought necessary for rigorous analysis. These variables include the discount rate or opportunity cost (k) and the invesment base $(P_{b}-1)$. Both, however, possess statistical and economic bias which no doubt affects the results. Details of the discussion on bias are discussed in E. Altman, *Potential*, pp. 897-898, but for this book's purposes, we will assert that if anything, the biases make the null hypothesis test *more* rigorous and strengthen our conclusions.

although not advocated here, is of some interest in a world where one of the most popular capital-budgeting techniques is still the payback period.

Testing of the Null Hypothesis

The next empirical investigation attempts to test whether or not a firm's equity value can be expected to fall (or rise) in bankruptcy. Statistically insignificant results will give us no evidence to dispute the null hypothesis and will, therefore, cast considerable doubt upon the generally accepted doctrine that bankruptcy and reduced values are complementary. If it is shown that the returns to stockholders of bankrupt firms are significantly below that of the average return on all securities, then we will have observed statistical evidence for what has been heretofore merely *a priori* theory.

Table 6-4 illustrates average year-by-year and total SPI performance and tests of significance. The number of observations falls from a high of 67 in the first year after bankruptcy to 18 in the tenth year due to (a) total stockholder loss in the earlier years; (b) liquidating dividends; and (c) less than 10-year-old bankruptcies. The discrepancy between the 67 firms listed for year #1 and the total of 76 firms examined is due to the fact that several companies had 100% stockholder loss recorded in some year after the first and those years in between had no data available at all. Firms with 100% loss were definitely included.

In order to test the null hypothesis, the mean SPI for the entire sample (0.76) is compared with the standard return of unity. This sample includes those firms

Table 6-3
Postbankruptcy Stockholder Experience, Absolute and Relative Measures

Years after Bankruptcy	N =	SPI ≥ 1.0 No.	Percent	Return ≥ Original Investment No.	Percent
1	67	11	16%	13	20%
2	50	8	16	9	18
3	39	6	15	9	23
4	29	4	14	9	31
5	22	2	9	10	45
6	22	5	23	12	55
7	20	5	25	12	60
8	20	6	30	12	60
9	19	5	26	14	74
10	18	5	28	13	72
1-5	207	31	15	50	24
6-10	99	26	26	63	64

Table 6-4
Average Year-by-Year and Total SPI Experience of Bankrupt Firms

Years	N =	Mean SPI	Test of H_0: $t =$[a]
1-10	306	.76	5.24*
1	67	.73	3.65*
2	50	.78	7.01*
3	39	.78	1.29***
4	29	.71	2.18**
5	22	.68	2.85*
6	22	1.05	0.17
7	20	.84	1.10
8	20	.95	0.22
9	19	.85	0.04
10	18	.86	0.72
1-5	207	.70	6.72*
6-10	99	.96	0.92

$$a_t = \frac{\bar{x} - \mu}{s/\sqrt{N}}, \quad s = \sqrt{\frac{\Sigma (x_i - \bar{x})^2}{N - 1}}$$

* Significant at .01 ⎫
** Significant at .05 ⎬ One tail
*** Significant at .10 ⎭

which suffered total stockholder loss as well as the remunerated ones. Since we are testing the difference between means in order to determine if bankrupt firms as a class of securities return significantly different amounts to their stockholders than average securities do, the test is as illustrated in Table 6-4.[h]

Based on the total sample results, the null hypothesis is rejected and we conclude that the mean SPI is significantly less than unity.[i] Therefore, returns

[h]An argument could be made for analyzing the results within a standard two-tail context since results above unity, as well as below, are theoretically possible. Returns above unity are also consistent with standard risk-return tradeoffs of investments. Since the risk involved with the class of bankrupt firms is greater than it is with the average listed company, one might also expect above average returns. Despite the above argument, a one-tail test is chosen for two reasons. The first reason is that below average returns and lower valuation conform with the usual assumptions about bankrupt securities. Secondly, and more important, the one-tail test is chosen here in light of the costs involved with the various types of errors. Acceptance of the null hypothesis when in fact it is incorrect (Type II error) appears to be potentially more costly than rejecting the null when it is true (Type I error). The latter error precludes investment in securities with bankrupt potential, but attractive alternatives are still available. The one-tail test places more stringent requirements on accepting the null or, stated alternatively, rejects the null slightly more frequently than the two-tail test.

[i]The entire sample's observations (306) are not all independent since they encompass many years experience for individual firms. Therefore, the test is subject to some criticism, but average values for the individual postbankruptcy years, especially the earlier years, tend to coincide with the overall performance.

from bankrupt securities as a class are expected to be below the average return, indicating a negative effect on equity valuation.

Of some additional interest is the year-by-year shareholder experience. The earlier postbankruptcy years all show significant below average returns between the mean SPI and investor opportunities. As noted previously, these earlier years include most of the 100 percent stockholder loss observations. The mean return for years 1-5 is only .70. The results are much different, however, in the later years. The average return is very close to unity (.96) for years 6-10, with one year (6th) showing an above unity average. Bankrupt firms whose old stockholders retain some equity in these years exhibit results which conform with the null hypothesis. Essentially, the empirical data show that bankrupt firms' equity *on average*, can be expected to fall in bankruptcy, but a surprising number of bankruptcy reorganizations result in favorable overall performance.

Investing In Bankrupt Entities

The prior section assessed valuation implications of firms and securities which go into bankruptcy. Here, we extend the analysis to include the option to act upon the news of bankruptcy and purchase bankrupt securities. The consideration of financially bankrupt firms as an investment alternative has usually centered on the debt obligations of the unfortunate firm. Recently, Baskin and Crooch[11] investigated the historical returns on investments in flat bonds and earlier studies by Hickman and Calkins[12] examined various aspects of the postbankruptcy experience of debt securities. Interestingly enough, all of these studies concluded that the continuing bondholders generally had favorable experience relative to returns on common stocks, as well as alternative debt securities, in the postdefault period. The purpose of this next empirical study is to examine the common stockholders' postbankruptcy experience.[13]

Empirical Test Methodology and Results

The model utilized to test postbankruptcy experience is the final version (3) of our prior model with the appropriate adjustments to include the two different base, or investment periods—one month and one year after bankruptcy declaration. The adjusted model now reads:

$$(4) \quad SPI = \frac{\displaystyle\sum_{t=0}^{n} \frac{D_t\,(1-.50)}{(1+k')^t} + \frac{P_n - .25\left(\dfrac{P_n - P_{b+1},\ \text{or}}{P_{b+12}}\right)}{(1+k)^n}}{P_{b+1},\ \text{or}\ P_{b+12}}$$

where,

SPI	=	Stockholder Profitability Index
D	=	Returns in the Form of Income
P_n	=	Price of New (or Old) Securities in the nth Year
k, k'	=	Stockholder Opportunity Costs
P_{b+1}	=	Price of Old Common Stock One Month after Bankruptcy
P_{b+12}	=	Price of Old or New Common Stock 12 Months after Bankruptcy.

As noted, the variables represent the same measures as before, thereby possessing the same attributes and biases. The companies involved were again scrutinized for every year of their existence up to 10 years after bankruptcy.

Table 6-5 illustrates how an investor who purchased a bankrupt security in the month following bankruptcy fared. His investment is taken as the mean between the high and low price in that month.

The results of this test are quite different from those found in Table 6-4 and reveal that the average SPI, both on a year-by-year and a pooled data basis, is *not* significantly different from 1.0. Recall that the average SPI for the 10-year period when the investment base date was one month prior to bankruptcy (P_{b-1}) was 0.76 compared to a 1.05 SPI for P_{b+1}. The impressive differential between P_{b-1} and the P_{b+1} is almost surely due to the "Bankruptcy Information Effect" (B.I.E.)

where,

$$(5) \quad (50 \quad \text{B.I.E.} = \frac{P_{b+1}}{P_{b-1}}$$

The effect measures the change in price from the average price during the month preceding bankruptcy, to the average price during the month following (in essence a two-month price change). The average B.I.E. for the bankrupt firms examined was 0.742 which interprets into a drop in price of slightly greater than 25%. This drop generally occurred in the days immediately preceding and slightly after bankruptcy declaration. Where we observe significant drops just prior to declaration, it is probably due to the fact that the market has anticipated the bankruptcy news and the price finally adjusts to some full-discounted value. Again, we find evidence where the market continually adjusts the common stock price of potential bankrupt firms as new information arises. This adjustment, however, does not appear to be complete until bankruptcy is declared formally and in some cases after the bankruptcy action.

The results using our model where the investment is measured at P_{b+12} (one year after bankruptcy) is quite similar to that reported in Table 6-5 for P_{b+1}. The average SPI in the one year lagged investment period is 1.09 vs. 1.05 for one month after bankruptcy. All of the SPI results for P_{b+12} are not significantly different from 1.0 (both overall and year-by-year SPI figures) and we can conclude that investors in these securities would not have experienced significantly different results than those who invested in a portfolio of New York Stock Exchange securities.

Table 6-5

Average Year-by-Year and Total SPI Experience of Bankrupt Firms, $I = P_b + 1$

Years	N =	SPI $\geq$ 1.0 No.	Percent	Mean SPI	Test of H_o: $t = *$
1-10	280	106	38%	1.05	.77
1	53	21	40	1.07	.57
2	45	15	33	.86	1.19
3	33	13	39	.80	1.08
4	28	9	32	.96	.23
5	22	10	45	.89	.83
6	22	9	41	1.30	1.04
7	20	8	40	1.10	.48
8	20	7	35	1.20	.72
9	19	7	37	1.24	.99
10	18	7	39	1.48	1.25

* Significant at .05, t $\approx$ 2.0.

Implications

To repeat, we found insignificant differences between returns on bankrupt equity securities and what were stockholder opportunity costs for the postbankruptcy period. These postbankruptcy returns were very much superior to those reported for the existing shareholders of bankrupt firms where the base period was *prior* to bankruptcy. Can we then assume that bankrupt firms' equity securities are a worthwhile investment alternative? The answer is *no*. Existing investment theory and common sense assessment of alternative investments tells us that there is a pervasive risk aversion propensity among investors. Therefore, where the expected risk of a class of securities is greater than alternative choices, investors will require a commensurate higher rate of return. Evidence presented by several other investigators (and some to be discussed in the next section) assert that the market-related risk on equities with a high bankruptcy potential is significantly greater than other equity alternatives. Since it is not likely that the risk class of bankrupt firms will change drastically (except perhaps in a few extreme cases) after bankruptcy, we can conclude with a good deal of confidence that risk and return expectation considerations among postbankrupt equity securities make their attractiveness extremely limited. Extreme caution and careful analysis is advised for those interested in searching for situations where a stock's price is temporarily undervalued just after bankruptcy. These situations do exist, however, and the bankruptcy process in the United States does foster rehabilitation and recovery for those economically viable firms.

Bankruptcy and Stock Market Risk

In Chapter 3, we analyzed the risk of firms going bankrupt by studying the characteristics of those manufacturing firms which eventually failed. One of the variables we examined contained a market value ratio, and thereby introduced a dimension which is not wholly endogenous to the particular firm. It was shown that the market adjusts to new information about potentially insolvent companies, but in general, the plight of these firms is underestimated. Beaver reported that the market reacts negatively to failure potential as much as five years prior to bankruptcy[14] while we show that equity values decline quite noticeably as bankruptcy approaches. While these results are quite indicative of the movement of share prices prior to bankruptcy and imply that the market itself is an accurate predictor of failure, it does not exhaust the possible information that can be derived from studying stock price behavior. Westerfield has taken the analysis one step further in his assessment of the market-risk component of share price behavior peculiar to bankrupt firms.[15]

Market and Systematic Risk

In an earlier chapter, we referred to Westerfield's work in his assessment of the monthly price performance of bankrupt companies over a ten-year period prior to failure. Utilizing the basic Sharpe-Lintner market model,

$$(6) \quad R_{it} = \alpha_i + \beta_i R_{mt} + e_{it}$$

where,

R_{it} = Return on asset i in period t.

R_{mt} = Return on market portfolio m in period t.

α_i = Constant parameter whose expected value is such that the expected value of e_{it} is zero.

β_i = Parameter (beta coefficient) unique to asset i and called a measure of systematic or nondiversifiable risk.

e_{it} = Random variable representing the error term.

he concluded that there were market reassessments of the solvency position of failed firms nearly six years before bankruptcy but that failure itself is not expected by the market until very close (during the last year) to the failure date.

The above market model was also utilized to assess the relationship between the systematic risk measure (β) and the rate of failure. The hypothesis is that firms whose common equity exhibit high systematic risk with market movements (high betas) experience a higher rate of failure than those assessed as low risk (low betas). Essentially, the beta coefficient's efficacy as a failure indicator is examined. This was done in the following manner. First, the period July 1926 to June 1954 was broken into four seven-year periods, i.e., July 1926-June 1933; July 1933-June 1940, etc., and beta coefficients were estimated for all firms with continuous price and dividend data during each sample period.

For each sample period, the risk estimates were broken into deciles and the ninety percent decile, the highest 10 percent, and the lowest decile were segregated for further analysis. For the first sample period, forty-one firms had systematic risk measures above 1.616 and qualified as the most risky securities. Of these forty-one firms, "sixteen failed, five merged, one was a war casualty, and two had miscellaneous capital changes. In contrast, only two of the low-risk firms failed while eight merged." Table 6-6 illustrates the results from Westerfield's study covering the four sample periods. In every sample period, the number of delisted firms in the high-risk category far exceeds the number in the low-risk category. Unfortunately, Westerfield does not list results for the eight other fractiles.j Can we expect a linear, or near linear, relationship between failure and risk measures broken down by fractile statistics? My intuitive feeling is that we cannot because of the expected random failure experience among firms making up the middle fractiles and perhaps extending all the way to the extreme fractiles.

Westerfield concludes that high-risk firms do experience failure at greater rates than low-risk companies. Also, he observes that the propensity to merge is greater in the high-risk category. A strong *normative* case was made for this very occurrence in Chapter 5 and perhaps, either knowingly or not, corporate managers of high-risk firms do seek out mergers to a greater degree than managers of low-risk firms do. An alternate theory could be that high-risk firms experience severe stock price declines which make them more attractive to the aggressive firms seeking sick companies for various motives. He also found that security delisting occurred more frequently for these same high-risk companies.

Implications

All of the prior mentioned studies, regardless of the time period and duration analyzed, conclude that bankruptcy risk and market price behavior are intimately related. The market appears to be somewhat able to adjust for increasing signs of corporate insolvency, but the fact that we observe the most serious declines in the last year prior to bankruptcy means that the ultimate failure reality is not fully discounted and the market as a predictor is therefore something less than perfect. This is certainly understandable, especially when you consider that many firms with high bankruptcy risk characteristics never go bankrupt and in these cases, the market was acting rationally and digesting information efficiently. The final section of this chapter examines just these very firms which exhibit failure characteristics but do not go bankrupt.

---

jA surprising result is that more firms failed from among the low-risk group than the high-risk group in the last sample period. Was this a statistical quirk or a structural change?

Table 6-6
Market Risk and Failure

Causes of Delisting	High Beta Firms				Low Beta Firms			
	7/26-6/33	7/33-6/40	7/40-6/48	7/48-6/54	7/26-6/33	7/33-6/40	7/40-6/48	7/48-6/54
1. Merger	5	16	28	30	8	8	16	10
2. Bankruptcy	16	10	11	4	2	2	3	5
3. Reclassification						3	1	
4. War Casuality	1	1	2			1		
5. Other	2	5	7	5	2	1	1	6
Total Delist	24	32	48	39	13	15	21	21
No Change	17	28	25	48	28	45	52	66
Total Firms	41	60	73	87	41	60	73	87
BETA of F.90	1.616	1.581	1.606	1.565				
BETA of F.10					0.498	0.436	0.500	0.473

Source: R. Westerfield, "The Assessment of Market Risk and Corporate Failure," (Wharton School of Finance, August, 1970).

Short-Sale Investment Strategy

The purpose of this last section is to utilize the bankruptcy prediction model we developed earlier in order to assess its efficacy as an investment device for common stocks. Time and again we have emphasized that investors appear to be somewhat capable of anticipating poor operating performance of certain companies, but there remains a pervasive tendency to underestimate the financial plight of firms which eventually go bankrupt. This behavioral pattern seems to be borne out by the stock price results discussed in the earlier sections of this chapter and in Chapter 3. Although prices tend to move down consistently as bankruptcy approaches, the greatest drop still occurs in the last year prior to bankruptcy. Therefore, there appears to be some potential for a model which is fairly accurate in predicting bankruptcy to also choose stocks destined for severe price depreciation. The potential for a short-sale investment strategy becomes evident under these considerations.

A crucial ingredient in our investigation, however, is that very few listed securities actually declare bankruptcy and the assumption that our short-sale investment strategy is applicable only to bankrupt firms would make its testing relatively meaningless. Our analysis must therefore go one step further. We will utilize the bankruptcy prediction model in order to select those firms which manifest similar financial and economic characteristics as those firms which went bankrupt (Chapter 3) but, for various reasons, remained in existence. Simply put, the mechanism will be to select candidates for short-sales when they first exhibit bankrupt characteristics and then simulate the one-year rate of return an investor would have received had he actually sold these securities short.

Results with Bankrupt Firms

The bankruptcy prediction model developed earlier is utilized in a short-sale investment strategy. Recall, the model was of the form:

$$Z = .012X_1 + .014X_2 + .033X_3 + .006X_4 + .999X_5$$

where,

Z	=	Overall Discriminant Score or Rating
X_1	=	Working Capital/Total Assets
X_2	=	Retained Earnings (Balance Sheet Item)/Total Assets
X_3	=	Earnings before Interest and Taxes/Total Assets
X_4	=	Market Value of Equity/Total Debt
X_5	=	Sales/Total Assets

We first assessed its investment strategy potential on the original sample of bankrupt firms. We suggest that the model has at least two investment strategy aspects. For those investors who hold securities in companies whose future appears dim, the natural course of action is to sell before its price declines, even if this decline has already started. This strategy is not very risky since we can visualize losses only if the owner is wrong in his assessment and the price actually *rises* after the sale. At the same time, however, he has the opportunity to reinvest those funds received from the sale. Therefore, the risk aspects take on the characteristics of any normal trading strategy.

The second and more provocative strategy implied by the model relates to short-selling. This operation is not usually basic to the overall portfolio strategy of the investor but often is the vehicle which provides a "hedge" for other types of strategies or is part of an arbitrage transaction. Regardless of the expressed purpose, most students of the market will agree that the risk aspects of short-selling are great. For one thing, the investor only risks his initial investment in a normal buy strategy, but his potential loss is infinite in a short-sale strategy. As for the positive return on investment, the reverse is true. If you sell short, you can only hope to double your return if the price goes to zero (not very likely), while theoretically the potential return from buying long is infinite. In addition, "The portfolio managers will tell you that, given the long-term trend of the market upward, their most difficult job is picking good short-sales. . . . as a result, he (Alfred Jones) and other hedge fund managers normally consider themselves lucky to break even on their short portfolios."[16]

The above comments on short-selling appear reasonable yet recent empirical evidence shows that the risk from selling short is not very great although the expected return is negative. Professors Richard McEnally and Edward Dyl presented interesting and useful statistics in their article on "The Risk of Selling Short" in the November-December, 1969 issue, *Financial Analyst Journal*. Essentially, they assessed the results of randomly selling short a large sample of over 500 common stocks listed on the New York Stock Exchange, for various short holding periods, during the years 1961 through 1965. Although the average expected return from such a strategy was negative, they found that the down-side risk was not very great. The results from their study will be used as one benchmark in assessing the performance of the bankruptcy prediction model.

As noted, we first scrutinized the bankrupt firms used in the construction of the model. Naturally, if the performance is not exceptional for these firms, we can hardly expect it to be profitable for general investment opportunities. We realize that there is a significant sample bias involved, but this is a necessary first step. Those firms which were correctly classified as future bankrupts in the original sample were scrutinized for their subsequent price performance from the time the model first predicted bankruptcy. Operationally, the point in time when the model predicts bankruptcy triggers the short-sale transaction.

The results are indeed impressive. The average change in the price of the bankrupt group's common stock from the prediction date to just prior to the actual bankruptcy date is a *negative* 45 percent. The average period for this drop in price was fifteen months. In only 2 cases out of 28, did the stock's price appreciate in value. Over the same relevant periods of time, the average

Dow-Jones Industrial Average movement was a *positive* 13 percent and the National Quotation Board's OTC Index *rose* 12.4 percent. Therefore, although the stock market in general was increasing substantially over the period of study, an investor who sold short could have realized a gross return over three times that of the market performance.

These results, although impressive, should not be considered conclusive. As noted earlier, the firms involved were all bankrupts whose price you normally would expect to fall as bankruptcy approached. Obviously, there are far more firms which remain solvent even though they may, at various points in time, exhibit characteristics which are similar to the group of bankrupt firms. The prospective investor or fund manager does not have the luxury of a controlled experiment as illustrated above. He can scrutinize hundreds or thousands of securities and the number of firms which are predicted to go bankrupt but remain solvent will no doubt increase in some proportional manner. Therefore, the number of stocks he could conceivably short will increase. In the above test, we compared the short-selling performance of a number of special stocks with the overall market index. A more meaningful test of short selling would be to compare performance of the bankruptcy prediction filter rule with some random short-selling strategy. The next empirical test will hopefully adjust for all of the above biases and criticisms.

Further Evidence

Thus far, we have shown that the short-selling investor would have realized significantly above average returns had he concentrated on future bankrupts. Since few large publicly traded firms fail these days, this information is interesting but not very indicative of the expected results if a large cross-section of firms are examined. With this in mind a final, more comprehensive test is devised in order to assess the MDA's overall short-selling investment potential. The following examination is performed.

For the years ending 1960 to 1963, every firm on the Compustat Data Tape is scrutinized and a discriminant score is attained for all firms which had the necessary balance sheet and income statement data available. Those firms whose Z score was equal to or less than 2.675 were segregated for further analysis. The following other criteria were used for final selection:

1. Only *manufacturing* companies (recall that the bankruptcy prediction model is for manufacturers only).
2. All firms whose year-end statements are at December 31. This was necessary because the short-selling strategy rates of return will be compared with yearly rates of return for short selling for a large sample of firms where the simulated short date was approximately at the time when the necessary financial statements were made available for the scrutiny of the investing public. In order to be sure that the statements would be available, we have

chosen April 30th, a full four months after the calendar year ends, as our simulated reference date.

3. A firm is selected only if its discriminant score $\leqslant 2.675$ for that year and was above that level in the preceding year. Therefore, we examine the firm when its failure potential is first detected—or at least was not evident the year prior to the observation.

From the more than 1,700 firms on the Compustat Data Tape, the remaining number of qualified companies ranged from a high of 43 in 1960 to a low of 10 in 1961. For these firms, we compute a simulated rate of return for the one-year period after the firm displayed its bankruptcy characteristics as evidenced by its relatively low Z score. Since the short seller is not entitled to any dividends and, in fact, must pay out the equivalent of the dividend, the rate of return formula utilized was:

$$R_S = -\left[\frac{P_{t+1} - P_t + D_{t+1}}{P_t}\right]$$

where,

R_S = Rate of Return on Selling Short.
P_{t+1} = Price One Year after the Short Sale.
P_t = Price on the Short-Sale Date.
D_{t+1} = Any dividends Paid during the One-Year Period.

For example, the rate of return on a security which sold for \$10 at t and \$8 at $t + 1$ and paid a \$1 dividend is equal to +10.0 percent. Transaction costs, differential tax treatments on capital gains from long and short positions, and any interest costs which may be present are not considered. Nor were they considered in our comparison test results (below).

The average rate of return (R_S) for the sampled firms in each of the four one-year holding periods April 1961-1965, is computed and compared with the average rate of return on selling short for 572 companies examined by Professors McEnally and Dyl (M & D) for comparable periods.[k] In fact, we chose this four-year period because of the availability of M & D's results. Their results will serve as the population mean (μ) and they also supplied the population standard deviation (σ) of their average returns. Therefore, we can now perform the standard statistical z test (no relation to the discriminant Z score) in order to test whether or not the results obtained in this analysis are significantly different from the expected population value.

---

[k]McEnally and Dyl utilized a different data source which contained only firms listed on the New York Stock Exchange while the Compustat Data Tapes largely contain firms listed on both the New York and American Stock Exchanges.[17]

Test Results

The results for the companies selected by the bankruptcy prediction model and the M & D results are presented in Table 6-7 along with statistical significance tests. The mean values (R_S) from our short-sale investment strategy compared with the population mean results (μ) indicate that the Multiple Discriminant Analysis ratio selection technique is significantly greater than the population mean in each of the one-year sample periods. That is, R_S is significantly greater than μ; the results are significant at the .01 or .05 level. Further, the results show that R_S is positive in two of the four one-year periods although the general market (S & P) was also positive in each of the four periods. Table 6-8 shows that the number of firms with positive R_S exceed the negative R_S in each of the periods. The reason for the negative R_S in the last two periods is that the absolute amounts of the negative returns in general were higher than the amounts of positive returns. In fact, there were three observations in these two periods where the R_S was greater than -100.0%.[1]

Table 6-7
Statistical Results - Short-Sale Strategy

Period	Sample Mean R_S	Population Mean μ	Population Standard Deviation σ	Statistical Test and Number of Observations z^* (n)
April '61-April '62	+19.10%	− 8.68%	24.66%	7.38** (43)
April '62-April '63	+18.50	+ 3.84	19.77	2.34***(10)
April '63-April '64	− 5.02	−21.86	29.38	3.03** (28)
April '64-April '65	− 6.06	−19.91	27.95	1.98***(16)

$$ z = \frac{\bar{R}_S - \mu}{\sigma} \cdot \sqrt{n} $$

** Significant at .01 level.
***Significant at .05 level.

---

[1] A final note on the statistical test and the data utilized concerns the nature of the Compustat Data Tapes. These tapes are updated weekly with new quarterly or annual data and include *only* those firms which are still in existence when the new information is added. For instance, a firm which did exist sometime during our 1960-1964 sample period but, for one reason or another, e.g., bankruptcy, is no longer in existence in 1968 (the last year our Compustat Tape covered) would not show up on the tape. This means that a potentially significant group of firms cannot be analyzed for their short-selling experience. How significant is this bias? According to Dr. Victor Niederhoffer, a financial consultant who has researched this very type of bias, the effect can be substantial. The above bias, however, if anything strengthens the results of this study. The reason is simple. A short-sale strategist is interested in potential big *losers* among the stocks he scrutinizes. Earlier, we showed evidence that the expected short-selling rates of return on firms which go bankrupt are substantial. This relatively infrequent but significant occurrence, along with other reasons of exclusion from the data tapes, obviously negates the potential contribution of these firms in our controlled experiment. Therefore, we conclude that the average rate of return (R_S) would probably have been higher had all firms in existence during the sample period been observed. The data source, however, for the M & D sample of firms (CRSP Stock Price Tapes) does not possess this bias and firms which are no longer in existence today will still have their prices represented for the years when the firm was in existence.

Table 6-8
Number of Positive and Negative Rates of Return (R_S) for Various Annual Periods

Sample Period (One Year)	n	Number of Positive R_S	Number of Negative R_S
April, 1961-1962	43	36	7
April, 1962-1963	10	9	1
April, 1963-1964	28	16	12
April, 1964-1965	16	9	7

Conclusions and Implications

Based on the above tests, we conclude that the investor who utilized a short-selling strategy based on the bankruptcy prediction model would have done significantly better than if the short-sale strategy results approximated randomly selected (population) results. While investors do not select stocks randomly, no other comprehensive short-sale strategy comparisons are available and the conclusions still are meaningful. It should be noted that the model used was not developed for stock selection, but for bankruptcy assessment, and the result bodes well for adjusting the ingredients to make the model more suitable for stock market purposes. We are not suggesting, however, that the bankruptcy model (adjusted or not) should be utilized for all common stock investment purposes. Rather, we are basing its usage on the belief that investors tend to underestimate the plight of distressed firms and we have shown this is also true, to an extent, for firms which manifest bankruptcy potential but do not in fact fail.

The subject of this chapter has been the common stock implications of corporate bankruptcy and we have covered this topic from several angles. No doubt, we have not exhausted all avenues of analytic research on the topic and, of course, the consequences dealing with other types of security holders, e.g., creditors, have not been examined. Still, the results very likely will contribute to the theory of business finance, the evaluation of the bankruptcy process and the dimensionality of the investment process.

7

Railroad Failures: The Penn Central Debacle and the Prediction of Railroad Bankruptcy

On June 21, 1970, the nation's economy, and to some extent the entire world's money and capital markets, was severely shaken by the news that the $5-billion Penn Central Transportation Company (P-C) had petitioned the courts and was granted the right to declare bankruptcy under the provisions of the National Bankruptcy Act. The bankruptcy of this company represents the largest single corporate failure in history. Because of this event, and its close timing with respect to this writing, we devote this last chapter to a discussion of three related aspects: (1) the history of railroad problems in the United States (in order to put the Penn Central case in its proper perspective); (2) the immediate events leading to the collapse and the significant repercussions in the first year subsequent to bankruptcy declaration; and (3) an attempt to develop a predictive tool in order to provide an early warning device for spotlighting potential railroad bankruptcies.

Railroad Industry Background

More than any other industry in the business history of America, the railroads have produced a long line of almost continuous corporate bankruptcies. Since this industry moreover, is subject to public interest qualities that have led to public regulation, one wonders how so many failures could continuously occur. One recent reporter observed that the number of railroad receiverships, bankruptcies, and liquidations during the period 1876-1970 exceeds 1100.[1] This compares with an Interstate Commerce Commission (ICC) report of approximately 840 failures during 1894-1942.

As noted above, the nation's railroads have almost continually had problems in staying solvent. During the depression years of the 1930s, approximately one-third of the nation's trackage was in the hands of receivers and going back into history, only slightly smaller proportions were in a similar state during the years just prior to World War I and the years subsequent to the panic of 1894. In point of fact, the 1969-70 recession is another period in this pattern of continuous railroad failure. To be sure, the number of large roads declaring bankruptcy in 1970 was not great, although three large roads did go under, but the proportion of the failed companies share of total railroad activity was very large indeed.

The history of railroad failure and receiverships has been classified by Arthur Stone Dewing into five periods up to and including the great depression years.[2]

The focus of attention is general economic distress in each of the periods. A discussion of these periods and other descriptive material on the history of railroad failures can be found in the appendix to this chapter. In the next section, we review the major problems that have faced railroads over the years.

Review of Railroad Problems

The large number of railroad failures has evolved due to a chain of unfavorable circumstances and poor management on a microeconomic level and also due to the regulatory nature of the industry. Due to the numerous legislative moves to regulate the transportation industry, from the Interstate Commerce Act (1887) to the Department of Transportation Act (1966), we now have an example of government regulated cartelization which has been characterized by its inability to adjust to change and, at times, grossly inefficient management. Rather than review the history of railroad progress in the United States, it will serve the purposes of our discussion to summarize the major problem areas.[3]

The major reasons for the railroad industry's periodic dismal performances are (1) its inability to meet competitive conditions due to an inflexible pricing and cost structure; (2) its acute susceptibility to large net income losses during periods of economic stress due to a fixed asset and liability structure which is heavily leveraged; (3) its excess capacity; (4) the acute labor and manpower rigidities; and (5) a shortage of innovative management. Many of these problems have resulted from government regulation and rigidities. These have produced an industry pricing structure dictated, in part, by political and noneconomic terms rather than comparative advantage considerations.[4] For instance, prices to shippers of agricultural goods have traditionally been favored compared to those charged to shippers of manufactured goods. Competition from other modes of transportation has left the railroads in an unfavorable competitive position on the potentially high profit manufactured goods. While it is not the intent of this discussion to suggest changes in the railroad industry's structure, it should be pointed out that several noted economists favor deregulation resulting in alleged desirable shifts in resource allocation in our transportation industries.

The railroad industry is a classic illustration of the magnification effect caused by high operating and financial leverage structures. The leverage concept, taught to beginning students in finance, affirms that during periods of economic downturns, those firms which are more heavily leveraged will experience greater negative returns on equity and be more vulnerable to failures than low fixed cost firms. Combine this situation with recurring liquidity problems common to railroads, and the reasons for the high incidence of railroad bankruptcies becomes clear. The macroeconomic influences on business failures, discussed in Chapter 2, are particularly relevant to railroads, especially the discussion of the correlation between poor overall national economic growth and failures.

In essence, the railroad industry is quite vulnerable to business cycle fluctuations but unlike other cyclical industries, the asset and capital structures do not reflect this high-risk situation. In the third section of this chapter, we observe that for those roads which went bankrupt, the percentage of total capital contributed by creditors, one statement prior to bankruptcy, averaged 91.2%, while the industry average was approximately 50%. The ability of firms to withstand even small declines in revenues in this highly leveraged condition is questionable. Combine this high-risk situation with historically low returns on invested capital and we have valid grounds for criticism of the industry's overall managerial efficiency.

The case for railroad overcapacity has been made on economic grounds many times with periodic reports advocating railroad mergers and abandonments. In Chapter 5, we made the case for well-conceived mergers obviating the need for bankruptcy declaration when the need for drastic action is realized early enough so as to effectively combine a sick company with one that is financially and managerially strong. Since the railroad industry has been marked by parallel and duplicative facilities, a strong case could be made for operating economies from mergers. Ironically, it was the merger of the two largest railroads in 1968 which helped plunge the merged Penn Central Transportation Company into bankruptcy. With this merger failure and the subsequent cancellation of merger discussions between the Chesapeake and Ohio and Norfolk and Western Railways (March 20, 1971), some analysts expect that the trend toward railroad mergers is temporarily and possibly permanently derailed.a

The industry's labor situation is critical. Although we do not take a definitive position on this controversial topic, it is fair to point out that union featherbedding and rigid work rules are often cited as contributions to the railroad's problems. While some analysts testify that labor costs are the industry's number one problem (including one of the primary causes of the Penn Central collapse and the failure of the unsuccessful merger),[6] others protest that the labor problems are exaggerated and not enough attention is given to high labor productivity.[7] Still, anytime a company is saddled with rigid cost structures, in this case due to labor contracts, it is at a distinct competitive disadvantage to other firms and other industries which have less rigid structures.

In the P-C bankruptcy aftermath, the road's trustees have appealed to Congress to permit them to reduce the crippling labor costs agreed upon just prior to the merger in 1968. They argued that P-C's labor costs account for 66

---

aTwo acknowledged railroad experts, Isabel Benham and Arthur Jansen, attested to the probable disappearance of railroad mergers, except in isolated cases, in a recent interview in *Barrons*. Reasons given for their position include the disabling effect of labor costs and rigidities which tend to erode any efficiency gains from mergers. Jansen commented that "any savings from mergers would go to the employees, and that the stockholders would never see any of the benefits." He also views the Penn Central bankruptcy as the industry "savior" because of the favorable legislation expected in its wake and the ridding of unprofitable passenger operations. Benham, on the other hand, views the railroads in 1971 as being at the crossroads and possibly headed toward nationalization. One of the Penn Central trustees, Jervis Langdon, advocates the merger of all of the over 70 large railroads in the United States into a single privately owned entity. He was recently quoted, however, as believing "that the day of the rail merger is probably over" due to Penn Central's failure.[5]

percent of total operating expenses—compared to 58 percent for other rail-roads—and these costs must be reduced if the road is to survive.[8]

One might argue that the regulatory and labor rigidities are not the fault of company management personnel but, in the case of labor, the contracts had to be signed by someone. Admittedly, however, a regulated industry like the railroads will have difficulty in attracting bright, new managerial talent when the prospect of rapid promotion and expanding markets is so limited. At least one analyst expects that this situation would be corrected in time with moves toward deregulation.[9]

The Penn Central Bankruptcy

The Penn Central Transportation Company and its predecessor companies had enjoyed a long and distinguished history since the Pennsylvania Railroad's incorporation in 1846. Investors in this company received continuous dividends from 1848 until P-C finally eliminated its cash dividend payout late in 1969; this impressive continuous dividend record is surpassed only by some 13 banks in North America. Ironically, the continued cash drain from cash dividend payments in 1968-69 hastened P-C's final collapse. At the time of its failure, the P-C Transportation Company (assets of approximately $4.5 billion) was one of two primary subsidiaries of the parent Penn Central Company (assets of about $7 billion). The Pennsylvania Company, essentially a conglomerate with interests in several diversified enterprises, is a subsidiary of the transportation company. In fact, only the transportation company declared bankruptcy, although the parent firm—listed on the New York Stock Exchange—is unquestionably on shaky ground also.

Penn Central's corporate structure at the time of its collapse was the result of a conscious plan to make the unprofitable rail business as palatable as possible and to diversify in order to offset the railroad burden. The result was the famous Pennsylvania R.R.—New York Central R.R. merger on February 1, 1968, formed to realize sizeable economies in an area where overcapacity, pointless competi-tion and duplicate facilities were serious problems.

Road to Bankruptcy

Since the P-C collapse of one year ago, countless articles and comments have been published regarding the causes and repercussions.[10] The bankruptcy, probably one of the most significant in history, has also prompted numerous Congressional and commission investigations, most of which are still in process. (Among the many groups investigating are the ICC, the Senate and House Commerce Committees, and the House Banking Committee.) Rather than attempt to completely review the agonized collapse, we will try to highlight the critical factors. These include the fundamental economic problems inherent in the railroad industry, and the immediate events preceding the June 1970 shock. The latter include (1) unfortunate consequences of the 1968 merger between two of the nation's largest railroads; (2) managerial and director conflicts, incompetencies and alleged fraudulent activities; and (3) severe liquidity problems combined with an untimely economic recession.

Merger Consequences

The primary motivation for the merger was the sizeable economies envisioned to result from combining these two competing giants. Estimates of the long-term savings exceeded $80 million and the merger was finally consummated after almost a decade of negotiation. These efficiencies were never realized. From the start, the merged company encountered problems. Service, instead of being vastly improved, seemed to deteriorate. In order to receive ratification for the merger, the companies had to agree upon a costly labor settlement which in the opinion of several analysts doomed the marriage from the very start.[11] In addition, the ICC required the merged entity to incorporate the bankrupt N.Y., New Haven and Hartford R.R. into its system. The latter had been in bankruptcy since 1961 and was (and still is) in such woeful shape that besides the $150-200 million P-C will finally be required to pay for the sick railroad, large capital outlays were required from the start.[b] Both of these forced agreements were a cash drain not only initially but on a continuous basis.

The consolidated company's profits appeared to be quite impressive in 1968 with reported earnings of $88 million, but these figures were propped up by the sizeable income from real estate operations and the alleged, and challenged, liberal accounting treatment. In actuality, the transportation end of the parent company lost a sizeable amount (over $5 million) and the cash flow was negative also. One account testifies that of the $88 million in reported income in 1968, $54 million came from extraordinary gains on security sales, $23.8 million from capitalized merger costs, $10 million of advances from affiliates, an $11.8 million dividend that is alleged to be merely a property exchange.[12] The accounting firm which certified the statements has countered each of these so-called "virtuoso" bookkeeping tactics.[13]

Managerial Problems

Usually, a bankruptcy can be traced to some kind of managerial incompetence and the P-C case is certainly no exception. The managerial philosophies of the

---

[b]The exact total for the purchase is still in dispute, with the case already submitted to and ruled upon once by a higher court of appeal. Since the P-C bankruptcy, the New Haven trustee, Richard Joyce Smith, has had to continually argue for the rights of his security holders in the federal courts.

top executives of the two companies were in conflict from the start. As is so often the case, growth through any means, especially mergers, requires superior managerial resources as well as financial strength. There is considerable evidence the P-C lacked both. Perhaps the primary problem was the lack of coordinated and compatible leadership from the top.

Since the bankruptcy announcement, several of P-C's top executives have been accused of plotting unjust personal enrichment in their financial manipulations especially on real estate operations. At least three of the top aides have been named in a law suit by the trustees.[14] Several other alleged scandalous activities have ensued from the many investigations and no doubt more will come. The ICC claimed that trading in P-C stock by inside officers and directors may have hurt the road.[15] This includes substantial insider selling *prior* to the unsuccessful $100 million debenture offering in May 1970. The House Banking Committee charged that the public was kept in the dark while banks and other insiders sold significant shareholdings prior to the bankruptcy date.[16]

The share volume and price activity of P-C stock prior to bankruptcy bears some analysis. P-C's stock took a precipitous drop in the months prior to failure, with the stock falling from 43 1/4 on September 1, 1969, to 11 1/8 on June 19, 1970 (the last trading date prior to bankruptcy declaration). This decline of approximately 74% was considerably more than the Standard & Poor 500 Index decline of 19% over a comparable period. A large proportion of the drop in P-C stock price occurred between April 1, 1970, and June 19 (from 23 1/2 to 11 1/8). During this latter period, volume on the stock totalled just under 5 million shares traded; a substantial increase in volume over the prior three-month period (January 1-April 1) when only 1.5 million shares changed hands. So we observe a large increase in activity prior to bankruptcy accompanied by significant price decreases. In fact, between May 12 and June 19, 19 of the 29 trading dates saw volume rise above the 100,000 share level. This is all the more impressive when you consider that the last date before May 12 when over 100,000 shares were traded in P-C stock was back in November 1969! Obviously, the rumors and news concerning P-C's worsening condition contributed to the increased volume prior to bankruptcy. Whether or not "inside information" precipitated large sales from certain individuals and institutions is something which deserves serious probing.

It is of additional interest to observe that P-C stock fell about 54% in the period May 21-July 21 which encompasses the one month prior to one month after bankruptcy period—the B.I.E. discussed in Chapter 6. Recall, that the average B.I.E. for those firms was considerably lower at 25%. Almost all of the B.I.E. P-C price decline took place on the trading date (June 22) following bankruptcy declaration, however. In the one year following bankruptcy, the price of Penn Central company common has traded mostly in the $5-7 range.

It is quite remarkable that the price investors settled upon after just one day of bankruptcy—$6.50 per share on June 22nd has not fluctuated very much since that date. Perhaps that is true because investors have remained uncertain about the expected common equity in P.C. upon reorganization. Although historical railroad experience indicates that rarely is the common equity continued, some analysts have speculated that the vast real estate interests of the Pennsylvania Corporation ensures a continued positive net worth. The results of recent efforts to sell off a large proportion of this property[17] can help to reduce the uncertainty about the economic value of Penn Central Company's assets. (Estimates of asset values involved in this sale exceed $1 billion.) Much of this real estate, however, is pledged as collateral on already existing debt.

Returning to the realm of managerial problems at P.C., a comment on the role played by the Board of Directors is appropriate. As in all corporations, the board of P-C had the ultimate responsibility for the policies and actions of the company. Throughout the period preceding bankruptcy, it appears that the board went along passively with management's policies, asking virtually no questions until the situation was essentially irreparable. News of the cancellation of a vital $100 million debenture issue in May 1970 and the subsequent board meeting in early June finally prompted the board to take some action—in this case, the firing of Saunders and Perlman who were two of the most influential leaders in the railroad industry for several decades.

It is not likely that this board, even if it had foreseen the serious operating and financial problems in 1969-70 could have done very much about it. One writer has presented an interesting thesis that the P-C Board of Directors were fundamentally incapable of guiding a company which had become a "one railroad" holding company.[18] Commenting on the bankruptcy, Professor Vance observed:

The situation boils down to this: Penn Central's top management and, in particular, its board of directors, just was not groomed and geared to venture the conglomerate way.... If any inference can be drawn that certain capacities, competencies, or characteristics lend themselves to success in certain lines of business endeavor, then it appears that Penn Central's directors, presumably adequate for railroading, were congenitally unsuited for conglomerate venture.[19]

In his "director-characteristic-profile," Vance concluded that P-C's members were most similar in their backgrounds and competencies to director's of commercial banks and strikingly dissimilar to board members of conglomerates. Whether such evidence is conclusive enough to partially explain P-C's failure is subject to some skepticism. Yet, it cannot be denied that in this instance, the Board of Directors did not exert any positive influence.

The Liquidity Crisis

As in almost all bankruptcies, the most immediate cause of failure is the debtor's inability to meet its obligations—essentially running out of cash. Penn Central ran out of cash because of fundamental economic pressures and a poorly managed finance function.

In the two and one-half years following the merger, P-C suffered huge cash flow deficits from its railroad operations which were only partially compensated by profitable real estate and other nonrailroad ventures. The latter efforts did not result in any tangible net cash flow gains, however, as capital was constantly flowing into these operations. In reality, only Great Southwest Corporation provided any sizeable profits, $34.4 million in 1969, and even here large capital advances of approximately $19 million were made to Great Southwest with dividends paid to the parent of only $2.2 million in 1969. Another venture, the Executive Jet Aviation Company which cost P-C some $22 million, deteriorated to such an extent that it was reported to be sold in April 1971 for just $1.25 million.

Despite the cash shortage, P-C continued its generous dividend policy. In 1968-69, almost $100 million in cash dividends were paid out. No doubt the cutting of the dividend and most assuredly the total discontinuance of this remarkable dividend record, would have adverse effects on P-C's stock price. This was unacceptable to a company which now had to constantly worry about price-earnings ratios and its effect on the conglomerate strategy. In all fairness, a 123-year dividend record is hard to snap. Yet, stockholders were receiving a costly short-run payout from the 1968-69 dividends.

As economic conditions in the country worsened and Penn Central's earnings fell drastically in late 1969, the company's financial officers found it increasingly difficult to raise needed capital. Any hope of buying capital through the acquisition route was dashed by the continuous deterioration in the stock market and the above average decline in P-C stock itself. From a high of $86 per share in mid 1968, the price fell to the mid 40's in September 1969 and continued down to a low of $11 just prior to bankruptcy declaration. The drop of approximately $75 per share is explained by investor overoptimism with the merger and their disillusionment over the subsequent poor performance. In Chapter 3, we observed that market price changes are an accurate predictor of corporate bankruptcy—this is borne out again in the P-C case.

Given the risky financial structure of the company and its acute cash shortage, the Nixon Administration's decision to use monetary policy to bring about a desired level of inflation further exacerbated the railroad's problem. The compound effects of a poor economic situation *and* tight money conditions were, in this writer's opinion, the most important causes of the P-C bankruptcy. In Chapter 2, we observed that negative changes in economic growth, stock market growth and credit availability all contribute to increased business failures. A classic example of these influences on a firm is the P-C debacle.

One of these aggregate aggravators—the change in economic growth—appears to be particularly relevant to the railroad industry. A casual analysis of post-World War II railroad bankruptcies is revealing. During this period, 1946-1970, there have been sixteen major railroad bankruptcies (either Class I or Section 77's) in the United States. During the same 25-year period, there have been five relatively mild recessions, if we include the 1969-1970 growth recession. The number of recessions becomes six if we also include the 1967 minirecession. These five (six) recessions encompassed approximately sixty (seventy) months out of the three hundred months making up the afore-mentioned postwar period. The number of railroad bankruptcies (not including local passenger-oriented roads) occurring within these recession months was ten (twelve). Therefore, approximately two-thirds of the postwar bankruptcies occurred during recession months, whereas the number of these poor economic performance months comprised only approximately one-fifth of the period. This is fairly strong evidence for the concurrent association between railroad failures and poor overall economic conditions.

Why then call the P-C failure a *debacle* if we can identify the fundamental economic causes? Probably the reasons for depicting this one failure, amongst the numerous other firms which were failing in 1969-71, as a debacle comes from (1) the sheer size of the company; (2) the fact that so many sophisticated investors were caught with their wallets exposed; (3) the political and social involvement; and (4) the serious consequences in the days following the bankruptcy announcement.

In 1968 and 1969, P-C managed to raise over $150 million in new capital through various means and also raised its line of credit with a banking consortium. In late 1969, however, traditional sources of capital began to dry up. Large sinking fund requirements had to be met shortly and the company's commercial paper required continuous turning-over and therefore an acceptable credit rating was mandatory. P-C's management vainly attempted to secure rate increases from the I.C.C. and new lines of bank credit were frantically sought.

Key administration officials in Washington began to come to the aid of the beleaguered company in the hopes of avoiding bankruptcy and a possible financial panic. Congressional bills were drawn up to provide huge Defense Department guarantees for railroad loans. A group of banks were willing to make loans of $200 million immediately upon receipt of government guarantees. The plan met staunch resistance, however, from members of Congress especially from Representative Wright Patman of the House Banking and Currency Committee. Considerable sympathy had emerged for government's noninterference in the affairs of private enterprises. This opinion was climaxed by Congressional nonsupport of the $750 million railroad loan guarantee bill and the bankruptcy was sealed with the Nixon administration's sudden withdrawal of its support for the $200 million immediate financing guarantee. Naturally, the bankers with-drew their offer and after several unsuccessful attempts to reverse this decision, P-C's management grudgingly petitioned the courts for bankruptcy.

Post-Bankruptcy Events

As mentioned earlier, the P-C bankruptcy set off a chain of events which bordered on financial panic. The commercial paper market went into shock and other leading companies whose operations and financial structures were of questionable investment quality suddenly found that they could no longer depend upon their commercial paper as a source of funds. For instance, Chrysler Corporation suffered considerably in this period but has since recovered. Fortunately, the admirable efforts of the financial and government communities managed to avert a serious crisis of confidence and liquidity in the money and capital markets. The recovery in the commercial paper market has been so complete that many believed the market just one year after the P-C disaster was in the best shape of its existence:

> It (commercial paper market) also appears to be stronger, thanks to the fact that it has received several qualitative shots in the arm. In place of one rating service, two credit checkers pass on the merits of commercial paper issuers. A number of big names with soggy balance sheets have quietly left the market and the firms that have remained are being subjected to the kind of thorough-going scrutiny the textbooks call for. 'Penn Central was a disaster but in the long run it was probably the best thing that could have happened to the commercial paper market.'[20]

While the recovery is indicative of the resiliency of our money and capital markets, it is undeniably true that public and private institution confidence was badly shaken as a result of just one firm's failure.

Certain creditors, particularly several of the nation's largest insurance companies, suffered huge losses in excess of $100 million on investments in P-C securities. Not only were creditors, customers, and suppliers confused, but many investors did not seem to realize that the Pennsylvania Company, the holding company of most of the nonrail assets, is actually a subsidiary of the bankrupt transportation company. Therefore, virtually all of the nonrail assets were pledged as security on the railroad obligations. Whether or not the cash realizable from these assets will be sufficient to repay even the secured creditors of P-C is not likely to be fully ascertained for many years.

Several other railroads moved to protect themselves from financial embarrassment in the wake of the P-C collapse. Rental payments on equipment owned by other roads were called, but due to the protective clauses of the Bankruptcy Act, many of these obligations and others were "frozen."[c] The Pittsburgh-Ft. Wayne Railroad omitted its regular dividend citing the uncertainty of securing rentals owed by P-C. Approximately one month after the bankruptcy, the Lehigh Valley R.R. (97% owned by P-C) followed its parent into the uncertain confines of the bankruptcy courts. In a related event, the Jersey Central R.R. itself a bankruptcy victim on several previous dates—told the I.C.C. it faced closing unless emergency aid was received.[22] In addition, the I.C.C. granted certain railroad petitions to raise rates on freight traffic. In October 1970, Congress gave approval for an intercity transit corporation (AMTRAK) to take over passenger traffic of those roads which join the system. P-C trustees estimate this new

---

[c]On occasion, however, the courts have ruled that P-C still had to pay certain obligations incurred before and since bankruptcy was declared. For instance, back taxes owed to New York City were deemed collectible and enforced by the city's nonpayment of rentals owed to P-C on some of its properties.[21]

system, started on May 1, 1971, will result in savings of approximately $267 million. Critics, however, remain skeptical.

One of P-C's problems prior to bankruptcy was its inability to raise funds. This situation continued for months after the petition and only because the Transportation Department guaranteed $100 million of trustee certificates in January 1971, did the road secure a new infusion of capital. Although it appears that the P-C will continue to operate for a while longer, its troubles continue. The road suffered a huge loss in 1970 of $431.2 million compared to a $91.6 million deficit in 1969 and no relief is in sight.

The new capital infusion to be issued on a priority basis, however, was not received well by all quarters. A group called the Institutional Investors Penn Central Group (IIPCG) threatened to begin liquidating their holdings if the government continued to back more loans to keep the railroad afloat. They testified that: "railroad losses should be borne by the public and not private investors...."[23] and any additional loans guaranteed on a priority basis over existing obligations would be grossly unfair.

This presents an interesting social issue as well as a tricky financial problem. Should private investors suffer in order to preserve a company (or industry) which functions, in part, in the "public interest." As was pointed out earlier in Chapter 1, certain bankruptcies already penalize the public indirectly due to higher tax burdens and diversion of government funds from alternative uses. While the argument that private investors in railroads should be compensated by the government is ludicrous (except, of course, in the event of nationalization of the nation's railroads), it cannot be denied that the quasigovernment nature of the industry should provide for close scrutiny by the ICC or the Transportation Department pertaining to the solvency and operating ability of individual roads.

It seems clear, at least to this writer, that with all of its railroad bankruptcy experience, the ICC should have developed tools for assessing the failure probability of its railroads. If such tools were present, an early-warning device could help to avert some of these disasters. It appears that the Commission has been extremely neglectful in this function both to the individual railroads and the public at large.

The Prediction of Railroad Bankruptcies

The propensity for failure among railroads has been demonstrated throughout its stormy history. The trend in failures has apparently not abated although the sheer number of bankruptcies has diminished as the industry consolidated its facilities. In 1970, four railroads petitioned the courts for bankruptcy under Section 77 of the National Bankruptcy Act. These roads encompassed over $5 billion in properties and have necessitated the temporary "freezing" of a large proportion of their assets and liabilities. In addition to the obvious costs to failing companies' creditors, the situation has resulted in sacrifices on the part of the roads' employees, customers, suppliers, investors and no doubt eventually by the public. As a result of the Penn Central collapse, a great hue and cry emerged from various interested parties with numerous Congressional investigations and hearings resulting. (It is an all too clear example of the so-called crisis principle.)[24] In essence, this is the notion that the only time any change is made or investigation begun is after some catastrophe has taken place.

In a way, this writer is also a "Johnny-come-lately" in an attempt to comment on the propensity of railroads to fail. This discussion attempts to analyze the advanced warnings, if any, in the P-C case and, more importantly, to investigate the efficacy of developing an accurate predictive tool for railroad bankruptcies.[25] The need for such a procedure was clearly articulated by ICC Chairman George Stafford in the P-C aftermath:

Mr. Stafford said that beyond the Penn-Central investigation, the ICC probably will develop a number of rulemaking procedures aimed at fashioning guidelines for providing "early warnings" of impending bankruptcies of other roads.[26]

It is precisely in the area of an early-warning device that this section places its major emphasis. To the extent that this study parallels ICC investigations, the value is perhaps even greater. This is an area that cannot be overlooked simply because there is suspicion of other similar studies. Whatever information is derived by the ICC and vice-versa, will no doubt be mutually beneficial.

The P-C bankruptcy supposedly caught most outside analysts, both sophisticated and not, by surprise. At least one noted financial analyst stated, and I agree with him but for slightly different reasons, that this epic failure should not have been unanticipated.[27] Professor Murray asserts that adequate credit worthiness was lacking in the P-C case, and probably in other instances where a large, heretofore solvent enterprise is involved. In his opinion, the present concepts and techniques of credit analysis are sufficient to foresee disasters like the P-C, only they must be used properly. For instance, a useful summary measure of railway efficiency—net operating income before federal income taxes/gross revenues—should have alerted investors to the deteriorating picture of the newly merged road in 1968. This ratio for P-C compared to all Class I railroads in the years preceding bankruptcy is described in Table 7-1. Murray concludes that this margin of safety measure clearly warned of approaching difficulties in the industry and in Penn Central.[28] My own statistical comparisons showed the P-C Transportation Co. in trouble after 1968 in most categories, but not all. Several of these ratios, described more fully in the next section, are summarized below in Table 7-2. While we agree with Professor Murray as to the deteriorating situation at P-C and for the most part its poor comparison with industry averages, on a ratio-by-ratio basis, we hesitate to put much faith in an univariate type of analysis. This line of reasoning was discussed at length in Chapter 3. For instance, although 5 of the 6 ratios listed in Table 7-2 illustrate P-C's inferior position vis-a-vis the industry average, the sixth ratio—Total Debt/Total Assets—shows P-C to be in a *superior* position. The potential ambiguity in this type of analysis is evident.

Table 7-1
Comparable Profit Margins, 1965-1969

	P-C Ratio	Class I Roads
1969	5.4% deficit	6.6%
1968	3.0 deficit	6.9
1967	0.7	7.2
1966	6.3	11.6
1965	5.7	11.0

Table 7-2
Penn Central Transportation Company Ratios Compared to Industry Averages*

	1968		1969	
	P-C	Industry	P-C	Industry
Net Current Assets/ Total Assets	−3.01%	0.44%	−2.37%	−0.36%
Earned Surplus/ Total Assets	16.1%	33.0%	12.6%	32.0%
Income after Fixed Charges/Operating Revenue	−0.9%	6.7%	−5.0%	6.4%
Cash Flow/Fixed Charges	0.95X	3.4X	.09X	3.4X
Operating Expenses/ Operating Revenues	88.6%	77.5%	85.6%	78.1%
Total Debt/ Total Assets	37.0%	45.8%	42.3%	47.1%

*Industry averages do not include Penn Central totals. Since P-C accounts for such a large proportion of the industry's activity, it is more instructive to compare its ratios with those of all other firms.

Murray commented further that the possible distracting elements of the diversification program at P-C added to the analysts' confusion. In addition, the commercial paper market attracted many new and untested firms in the period 1967-69 and conceivably could have diverted the credit analyst from careful scrutinization of each account. The giant Penn Central which had never defaulted on its obligations and was still paying cash dividends through the first half of 1969 could easily have been overlooked. Unfortunately, this is not a convincing argument to the president of a large life insurance company which was caught holding millions of dollars of P-C paper in the spring and summer of 1970.

Among the conclusions reached by Murray in his examination of the P-C debacle are (1) that financial analysts had become "too casual" in their acceptance of bottomline earnings figures; (2) that there is no substitute for careful appraisal of the economics of the business; (3) that sheer size and corporate complexity especially through diversification have no inherent value; and (4) that perhaps new analytical techniques need to be developed from financial statements such as sources and uses of funds.

While we do not quarrel with most of the conclusions stated above, we do question the efficacy of traditional tools of financial analysis used in traditional ways. We wholeheartedly embrace the conclusion that new analytical techniques are needed and in the next section of this chapter we proceed to develop a technique of this genre.

A Specialized Railroad Industry Model

The explicit methodology proposed for the investigation of predicting railroad bankruptcies is almost identical to the one used in Chapter 3. In that analysis, financial and economic ratios were utilized within a multivariate statistical technique, called multiple discriminant analysis, in order to predict bankruptcy in several samples of *manufacturing* firms. The analysis proved extremely fruitful with accurate predictions of bankruptcy up to two years prior to the event.

Railroad Industry Advantages

One particularly fortunate ingredient of a multiple discriminant or even an univariate *railroad* bankruptcy analysis is that we now have a project where the comparative analysis can be concentrated within a relatively homogeneous group of sample firms. As we have pointed out several times, the prior manufacturing study suffered from one potentially serious drawback for broad practical application. The heterogeneous nature of the sample cast suspicion as to its accuracy in predictions of firms within industries where the nature of business operation differs greatly from the average manufacturing firm. The ideal would be to construct individual models for specific industries, or lines of business, so as to remove this drawback. The railroad industry study, therefore, provides an ideal framework from which we can apply a proven technique to an even more appropriate problem area. Specifically, we will match results drawn from a group of bankrupt railroads and compare them with average industry measures drawn from the same time periods as the prior-to-bankruptcy financial ratios. More detailed discussion of this procedure follows shortly. The beauty of this homogeneous type of analysis is that we can be confident that any new firm tested in the model will have similar characteristics that were present in the group of firms used to construct the model. Concentration can be directed specifically to bankruptcy potential without fear of distorted ratio comparisons due to industry differentials. We might add that there are few industries with sufficient bankruptcy experience to provide adequate readily available sample data. A dubious distinction for railroads—but one which can be exploited.

This brings us to another positive reason for our optimism that a viable bankruptcy predictive model in the railroad industry is feasible. Due to ICC reporting requirements, accounting data, both present and past, is for the most part available and quite comprehensive. Although these ICC requirements have changed from time to time, and have been criticized especially for "inflating earnings,"[29] the comprehensiveness of data has remained at a high level and continuity of accounting reporting has only been moderately difficult to interpret.[d] The uniformity of accounting systems required of railroads offers relatively comparable financial and operating data, but at the same time puts a burden on the analyst to be selective in his choice of indicators. In addition to the individual firm reporting standards, the ICC provides aggregate annual statistics for the entire railroad carrier industry which is published along with firm data in *Moody's Transportation Manual* on an annual basis.

One of the characteristics of the railroad industry which distinguishes it from most other businesses is its regulatory nature. An appropriate question can be asked as to whether or not a statistical predictive tool can be successfully developed and implemented in such an environment. Substantial evidence from several similar types of industries, in terms of regulatory governing bodies, appears to point favorably for the accomplishment of this task. The Savings and Loan industry for one has experimented with a multiple discriminant model to be used by their examiners in order to assess the solvency of the member associations around the country. One system, developed at the Federal Home Loan Bank Board, utilized annual and semiannual reported financial data and combined key measures to predict problem areas.[30] The entire federal process is now under review, however, due to data source and timing problems. In the commercial bank sector, an accurate predictive model was developed for assessing bank insolvencies utilizing a type of bivariate regression analysis which is essentially identical to multiple discriminant analysis for a two-group analysis. The model, developed by Professors Meyer and Pifer at the Federal Deposit Insurance Corporation, combines reported financial data ratios with local bank characteristics in order to make solvency predictions.[31] In the above instances, the motivation for developing an early warning device was due to the widespread public interest involved as well as making the economic system as stable as possible. Nothing shatters the public confidence in their financial institutions like insolvencies, potentially causing losses of hard earned savings and deposits. Currently, the Wall Street community is undergoing a crisis of confidence due to insolvencies, liquidations, and involuntary bankruptcies. Clearly, here is another area that needs remedial action fast. The railroad industry and its governing bodies simply cannot sit back and let roads go bankrupt without attempting to provide emergency measures when insolvency becomes a real possibility. To summarize then, the railroad industry possesses three powerful characteristics which leads us to conclude that there is a distinct possibility for successful

---

[d]We are fully aware, however, of the possibility of misrepresented, mistaken and manipulative reporting standards. Since we are using secondary data sources, there is little that can be done about this problem.

development of an early warning bankruptcy prediction tool. The industry's homogeneity provides a basis for nonambiguous comparison of past bankrupt carriers with their healthy counterparts. Second, the availability of data on a comprehensive and continuous basis reduces input problems to technical interpretation. Finally, other regulatory or quasiregulatory industries have been experimenting with techniques similar to the one advocated in this book with various degrees of success. The road ahead is obviously not one without possible setbacks in the development of a viable prediction tool, but unless there *is* a road, we can expect periodic railroad catastrophies, especially when general economic conditions are lagging.

The Data

A group of twenty railroads that went bankrupt between the years 1939-1970 was compiled and scrutinized, (listed in Table 7-3). This list includes those bankruptcies where sufficient data were available on their prebankruptcy operations. For the most part, they are comprised of Class I roads (greater than $5 million in revenues) and/or those which have filed under Section 77 of the Bankruptcy Act. Balance sheet and income statement data were then gathered for one statement and two statements prior to actual bankruptcy. *Moody's* also publishes extremely comprehensive industry data on an annual basis and the next step was to gather financial statistics for the industry as a whole for the same years that we have bankrupt data. It is even possible to gather industry data on a regional basis but this was not attempted. The objective at this point is to compile a list of ratios for the bankrupt group sample in order to compare average results with that of the aggregate industry data. We expect to find significant differences in most of our ratios which would indicate that it is feasible to develop an analytical tool for early warning detection of impending railroad problems.

The actual ratios compiled encompass three overall groupings of financial measures including (a) those found to be meaningful in prior studies; (b) some popular measures found in the literature; and (c) ratios thought to be particularly relevant to the railroad industry. The ratios are listed in Table 7-4. The measures encompass three overall groupings of financial indicators: (1) liquidity measures; (2) profitability and efficiency measures; and (3) solvency and leverage measures.[e] Several of the ratios are quite similar and any multivariate analysis would, of course, not include all of these measures.

Our *a priori* feeling is that the liquidity, profitability and solvency measures of the bankrupt sample will show significantly worse results than the industry averages and that these differentials will increase as bankruptcy approaches. That

---

[e]The market value equity/total debt ratio, which was found to be an important contributor to bankruptcy discrimination in Chapter 3 was not included because of the unavailability of figures in the industry sector. However, market value data are expected to be an extremely efficient indicator of impending problems.

Table 7-3
Bankrupt Railroad Sample

Company Name	Bankruptcy Year
1. Lehigh Valley R.R.	1970
2. Penn Central Transportation Company	1970
3. Boston & Maine Corporation	1970
4. Tennessee Central Railroad	1967
5. Central R.R. of New Jersey	1967
6. New York, New Haven & Hartford R.R.	1961
7. Atlantic & Danville Railway	1960
8. Tennessee Railroad	1959
9. Sacramento Northern Railway	1953
10. Long Island Railroad	1949
11. Huntington & Broad Top Mountain R.R.	1947
12. Missouri & Arkansas Railway	1946
13. Pittsburgh, Shawmut & Northern R.R.	1946
14. St. Johnsbury & Lake Champlain R.R.	1945
15. Wisconsin Central Railway	1943
16. Rutland R.R.	1942
17. Alton R.R.	1942
18. Central of Georgia Railway	1940
19. Florida East Coast Railway	1939
20. Central Railroad of New Jersey	1939

Table 7-4
Financial Ratios for the Railroad Bankruptcy Study

I. Liquidity Measures
    (1) Net Current Assets/Total Assets
    (2) Net Current Assets/Total Operating Revenues

II. Profitability and Efficiency Measures
    (3) Income before Interest and Taxes/Total Assets
    (4) Operating Revenue/Total Transportation Property
    (5) Operating Revenue/Net Transportation Property
    (6) Operating Expenses/Operating Revenue (Operating Ratio)
    (7) Transportation Expenses/Operating Revenue
    (8) Income after Taxes and Fixed Charges/Operating Revenue
    (9) Total Maintenance/Total Transportation Property
    (10) 3 Year Compound Growth Rate of Operating Revenue

III. Solvency and Leverage Measures
    (11) Earned Surplus (Balance Sheet)/Total Assets
    (12) Total Debt/Total Assets
    (13) Fixed Charges Earned (Before Taxes)
    (14) Cash Flow/Fixed Charges

is, the two statements prior to bankruptcy measures will be more healthy than the one statement prior results. Railroad analysts who are cognizant of these deteriorations may now have the ability to foresee eventual failure.

Railroad Bankruptcy Duration and Delays

At the time of the enactment of Section 77, advocates proclaimed that the new procedure would shorten the reorganization period and thereby lower its costs. In addition, the old friendly receiver would be replaced by an unbiased trustee. Furthermore, it would lead to sounder and more permanent financial structures and thereby lower the probability of future railroad bankruptcies. While the number of railroad bankruptcies has decreased substantially since 1940, even this fact is illusory. This writer observed approximately 15 significant railroad bankruptcies during the period 1946-70, with no more than 8 which could be considered major (Class I roads). These figures are misleading, however, if you consider that prior railroad liquidations and recent mergers had reduced the number of Class I roads to approximately 70. Also, several of these more recent bankruptcies have occurred in the year 1970 and with continued economic distress many additional roads could be on the path to disaster.

The first proclamation that reorganization time would be reduced, and so the consequent costs, has been clearly shown to be invalid. The ICC, which was established in 1887 to prevent discriminatory rates and give more reasonable rates to shippers has, in its expressed desire to be perfectly fair and thorough, probably been the prime contributor to lengthy, drawn out proceedings.

The finding that the Section 77 bankruptcy proceedings are significantly longer than the prior equity receiverships and also longer than comparable Chapter X proceedings for manufacturing firms has significant statistical documentation. Guthmann and Dougall examined 31 major equity receiverships between 1916-1933 and found the average length to be between three and four years.[32] They speculated in the 1950s that with the lengthy proceedings already observed, the average time for Section 77 proceedings would be double the pre-1933 experience (6 to 8 years). In my own studies of railroad reorganizations, I have found the Guthmann and Dougall estimate to be essentially correct. A total of 36 bankruptcies during the period 1938-1970 were traced from their actual petition date to the time the railroad came out of reorganization either to resume operations, be liquidated or merged. The *mean* bankruptcy reorganization period was *seven years and seven months*, with the median period being *seven years and two months*.[33] This is significantly greater than the pre-1933 period and also compares quite unfavorably with an average two years and three months period for manufacturing companies in bankruptcy.[34]

Admittedly, there should be some tradeoff between the positive effects of reaching a fair and equitable solution and the desire to reduce time and costs of the bankruptcy process. In this writer's opinion, the lengthy delays are not necessarily to the benefit of anyone (except perhaps the legal profession and expert witnesses), and I would advocate some upper time limit on reorganizations; for instance, a five-year maximum for reorganization proceedings. In the event that the time limit expires, the various security holders would be compensated according to traditional priority patterns based only on the *net liquidation value* of the firm's assets. Obviously, the difficulties in implementing such a limitation and the possible problems due to timing strategies of the various parties involved present serious obstacles to this proposal. I merely submit this notion in the hope that the additional costs involved, which usually exceed several millions of dollars, could be significantly reduced.[f]

As for the so-called "fairness" attribute, I wonder if this is the case. The longer a company remains in the uncertain condition of trusteeship, the greater the probability that economic values will be eroded—assuming, of course, that the firm could have emerged in a healthy condition at an earlier date. For one thing, new financing is not likely to be forthcoming except on a government guaranteed and priority basis. This is especially likely as long as the future survival of the company is uncertain. A noted railroad analyst, Oscar Lasdon, recently observed that in 57 postdepression bankruptcies, common stockholders had their total equity wiped out in all but two cases. This compares quite unfavorably to the 55 out of 92 cases of 100% stockholder loss in manufacturing companies (Chapter 6). While we realize that railroads have considerably more complex financial structures than do manufacturers, usually with many layers of debt obligations, the great difference in common stockholder experience could conceivably be due in part to the costs of prolonged railroad reorganizations. Also, many recent railway bankruptcies were petitioned at a time when their internal situation was so dire that successful rehabilitation with a continuing equity interest was highly unlikely. This would seem to be the case in the Penn Central situation, yet stockholders—mainly small investors—continued to purchase P-C stock in surprisingly great numbers.[36]

Long delays in railroad proceedings are primarily due to (1) lengthy courtroom hearings and appeals; (2) complexity in railroad capital structures; (3) reluctance of all parties to face the economic situation realistically in the hope for higher earnings; (4) difficulty in arriving at accurate earnings estimates; (5) an overburdened and sometimes overrigid ICC; and (6) the sheer time involved in court review of reorganization plans. These and other reasons were called to the attention of law makers as early as 1940 by Florence Dembitz[37] and there is no evidence that conditions have improved since then. (Her thesis was that the blame should primarily be placed on corporate managers and not the ICC.) In conclusion, it is felt that further legislation is needed to effect railroad reorganizations on a more rapid basis.

---

[f]The Bureau of Finance of the ICC computed, as of May 1947, that the average allowance for compensation in eleven prior railroad reorganizations was just under $2 million. While we are not aware of any recent statistics, it is fair to assume that these average costs have increased.[35]

Ratio Differentials

The next step in our empirical investigation is to examine the average ratios for the bankrupt group of firms and statistically compare them to the average railroad industry ratios. More precisely, we calculated averages for the 14 ratios listed in Table 7-4 for the bankrupt group sample of 20 firms based on data drawn from one and from two annual statements prior to bankruptcy. Industry averages were calculated from the same periods. For instance, the sample of bankrupt firms includes three firms who declared bankruptcy in 1970 and therefore data were collected as of the end of 1969 and 1968 for each firm. Likewise industry average ratios are calculated by giving proportional weighting to the 1969 and 1968 years (3 out of 20). Since the bankrupt groups' petitions covered a relatively long span of time, the proportional weighting helps to remove any bias due to trend movements in the variable values. Ideally, we would prefer bankrupt firm sample points falling within a relatively short period of time especially for a discriminant parametric model.

The ratio results listed in Table 7-5 conform with our *a priori* expectations and indicate that a multivariate prediction model is a viable possibility. The bankrupt group's ratios show significantly worse (F-ratios significant at .01 or .05 level) measures than the industry averages (with 3 exceptions) for both one and two statements prior to failure. In addition, the bankrupt averages all show deterioration as failure approaches. Since this analysis only includes two years of data, it is possible that these deteriorations, starting at statistically significant levels, could yield even longer term indications of eventual failure. Another consideration of future analysis involves the accumulation of some other group of *nonbankrupt* sample firms to compare with our bankrupt group in a multivariate context. The reason being that the assumption of sample variability homogeneity necessary for MDA is less likely to be violated than if we utilize the industry data.

Since each of the ratios show discriminating potential, we will briefly mention just a few of these measures and their characteristics. Both liquidity measures exhibit large bankrupt vs. industry differentials with this writer favoring ratio (1) Net Current Assets/Total Assets. Only two of the 21 bankrupts showed this ratio being greater than the industry average while as many as six displayed greater than the industry average for ratio (2). Therefore, the greater volatility of operating revenues, the denominator, leads us to believe ratio (1) will prove to be a more dependable discriminator. In the profitability sector, ratios number (3) and (8) appear to be providing comparable information. Both measures contain only one bankrupt firm which possessed a profitability ratio greater than the industry average of one and two statements prior to bankruptcy. We also have confidence that an extremely important railroad measure of efficiency—the operating ratio (6)—will provide important discriminating power. This measure, which compares operating expenses with operating revenues, was 12 percent greater in the bankrupt group vs. the industry level and extremely significant due to the relatively small intragroup variation. Sur-

Table 7-5
Bankrupt Firms and Railroad Industry Ratios

Ratio Name and Number*	One Statement prior to Bankruptcy			Two Statements prior to Bankruptcy		
	Average for Bankruptcy Group	Average for Industry	F Ratio**	Average for Bankruptcy Group	Average for Industry	F Ratio**
I Liquidity						
(1) NCA/TA	−11.0%	2.8%	10.4	−7.3%	2.9%	8.8
(2) NCA/OR	−42.0	5.7	7.7	−36.6	6.8	6.2
II Profitability & Efficiency						
(3) EBIT/TA	−3.0%	5.0%	10.3	−2.0%	5.0%	9.9
(4) OR/TTP	24.8	31.8	5.7	25.2	31.4	4.1
(5) OR/NTP	30.5	41.5	0.2a	32.0	40.9	0.4a
(6) Operating Ratio	87.4	75.4	15.5	85.3	75.1	18.9
(7) TE/OR	44.3	37.2	30.9	45.4	37.1	44.8
(8) EAIT/OR	−15.0	6.4	56.2	−11.0	6.1	75.5
(9) MAIN/TTP	7.3	8.7	0.3a	7.3	8.7	0.5a
(10) Growth Rate in OR	1.6	3.9	0.9a	2.7	3.7	0.2a
III Solvency and Leverage						
(11) ES/TA	−31.8%	18.6%	22.4	−27.3%	18.1%	17.3
(12) TD/TA	91.2	50.5	13.8	88.2	50.7	10.9
(13) Cash Flow/Fixed Chgs.	−0.5X	2.3X	65.8	−0.4X	2.2X	74.5
(14) Charges Earned	−0.6X	2.3X	54.1	−0.5X	2.2X	59.4

*Due to space limitations these ratios appear in abbreviated form and for their full definition please refer to Table 7-3.
**This ratio measures the significance of the mean values between the two groups.
aNot significant on a univariate basis.

prisingly, however, four bankrupt firms showed slightly lower than industry average operating ratios which indicates that further analysis on a multivariate basis is required to determine its overall contributory power to bankruptcy prediction.

In the solvency and leverage sectors, all four measures appear to be powerful discriminators. The Earned Surplus/Total Asset ratio (11) which is a measure of cumulative profitability over time, did not contain a single bankrupt firm that even approached the industry average. The Debt/Asset ratio (12) also proved to be extremely powerful, with several of the bankrupt firm ratios rising well over 100%. There appeared to be little to choose from between the fixed charges earned ratio (14) and the cash flow coverage ratio (13) in their ability to add to a multivariate model. Both appear to be excellent discriminators.

Discrimination Results

From the original list of 14 variables, listed in Table 7-4, the discriminant profile of variables which is selected as providing an accurate railroad bankruptcy prediction model is:

$$Z = f(X_{13}, X_7, X_{11}, X_{10}, X_8, X_6, X_3).[g]$$

where,

X_{13} = Cash Flow/Fixed Charges
X_7 = Transportation Expenses/Operating Revenues
X_{11} = Earned Surplus/Total Assets
X_{10} = 3-year Growth Rate in Operating Revenues
X_8 = Earnings after Taxes/Operating Revenues
X_6 = Operating Expenses/Operating Revenues
X_6 = Earnings before Interest and Taxes/Total Assets.

The ordering of these seven variables is derived from the discriminant computer program which selects variables in the order of their contributory importance. The process, a stepwise discriminant analysis,[h] first chooses the variable with the greatest F-value (in this case X_{13} with an F = 65.8; see Table 7-4) and then includes other variables such that the resulting multivariate F-ratio is maximized for that number of degrees of freedom. In the seven-variable profile, the resulting F-ratio = 20.1, significant at the .01 level.[i] This test rejects the null hypothesis that the observations come from the same population.

[g]The subscript numbers refer to Table 7-5.

[h]The computer program is called BMD-07M and is one of the standard statistical packages available in most computer centers.

[i]For F = 7, 34 degrees of freedom, the .01 significance level = 3.21. The F-statistic falls as the number of variables in the profile increases. We observe that the F-ratio equals 65.8 with a one variable profile (#13) and diminishes as follows: 50.0, 36.3, 28.1, 23.4, 20.2 until we achieve the 20.1 figure for the entire 7-variable structure.

This seven-variable profile, and other smaller variable groupings were quite accurate in predicting the group membership in the forty-firm, two-group sample. In fact, only one firm, #15—Wisconsin Central Railway (1942) of the bankrupt railroad group was incorrectly classified. That is, the more costly Type I error is only 5 percent (one misclassification out of 20) and there are no errors of the Type II variety. As discussed in Chapter 3, a Type I error is where a member of the bankrupt group is classified as a nonbankrupt; vice-versa for the Type II variety.

The Type I error is obviously the more serious of the two. In this event, a railroad destined for bankruptcy will go undetected and no remedial action will be forthcoming. The Type II error will result in a false bankruptcy specification and if remedial action is specified, it quite probably will prove unnecessary.[j]

Variable Description

X_{13}—**Cash Flow/Fixed Charges**. This variable is a slight variation on the traditional fixed charges earned ratio (#14) and its denomination is in number of times (X). Although the mean differential between groups is not exceptional (Table 7-4), the relatively small standard deviation among the firms in the sample accounts for its powerful significance. The measure shows the number of times that the firm's *cash flow*— earnings after taxes plus depreciation and amortization expenses—exceeded all fixed charges for a one-year period. It is a type of a margin-of-safety variable so common in fixed income security analysis. Actually, the ratio is not a true safety margin measure because the cash flow total already incorporates fixed charges and also is adjusted for taxes which itself is affected by the tax deductible nature of fixed expenses. Since it was not possible, in many cases, to fully adjust the numerator of this ratio, the ratio we used essentially stands as a close proxy for the theoretically correct measure. In an industry where fixed charges play such an important role in the performance of its member firms, it is not surprising to find X_{13} to be such an important indicator of railroad bankruptcy.

X_7—**Transportation Expense/Operating Revenue**. This is a measure particularly unique to the railroad industry as a performance indicator. The higher the ratio, the less efficient the road is operating. For the most part, the numerator represents expenses which are variable in nature and therefore fall within the province of operating and managerial related costs. It is quite similar to the so-called operating ratio (X_6) which also appears in our bankruptcy profile. Although the differential between the two group averages for X_7 is *less* than that

---

[j]Recall that the observations in the nonbankrupt group are in fact industry averages for various years and not individual firms. The excellent classification results are not surprising and we would expect less accurate overall results if we had used actual firms in this group.

for X_6 (12.0% vs. 7.1%), the *greater* significance, F-ratio in Table 7-4, shown by X_7 is due to a considerably smaller standard error (approximately 9.0% for X_6 and 4.0% for X_7).

X_{11} –**Earned Surplus/Total Assets.** This ratio was also found to be a prime indicator of manufacturing bankruptcies. It is a measure of the cumulative profitability of the enterprise and indicates in part, the book value net worth position. The bankrupt railroad average is -31.8%, indicating that those roads prone toward failure have suffered considerable operating losses. This average ratio, however, is not as drastic as the -61.6% average for our manufacturing bankrupt group. This can be explained partly by the fact that the average railroad firm in our sample is considerably larger than its manufacturing counterpart and therefore cumulative operating losses, although often large in absolute amounts, are not as significant relative to total assets. The significance given to this ratio's relationship to the age of the firm among manufacturers is not as great in our railroad analysis since most of the roads today have been in existence for several decades, and in many cases, for a century and more. The public interest nature of this industry explains the continued existence of many roads which under less rigid regulatory circumstances, would no doubt result in more numerous liquidations.

X_{10} –**Three-Year Compound Growth Rate in Operating Revenues.** This flow measure represents an attempt to capture the critical combined effects of high fixed costs and insufficient revenues. The debilitating magnification effect can result in railroad failures despite a road's long existence and supposedly established reputation. The three-year span is purely arbitrary and is chosen to examine the relatively short-run effects of poor operating performance. Of all the variables included in the variable profile, this one is by far the least significant on a univariate basis. Yet, we find it does contribute to the overall discriminating ability of the entire function. We observed a similar occurrence for one variable in Chapter 3.

X_8 **and** X_3: **Earnings Ratios.** Both measures report on the one-year earning performance of the firm. While X_{11} represents a type of after tax return on sales (traditionally called a profit margin), X_4 measures the pure earning power of the firm's assets. Since several railroads diversified in the 1960s in an attempt to protect themselves against economic downturns, X_3 and X_8 do not measure the return on *railroad* assets alone. The analyst must be careful, as Professor Murray attests, to realize this distinction.

Parameters of the Model

The reader is possibly wondering why this railroad model is not described complete with variable coefficients, individual firm discriminant scores, cut-off points and other documentation found in the aforementioned manufacturing model. The reason for this is that, although we are convinced that a viable and accurate prediction model for railroads is likely to be developed, we are not convinced that the seven-variable profile is necessarily the proper one. We do not have sufficient data on enough railroad failures to construct a large secondary sample. The latter could be used to *test* the model and its parameters and provide an unbiased estimate of its overall accuracy. No doubt the results reported thus far are biased upward since the classifications are made on the same firms which are used to construct the model.

There is also the possibility that the seven-variable profile may not be the best one in terms of more qualitative reasons. A six-variable grouping (with X_3 eliminated) results in the same classification accuracy and a slightly higher overall F-ratio. Since X_3 and X_8 are quite similar, we might just as easily accept the shortened version. Also, we are surprised to observe that variable X_{12}—total debt/total assets—is not included. Since financial leverage is thought to be so crucial to railroad failures, we had expected to find X_{12} to be a significant contributor. It is likely that X_{12}'s high negative correlation with X_{11} accounts for its conspicuous absence. In fact, these two variables have an overall correlation coefficient of -0.86. In other words, the less favorable the earned surplus to asset ratio, the greater the debt ratio.

Penn Central's Classification

Earlier in this section, we observed that the situation at P-C was indeed quite critical at the end of 1969 and that a careful analysis of the overall picture would have provided sufficient evidence for classifying P-C in the poor investment quality category. The multiple discriminant model discussed in this section reinforces this to such an extent that it was clear that P-C was a likely candidate for bankruptcy not only on December 31, 1969, but also at the end of 1968. P-C ranked #15 out of 20 in the bankrupt group in terms of its overall discriminant score in the one statement prior to bankruptcy analysis and #14 two statements prior (1 1/2 years) to the fateful event.

Concluding Remarks

The purpose of this analysis has been to suggest the need and examine the efficacy of a bankruptcy predictive model in the railroad sector of our economy. Several characteristics of the nature and content of railroad data are discussed with the expressed interest of eventually developing an accurate predictive tool. Preliminary empirical results comparing bankrupt railroad financial ratios with industry averages for the prebankruptcy period were indeed encouraging. A multivariate model combining several financial measures was developed with exceptionally accurate predictive results. Subsequent tests utilizing expanded sample data should ultimately result in a most acceptable statistical, early warning technique in the railroad bankruptcy area.

What would be the benefits of such a system? We suggest that internal management control systems would be enhanced by a model which clearly showed distressing indications. The crisis principle could be pushed several "leaps" forward and encourage changes, e.g., liquidity reserves, not thought necessary under normal control procedures. Another possible outgrowth of a practically acceptable model would be to guide the state and federal regulatory commissions in their evaluations of individual road petitions for issuance of fund-raising equipment trust certificates to improve the railroads profit potential. It could also provide the catalyst for intensified merger negotiations or perhaps even be used as evidence for abandonment petitions. The Transportation Department itself could be stimulated to institute emergency actions early enough to be meaningful and *not* construed as a last second stopgap procedure merely forestalling inevitable failure. Both present and prospective creditors and investors could add one more weapon to their arsenal of investigative tools for decision making. Finally, railroad financial disasters, especially ones of such overall significance as the P-C collapse, might be tempered or possibly eliminated completely.

Appendix B
Railroad Bankruptcy History

As noted in the introduction of Chapter 7, railroad bankruptcies can be grouped into several periods:

Period 1. The initial period comprises the attempts to rehabilitate those failures prior to the panic of 1857 and concerns local railroads in the main. These failures were usually due to poor promotion and not inefficient operations. The main source of financing was capital stock with little or no usage of debt instruments.

Period 2. This segment extends from the failures following 1857 to those prior to the railroad panic of 1884. This period was marked by many failures of relatively large intrastate railroads, with the primary one being the New York and Erie R.R. in 1859. This road suffered from poor maintenance, floods, labor problems, and of course, reduced revenues during the 1857 recession. Although the road was in deplorable shape and a complete overhaul was necessary, the reorganization was consummated in three years with little sacrifice on the part of the debt and equity holders, most of whom were powerful British investors. It was not surprising therefore, to witness the same roads' collapse again in 1875 followed by another lenient reorganization. Clearly, the receivers, at that time, were merely puppets of the more powerful security holders. In fact, many railroad presidents actually welcomed a temporary dose of receivership to forestall payment of obligations while at the same time ascertaining favorable rate changes.

Period 3. The reorganizations following the panic of 1884 comprise the next period. Many failures were on partially completed roads in all sections of the country. In many cases, these roads were built not for operation but with the hope of being brought out by strong, more established railroads. The most significant reorganization during this period was the Wabash, St. Louis and Pacific Railway which failed in 1884 and was the first of the large interstate railroads to be put in the hands of a receiver. The causes were quite simple—overexpansion and the inability to meet fixed charges. The significance of this failure, besides its size, was in the theory that the road should be reorganized as a whole entity rather than be fragmented into smaller sections based on the mortgage indentures held by various investors. The practice of a friendly receivership was now firmly established.

Period 4. The next group of railroad failures followed the panic of 1893 and lasted up to the great depression. These failures, however, were mainly of completed, well-established railway systems. In the period following the 1893-97 depression, one-sixth of the mileage and one-quarter of the total capitalization were in receivership, and in all, 57 companies were reorganized. Later, in the years prior to World War I, many roads failed for reasons similar to those of the bankruptcies in 1970—soaring labor and operating expenses, inflexible rates and the onset of an economic recession. In all, about 90 roads were in receivership by 1916. The earliest reorganization in this period of any consequence was the giant Atchison, Topeka and Sante Fe R.R. in 1894. This railroad expanded like wildfire in the years preceding its collapse without regard to future solvency. The importance of this reorganization was in the toughening of the terms and not the traditional no-sacrifice plans promulgated by foreign investors. For the first time, it was felt that a reorganization must be far reaching and well planned with considerable sacrifice from existing security holders. The prior leniency could be partially explained by the lack of realistic expectations as to the possibility of poor or negative earnings by railroads. That is, railroads were considered to be inherently profitable and the increase in revenues could be expected to absorb all fixed charges. For the first time, the possibility that railroads could have continuous problems was realized by investors. As a result of the drastic reorganizations of the late 1890s, the nation's railroads emerged in a more healthy state, although this new found health did not last for long. The pattern of railway reorganization established in these years was followed to a great extent until the depression years. During this long period, there were three years (1917-1920) when the railroads were operated by the federal government whereby the roads were guaranteed a return equal to prewar earnings. The results were continued deficits with the difference paid by the government. The Transportation Act of 1920 returned the roads to private control with substantially increased powers given to the ICC.[1]

Period 5. With the onset of the dismal economic period starting in 1930, the old equity receivership procedure proved inadequate. By the start of 1933, several large railroads had already failed and railway credit dropped to the level of the panic years of the 1890s. The wave of failures continued, just as in most lines of business, with statistics showing that 44 out of the 138 Class I railroads (gross revenues greater than $1 million—changed to $5 million under present lawmaking rules) were in receivership. The decrease in traffic because of general economic declines and increasing competition from truckers, combined with the pressure of excessive fixed charge obligations, caused the net profit of the industry to decline over $1 billion in the years 1930-32. In 1932, 81 percent of the Class I railroads failed to earn enough to meet their fixed charges. Those critics who had continually attacked the old equity receivership procedures as unfair, favoring the most powerful creditors, excessively long and drawn out, and without proper court supervision finally gained new strength as the number of failures increased.

In order to "strengthen" and give a statutory basis for the court proceedings, a Congressional bill was introduced in 1932 followed by a reform bill in 1933. Under these bills, any efforts to relieve a railroad of its problems had to be initiated, planned, and consummated by the ICC—supposedly because it was expert in all railroad matters. The legislation finally acted upon included Section 77 of the Federal Bankruptcy Act in 1933. This act was considered by its advocates to be a compromise between the old unencumbered equity receivership procedure and governmental regulation of the entire procedure. The federal courts were thereby given full responsibility to confirm any reorganization plan with direct participation by the ICC. Critics of this plan were vehement in their accusation that it was a sellout toward government control. Due to ambiguities in interpretation, the original Act was amended slightly within two years of its inception and again in 1943.

The steps in the granting and approval of bankruptcy reorganization plans under Section 77 of the act are as follows:

(1) A voluntary or involuntary petition for bankruptcy is submitted and either approved or not by the federal courts. This procedure took less than one day in the Penn-Central case.
(2) If approved, reorganization plans are submitted to the court and the ICC, generally by the court-appointed trustee(s)—in the Penn Central case there are four trustees. In fact, any group with substantial interest or ICC permission can submit a reorganization plan to the court.
(3) The ICC, unless it finds the plan to be obviously impractical, holds public hearings at which interested parties are heard.
(4) After the hearings, the Commission either approves the plan or substitutes one of its own. The plan must be compatible with the public interest. The exact meaning of this phrase is not completely clear to this writer but presumably means continued service.
(5) The plan is then certified by the courts and, after the interested parties have had a chance to file objections, the court approves it as fair and equitable. As in Chapter X proceedings, fair and equitable as well as feasible means that all creditors and investors are compensated according to their remaining equity and the plan provides for fixed charges which are expected to be covered by prospective earnings. If the plan is not approved, it is dismissed or referred back to the Commission.
(6) The approved plan is submitted for a vote to all stockholders and creditors who are deemed by the Commission to possess a continuing interest in the company. The plan must be ratified by two-thirds of each class of debt and stock to which submission has been allowed. Even if the plan has not been accepted by each class of investor, the court, after another public hearing, may confirm it on the grounds that it is still fair and equitable to all. Dissident interests, however, still retain the right to appeal the court's decision as did the New York, New Haven R.R. bondholders in the bankruptcy reorganization merger agreement with Penn Central in 1968-69. In this case, the Court of Appeals upheld, to some extent, the petition by the bondholders and ruled that P-C must pay a larger sum for the New Haven which itself had been in bankruptcy under Section 77 since 1961. Ironically, the improved verdict for these creditors may never be realized in view of the subsequent P-C collapse.

(7) Finally, the properties are removed from the trustee's control and transferred to the reorganized company without mortgage foreclosures as was sometimes the case under equity receivership.

Period 6. The most recent economic recession, 1969-70, has seen a revival in the seriousness of railroad problems and failures. Soaring labor and operating costs along with decreasing revenues accounted for the bulk of railroad losses. The relative neglect of many roads' physical condition also contributed to several collapses. The absolute number of roads failing in this two-year period is not large, but many other railroads remain on the brink of failure. Assets of the failed companies, however, are a significant proportion of the industry's total. In fact, the three largest failures in this period had combined assets of $5.1 billion, compared to the industry total of $33.1 billion (15%). Of course, P-C's share of over $4.5 billion in railroad assets accounts for the bulk of these assets. There is every reason to believe that the number of railroad bankruptcies will increase in the 1970s.

Notes

Notes to Chapter 1

1. For a discussion of the Schumpeterian system see Joseph Schumpeter, *Business Cycles*, Vol. I and II, (New York: McGraw Hill, 1939), and more specifically R. Clemence and F. Doody, *The Schumpeterian System* (Cambridge, Mass.: Addison Wesley Press, 1950), pp. 10-11.

2. For a comprehensive statistical analysis and presentation of failure statistics, see *The Failure Record* (Annually), Dun & Bradstreet, New York.

3. For a discussion of this insolvency condition, see J. Fred Weston and Eugene Brigham, *Managerial Finance*, 2nd ed. (New York: Holt, Rinehart & Winston), p. 714.

4. James Walter, "Determination of Technical Solvency," *Journal of Business* (January 1957): 30-43.

5. See M.J. Gordon, "Towards a Theory of Financial Distress," *Journal of Finance* (May 1971): 346-347; Lawrence Fisher, "Risk Premiums on Corporate Bonds," *Journal of Political Economy* 67 (June 1959): 217-237.

6. For a detailed discussion on equity receiverships, see Guthmann and Dougall, *Corporate Financial Policy*, 3rd ed., Prentice-Hall, 1955, Chapter 29.

7. Chandler Act, Pub. L. No. 696, 75th Congress, 3d Session, approved by the President, June 22, 1938.

8. A discussion of railroad bankruptcy reorganizations will be deferred until Chapter 7 of this volume. The reader is referred to the comprehensive and insightful material on this type of reorganization in A.S. Dewing, *The Financial Policy of Corporations*, Volume II, The Ronald Press Company, New York, Ch. 39.

9. For a technical discussion of the changes instituted under Chapter X see J. Gerdes, Corporate Reorganizations: Changes Effected by Chapter X of the Bankruptcy Act, *Harvard Law Review* (November 1938).

10. The two Bankruptcy Chapters are discussed, from a legal viewpoint in S. Krause, "Chapters X and XI — A Study in Contrasts," *Business Lawyer* 19 (January 1964): 511-526, and "Allocation of Corporate Reorganization between Chapters X and XI of the Bankruptcy Act, *Harvard Law Review* 69 (December 1955): 352-362.

11. Weston and Brigham, *Managerial Finance*, pp. 724-726.

12. See Chapter III, Sec. 3a, of the Bankruptcy Act for a listing of the six acts of bankruptcy.

13. See for example, *The Failure Record*, 1970, p. 5.

14. Probability density functions by age, for business failures are illustrated clearly by K. Lewis, "Business Failures — Another Example of the Analysis of Failure Data," *American Statistical Association Journal* (December 1954): 847-52. For a discussion of failure rates among small, young companies, see H.N. Broom, and J.G. Longenecker, *Small Business Management* (Cincinnati: South-Western Publishing Co., 1971), Chapter 5.

15. For example, see V. Sadd and R. Williams, *Causes of Commercial Bankruptcies*, U.S. Department of Congress, 1932; Guthman and Dougall, pp. 628-631; and M. Ulmer & A. Nielsen, *Survey of Current Business* (April 1947): 10-16.

16. Sadd and Williams, *Causes*, p. 1.

17. Dewing, *Corporations*, Chapter 38.

Notes to Chapter 2

1. See A.S. Dewing, *The Financial Policy of Corporations*, Vol. 2, Fourth ed., (New York: Ronald Press, 1941).

2. V. Zarnowitz and L. Lerner, "Cyclical Changes in Business Failures and Corporate Profits," Chapter 12 in *Business Cycle Indicators – Volume I*, edited by G. Moore, (New York: National Bureau of Economic Research, 1961).

3. P. Simpson and P. Anderson, "Liabilities of Business Failures as a Business Indicator," *Review of Economics and Statistics* (May 1957): 193-199.

4. See, G. Moore and J. Shishkin, *N.B.E.R. Occasional Paper #103*, New York, 1967.

5. For a monthly report of business failures, see *Dun's Review* and annual statistics are reported in *The Failure Record*, Dun & Bradstreet, New York.

6. See Zarnowitz and Lerner, *Cyclical*, pp. 371-383, and Simpson and Anderson, *Review*. The latter suggest that profit margins per dollar of sales may lead business cycles and since these margins are of critical importance to "submarginal" firms, they also affect failure liabilities. The authors, however, are doubtful of results using quarterly profit margins (pp. 197-198) due to seasonal variation which is difficult to measure and interpret.

7. See G. Moore and J. Shishkin, *N.B.E.R.*, p. 48.

8. A recent paper by W. Silber and M. Polakoff, "The Differential Effects of Tight Money: An Econometric Study," *Journal of Finance* (March 1970) concludes that in tight money conditions, the small business borrower suffers to a greater extent than the larger entity. This study disputes the earlier findings reported by G.L. Bach and C.J. Huizenga, "The Differential Effects of Tight Money," *American Economic Review* (March 1961): 52-80. A recent study by D.M. Jaffee and F. Modigliani, "A Theory and Test of Credit Rationing," *American Economic Review* (December 1969): 850-872, presents further evidence of a type of credit rationing which considers commercial bank objectives as well as supply and demand conditions.

9. See K. Brunner and A. Meltzer, "The Federal Reserve's Attachment to Free Reserves Concept," Washington, D.C., 1964; M. Friedman and A. Schwartz, *A Monetary History of the United States 1867-1960* (Princeton, N.J., 1963); and A. Meltzer, "The Appropriate Indications of Monetary Policy," in *Savings and Residential Financing*, 1969 Conference Proceedings (Chicago, 1969), pp. 11-31.

10. For example, see Beryl Sprinkle, "Money Matters," *Barrons*, December 2, 1969, p. 5.

11. For instance, see L. Anderson and J. Jordan, "Monetary and Fiscal Actions: A Test of their Relative Importance in Economic Stabilization," and M. Keran, "Monetary and Fiscal Influences on Economic Activity–The Historical Evidence," both in *Review, Federal Reserve Bank of St. Louis*, November 1968 and November 1969, respectively.

12. G. Moore and J. Shishkin, *N.B.E.R.*, Table 6, pp. 36-45.

13. All series are reasonably adjusted with the exception of the Standard & Poor Index. Data sources for quarterly GNP, S&P, and money supply are, respectively: *National Income and Product Accounts of the United States and Survey of Current Business* (U.S. Department of Commerce); Standard & Poor Trade and Securities *STATISTICS*: and Federal Reserve Bulletin, October 1969, and April 1971. The latter source presents the most recent revised series of money supply data and reflects adjustments for Eurodollar transactions, recent benchmarks and seasonal factors. Quarterly failure rate and number-of-enterprises data are available in *Dun's Statistic Review* until 1957 and in *Dun's Review* thereafter.

14. Zarnowitz and Lerner, *Changes*, pp. 371-383 and Simpson and Anderson, *Liabilities*.

15. See *Failure Record Through 1969*, Dun & Bradstreet, New York, p. 6.

Notes to Chapter 3

1. The following material was originally discussed by the author in an article, "Financial Ratios, Discriminant Analysis and the Prediction of Corporate Bankruptcy," *Journal of Finance* (September 1968): 589-609.

2. For an interesting and informative discussion on the development of credit agencies and financial measures of company performance, see, Roy A. Foulke, *Practical Financial Statement Analysis*, 5th ed. (New York: McGraw-Hill, 1961).

3. R.F. Smith and A.H. Winakor, *Changes in the Financial Structure of Unsuccessful Corporations* (University of Illinois, Bureau of Business Research, 1935).

4. For instance, a comprehensive study covering over 900 firms compared discontinuing firms with continuing ones; see C. Merwin, *Financing Small Corporations* (New York: National Bureau of Economic Research, 1942).

5. W.B. Hickman, *Corporate Bond Quality and Investor Experience* (Princeton, N.J.: Princeton University Press, 1958).

6. W.H. Beaver, "Financial Ratios as Predictors of Failure," *Empirical Research in Accounting, Selected Studies, 1966* (Institute of Professional Accounting, January 1967), pp. 71-111. A more recent study by Beaver considers ratios and stock price performance of bankrupt firms; see W.H. Beaver,

"Market Prices Financial Ratios and the Prediction of Failure," *Journal of Accounting Research*, Autumn 1968, pp. 179-192. Also, an attempt was made to weigh ratios arbitrarily; see M. Tamari, "Financial Ratios as a Means of Forecasting Bankruptcy," *Management International Review*, Vol. 4 (1966), pp. 15-21.

7. Exceptions to this generalization were noted in works where there was an attempt to emphasize the importance of a group of ratios as an indication of overall performance. For instance, Foulke, Chapters XIV and XV, and A. Wall and R.W. Dunning, *Ratio Analysis of Financial Statements* (New York: Harper and Row, 1928), p. 159.

8. R.A. Fisher, "The Use of Multiple Measurements in Taxonomic Problems," *Annals of Eugenics* (September 1936): 179-188.

9. For a comprehensive review of studies using MDA, see W.G. Cochran, "On the Performance of the Linear Discriminant Function," *Technometrics* 6 (May 1964): 179-190.

10. The pioneering work utilizing MDA in a financial context was performed by Durand in evaluating the credit worthiness of used car loan applicants; see D.D. Durand, *Risk Elements in Consumer Installment Financing*, Studies in Consumer Installment Financing (New York: National Bureau of Economic Research, 1941), pp. 105-142. More recently, Myers and Forgy analyzed several techniques, including MDA, in the evaluation of good and bad installment loans; see H. Myers and E.W. Forgy, "Development of Numerical Credit Evaluation Systems," *Journal of American Statistical Association* 50 (September 1963): 797-806.

11. J.E. Walter, "A Discriminant Function for Earnings Price Ratios of Large Industrial Corporations," *Review of Economics and Statistics* 41 (February 1959): 44-52.

12. K.V. Smith, *Classification of Investment Securities Using MDA*, Institute Paper #101 (Purdue University: Institute for Research in the Behavioral, Economic, and Management Sciences, 1965). Also in the investment area, Carleton and Lerner established a discriminant model to classify municipal bonds into their various bond ratings; see W. Carleton and E. Lerner, "Statistical Credit Scoring of Municipal Bonds," *Journal of Money Credit Banking* (November 1969). Another study utilized a similar technique to classify industrial bonds; see T. Pogue and R. Soldofsky, "What Is a Bond Rating?" *Journal of Financial and Quantitative Analysis* (June 1969): 201-228.

13. P. Meyer and H. Pifer, "Prediction of Bank Failures," *Journal of Finance* (September 1970): 853-879. Other recent works on predicting bankruptcies are Marc Blum, "The Failing Company Doctrine," Unpublished Ph.D. dissertation, Columbia University (1969), and Robert Edmister, "An Empirical Test of Financial Ratio Analysis for Small Business Failure Prediction," paper presented at the *Western Finance Association Meetings*, August 30, 1971.

14. For a formulation of the mathematical computations involved in MDA, see J.G. Bryan, "The Generalized Discriminant Function, Mathematical &

Computational Routine," *Harvard Educational Review* 21 (Spring 1951): 90-95, and C.R. Rao, *Advanced Statistical Methods in Biometric Research* (New York: John Wiley & Sons, Inc., 1952).

15. See Beaver, *Ratios*, p. 89.

16. Merwin, *Small*, p. 99.

17. Statistics taken from *The Failure Record, Through 1968* (New York: Dun & Bradstreet, Inc., 1966), p. 11.

18. See Lawrence Fisher, "Determinants of Risk Premiums on Corporate Bonds," *Journal of Political Economy* 67 (June 1959): 217-237.

19. For an excellent discussion of how a seemingly insignficiant variable on a univariate basis can supply important information in a multivariate context, see, W.W. Cooley and P.R. Lohnes, *Multivariate Procedures for the Behavioral Sciences* (New York: John Wiley & Sons, Inc., 1962), p. 121.

20. Cochran, *Linear*, p. 182.

21. R.E. Frank, W.F. Massy, and G.D. Morrison, "Bias in Multiple Discriminant Analysis," *Journal of Marketing Research* 2 (August 1965): 250-58.

22. A similar method proved to be useful in selecting cut-off points for marketing decisions; see R.E. Frank, A.A. Kuehn, W.F. Massy, *Quantitative Techniques in Marketing Analysis* (Homewood, Ill.: Richard D. Irwin, Inc., 1962), pp. 95-100.

23. William H. Beaver, "Market Prices, Financial Ratios, and the Prediction of Failure," *Journal of Accounting Research* (Autumn 1968): 179-192.

24. The Fisher Index is described in L. Fisher, "Some New Stock Market Indices," *Journal of Business* 39 (January 1966): 191-225.

25. A critique and discussion of financial ratios in a prediction context is presented by C. Johnson, "Ratio Analysis and the Prediction of Firm Failure," and replied to by E. Altman, *Journal of Finance* (December 1970): 1166-1172.

26. Randolph Westerfield, "Pre-Bankruptcy Stock Price Performance," University of Pennsylvania working paper, Fall 1970.

27. William Sharpe, "A Simplified Model for Portfolio Analysis," *Management Science* 9 (January 1963): 277-293.

Notes to Chapter 4

1. D. Durand, *Risk Elements in Consumer Installment Financing*, Study No. 8, (New York: National Bureau of Economic Research, 1941).

2. For instance, see H. Myers and E. Forgy, "Development of Numerical Credit Evaluation Systems," *Journal of American Statistical Association* 50 (September 1963): 797-806; and R. Biborosch, "Credit Scoring Systems Have Built-In Bonuses," *Bankers Monthly* (March 1967): 40-44.

3. R. Abate, "Numerical Scoring Systems for Commercial Loans," *Journal of Commercial Bank Lending* 51 (July 1969): 32-36.

4. *Annual Report of the Federal Deposit Insurance Corporation*, 1968, Washington, D.C., p. 208.

5. R. Abate, *Scoring*; F. Hammer and Y. Orgler, "Developments in Credit Scoring for Commercial Loans," *Journal of Commercial Bank Lending* 51 (July 1969): 25-31. Other recent articles on the same theme which have appeared in this Journal are N. Connelly, "Automation and Computers in Commercial Lending," (September 1967): 21-66; G. Work, "Loan Decision Making and the Critical Assumption," (October 1967): 17-23; and R. Long, S. Overton, and J. Holt, "Automation: Guidelines for Designing an Automated Commercial Loan Information System and the Use of Computers in Loan Decision Making (January 1969): 13-31.

6. J.B. Williams, "Survey of Commercial Loan Charge-Offs for the Year Ending December 31, 1968, *Journal of Commerical Bank Lending* (August 1969): 42-47.

7. *Annual Report of the Federal Deposit Insurance Corporation, 1968*, Washington, D.C., p. 200.

8. J.B. Williams, *Survey*, p. 46.

9. M. Mitchner and R. Peterson, "An Operations-Research Study of the Collection of Defaulted Loans," *Operations Research* (August 1957): 522-545.

10. K. Cohen, T. Gilmore, and F. Singer, "Bank Procedures for Analyzing Business Loan Applications," included in K. Cohen and F. Hammer, eds., *Analytical Methods in Banking* (Homewood, Illinois: Richard D. Irwin, Inc., 1966), pp. 218-251.

11. See J. Van Horne, *Financial Management and Policy* (Englewood Cliffs: Prentice-Hall, 1968), pp. 381-383; and W. Beranek, *Analysis for Financial Decisions* (Homewood, Illinois: Richard D. Irwin, 1963), pp. 327-335.

12. Rather than go through a detailed development of such a procedure, we refer the reader to W. Beranek, *Analysis*, Chapter 10, particularly pp. 333-35.

13. W. Newman and J. Logan, *Management of Expanding Enterprises* (New York: Columbia University Press, 1955).

14. A.S. Dewing, *Financial Policy of Corporations – Vol. II* (New York: Ronald Press, Inc., 1953), p. 1225.

15. Examples of the various types of quasireorganizations can be found in J.F. Weston and E.F. Brigham, *Managerial Finance*, 2nd ed. (New York: Holt, Rinehart & Winston), pp. 716-19. For a more technical discussion, see W. Karrenbrock and H. Simons, *Intermediate Accounting*, 3rd ed. (Cincinnati: South Western, 1958), pp. 693-96.

16. SEC Corporation Release #95, June 1955, p. 4.

17. F. Calkins, "Corporate Reorganization under Chapter X – A Post-Mortem," *Journal of Finance* (June 1948): 19.

18. Ibid., p. 20.

Notes to Chapter 5

1. Virtually all means at least 90% of fair market value of net assets and at least 70% of gross assets. For an excellent nontechnical discussion of tax

considerations in mergers, see A. Wyatt and D. Kieso, *Business Combinations: Planning and Action* (Scranton, P.A.: International Textbook Co., 1969), Chapter 6.

2. Probably the most comprehensive discussion on this subject can be found in R. Holtzman, *Tax-Free Reorganizations*, (Lynbrook, N.Y.: Farnsworth Publishing, 1967).

3. The entire code on loss carry-overs is contained in *Federal Taxes*, Vol. 3, (Englewood Cliffs, N.J.: Prentice-Hall, 1970), pp. 18501-18634 and is well interpreted in R. Holtzman, Chapter 12. Also see R. Baldwin, "Carryovers in Certain Corporate Acquisitions," *Taxes*, XLI, August 1963, pp. 474-481, and J. Van Horne, "A Look at the Loss Carry-Forward," *The Accounting Review* (January 1963): 56-60.

4. "Corporate Reorganization under Chapter X: A Post Mortem," *Journal of Finance* (June 1948): 19-28.

5. Again, we arbitrarily utilize the average return on investment in common stock on the New York Stock Exchange in order to discount future returns—dividends plus stock price—during the postmerger years.

6. *New York Times*, 4 September 1957, p. 50:7.

7. SEC Corporation Release #105, p. 5.

8. *Moody's Industrial Manuals*, 1957-1969, and Jessop Steel Annual Reports.

Notes to Chapter 6

1. Much of this discussion and results are presented by this author in, Edward I. Altman, "Corporate Bankruptcy Potential, Stockholder Returns, and Share Valuation," *Journal of Finance*, 24 (December 1969): 887-900.

2. Franco Modigliani and Merton Miller, "The Cost of Capital, Corporation Finance, and the Theory of Investment," *The American Economic Review*, 48 (June 1958): 268.

3. Lawrence Fisher, "Determinants of Risk Premiums on Corporate Bonds," *Journal of Political Economy*, 67 (June 1959): 217-237.

4. Alexander Robichek and Stewart Myers, "Problems in the Theory of Optimal Capital Structure," *Journal of Finance and Quantitative Analysis* (June 1966): 1-35.

5. Nevins Baxter, "Leverage, Risk of Ruin and the Cost of Capital," *The Journal of Finance*, 22 (September 1967): 395-403.

6. This same conclusion was actually reached earlier by Modigliani and Miller in their parenthetical discussion of temporary business failures cited in footnote number 18 of their 1958 article; see Modigliani and Miller, *Cost*, p. 274.

7. Two decades ago, Calkins examined the postbankruptcy experience of a small number of firms; see Francis Calkins, "Corporate Reorganization under Chapter X: A Post Mortem," *Journal of Finance* (June 1948): 19-28.

8. The vast majority of these firms, with the exception of two or three, reorganized under Chapter X, and the major sources for this list are the *Security & Exchange Commission Annual Reports, Moody's Industrial Manuals*, and the *Financial Daily Card Service*.

9. Table 2, Part F from Lawrence Fisher and James Lorie, "Rates of Return on Investments in Common Stock: The Year-By-Year Record, 1926-65," *The Journal of Business*, 40 (July 1968).

10. Various works have studied marginal stockholder tax-brackets with estimates of 38 percent, 46 percent, and 52-63 percent. See Edwin Elton and Martin Gruber, "An Inferential Model for Determining Stockholder Marginal Tax Brackets," *Review of Economics and Statistics* (February 1970): 68-74; J.F. Weston and Eugene Brigham, *Managerial Finance*, 2nd Ed., New York: Holt, Rinehart and Winston, 1966, p. 309; and Gordon Donaldson, "In Defense of Preferred Stock," *Harvard Business Review*, 40 (July-August 1962): 128.

11. Baskin and Crooch, "Historical Rates of Return on Investments in Flat Bonds," *Financial Analysts Journal* (November-December 1968).

12. W.B. Hickman, *Corporate Bond Quality and Investor Experience* (Princeton, N.J.: Princeton University Press, 1958) and F. Calkins, *Reorganization*.

13. A more detailed exposition of these tests can be found in Edward Altman, "Bankrupt Firms' Equity Securities As An Investment Alternative," *Financial Analysts Journal* (July-August, 1969).

14. W.H. Beaver, "Market Prices, Financial Ratios and the Prediction of Failure," *Journal of Accounting Research* (Autumn 1968): 179-192.

15. R. Westerfield, "The Assessment of Market Risk and Corporate Failure," (Wharton School of Finance, August 1970).

16. "The Jones Nobody Keeps Up With," *Fortune* (April 1966): 247.

17. For a complete description of their study, see R.W. McEnally and E. Dyl, "Risk of Selling Short," *Financial Analysts Journal* (November-December 1969): 73-76.

Notes to Chapter 7

1. S.C. Vance, "Penn Central–A Lesson for Bank Boards and One-Bank Holding Companies," *The Bankers Magazine* (Winter 1971), p. 78.

2. A.S. Dewing, *Financial Policy of Corporation–Fifth Ed., Vol. II* (New York: Ronald Press Co., 1953), pp. 1238-63. The footnotes in this section and in the entire volume are, in my opinion, a great contribution to knowledge of business finance.

3. An excellent review of the industry's development and the resulting problems can be derived from the following sources among others: T. Bray, "Bankruptcy: A Chronic Ill for Railroads," *Wall Street Journal*, September 14, 1970, p. 16; G. Hilton, "The Consistency of the Interstate Commerce Act,"

Journal of Law and Economics (October 1966), pp. 87-114; J. Meyer, M. Peck, J. Stenason, and C. Zwick, *The Economics of Competition in the Transportation Industries* (Cambridge, Mass.: Harvard Univ. Press, 1959); M. Peck, "Transportation in the American Economy," in S. Harris, ed., *American Economic History* (New York: McGraw-Hill, 1961), pp. 340-65; and J. Fred Weston, "Economic Background of the Penn Central Bankruptcy," *Journal of Finance* (May 1971), pp. 311-326. The latter source has the most recent comprehensive bibliography for railroad study and analysis.

4. Meyer, et al., *Economics*, p. 8; Weston, *Penn Central*, pp. 314-315.

5. *Barrons*, 29 March; 5 April, 1971, p. 20; *New York Times*, 12 March 1971.

6. Benham, 5 April, p. 1.

7. Peck, *Competition*.

8. *New York Times*, 21 June 1971, Sec. 3, p. 1.

9. Weston, *Penn Central*, p. 324.

10. Probably the most controversial were the *Fortune* magazine articles; R. Loving, Jr., "Penn Central's Bankruptcy Express" (August 1970), and "Peat, Marwick, Mitchell & Company Replies" (September 1970). Also the American Finance Association devoted one full session at its 1970 Annual Meetings in Detroit, Michigan (December 28, 1970) to the "Penn Central Debacle" of which this author was a participant—the Proceedings have been published in the May 1971 issue of the *Journal of Finance*.

11. *Barrons*, 5 April 1971, p. 5.

12. Loving, *Express*, pp. 164-65.

13. Peat, Marwick and Mitchell, *Replies*.

14. *Wall Street Journal*, 9 April 1971, p. 2.

15. *Wall Street Journal*, 10 October 1970, p. 3.

16. *Wall Street Journal*, 29 March 1971.

17. *New York Times*, 4 June 1971.

18. Vance, *Penn Central*.

19. Ibid., pp. 78-79.

20. *Barrons*, 21 June 1971, p. 3.

21. *Wall Street Journal*, 31 December 1970.

22. *Wall Street Journal*, 30 July 1970.

23. *New York Times*, 5 May 1971.

24. This principle has been stressed many times in the past with particular emphasis given by W. Newman and James Logan, *Management of Expanding Enterprises* (New York: Columbia University Press, 1955).

25. *Wall Street Journal*, 3 July 1970, p. 2.

26. *Wall Street Journal*, 3 July 1970, p. 2.

27. Roger F. Murray, "The Penn Central Debacle: Lessons for Financial Analysis," *Journal of Finance* (May 1971), pp. 327-32.

28. Ibid., pp. 327-28.

29. *Business Week*, 26 April 1971, pp. 77-78.

30. An early description of the Federal Income Home Loan Bank Board's Office of Examinations and Supervision efforts in this area is detailed in Harry Leavy, "Early Warning System–New Supervisory Tool," *Federal Home Loan Bank Board Journal* (September 1969), pp. 12-14. A similar study has been worked out utilizing nonparametric techniques for association ratings in a recent comprehensive work by Ernest Bloch, "The Settings of Standards of Supervision of Savings and Loan Associations"–part of *A Study of the Savings and Loan Industry*, Irwin Friend, director, (Washington, D.C., July 1969). Significant strides have also been made in the California sector of the Savings and Loan Industry; see, "A Proposed Analytical System to Provide an Objective Basis for Supervision," *State of California Division of Savings and Loan*, Price Waterhouse & Co., December 21, 1967.

31. P. Meyer and H. Pifer, "Prediction of Bank Failures," *Journal of Finance* (September 1970), pp. 853-868.

32. Guthmann and Dougall, *Corporate Financial Policy*, 3rd ed. (Englewood Cliffs, N.J., 1955), p. 653.

33. Edward I. Altman, "Railroad Bankruptcy Potential," *Journal of Finance* (May 1971), p. 339.

34. Edward I. Altman, "Corporate Bankruptcy Potential, Stockholder Returns, and Share Valuation," *Journal of Finance* (December 1969), p. 895; also see Chapter 6 of this volume.

35. Hearings, Committee on Interstate Commerce: H.R. 2298, 80th Congress; 1st Session (1947).

36. *Wall Street Journal*, 17 March 1971, p. 1.

37. F. Dembitz, "Progress and Delay in Railroad Reorganizations since 1933," *Law and Contemporary Problems*, Summer 1940.

Bibliography

Abate, R. "Numerical Scoring Systems for Commercial Loans," *Journal of Commercial Bank Lending*, Vol. 51, No. 11 (July 1969), pp. 32-36.

Altman, Edward I. "Financial Ratios, Discriminant Analysis and the Prediction of Corporate Bankruptcy," *Journal of Finance* (September 1968), pp. 589-609.

_____. "Bankrupt Firms' Equity Securities as an Investment Alternative," *Financial Analysts Journal* (July-August 1969), pp. 129-133.

_____. "Corporate Bankruptcy Potential, Stockholder Returns, and Share Valuation," *Journal of Finance*, Vol. XXIV, No. 5 (December 1969), pp. 887-900.

_____. "Reply to C. Johnson's Ratio Analysis and the Prediction of Firm Failure," *Journal of Finance* (December 1970), pp. 1169-72.

_____. "Railroad Bankruptcy Potential," *Journal of Finance* (May 1971), pp. 333-345.

Armour, Lawrence A. "Out of the Storm Cellar," *Barrons* (June 21, 1971), pp. 3 and 19.

Anderson, L., and J. Jordan. "Monetary and Fiscal Actions: A Test of their Relative Importance in Economic Stabilization," *Review, Federal Reserve Bank of St. Louis* (November 1968).

Bach, G.L., and C.J. Huizenga. "The Differential Effects of Tight Money," *American Economic Review* (March 1961), pp. 52-80.

Baldwin, R. "Carryovers in Certain Corporate Acquisitions," *Taxes*, XLI (August 1963), pp. 474-481.

Baskin and Crooch. "Historical Rates of Return on Investments in Flat Bonds," *Financial Analysts Journal* (November-December 1968), pp. 95-97.

Baxter, Nevins. "Leverage, Risk of Ruin and the Cost of Capital," *The Journal of Finance*, Vol. XXII, No. 3 (September 1967), pp. 395-403.

Beaver, W.H. "Financial Ratios as Predictors of Failure," in *Empirical Research in Accounting, Selected Studies, 1966* (Institute of Professional Accounting, January 1967), pp. 71-111.

_____. "Market Prices, Financial Ratios, and the Prediction of Failure," *Journal of Accounting Research* (Autumn, 1968), pp. 179-192.

Beranek, W. *Analysis for Financial Decisions*. Homewood, Illinois: Richard D. Irwin, 1963.

Biborosch, R. "Credit Scoring Systems Have Built-In Bonuses," *Bankers Monthly* (March 1967), pp. 40-44.

Bloch, Ernest. "The Settings of Standards of Supervision of Savings and Loan Associations"—part of *A Study of the Savings and Loan Industry*, Irwin Friend, director, Washington, D.C., July 1969.

Bray, T. "Bankruptcy: A Chronic Ill for Railroads," *Wall Street Journal*, September 14, 1970, p. 16.

Broom, H.N., and J.G. Longenecker. *Small Business Management*. Cincinnati: South-Western Publishing Co., 1971.

Brunner, K., and A. Meltzer. "The Federal Reserve's Attachment to Free Reserves Concept," Washington, D.C., 1964.

Bryan, J.G. "The Generalized Discriminant Function, Mathematical & Computational Routine," *Harvard Educational Review*, Vol. XXI, No. 2 (Spring 1951), pp. 90-95.

Calkins, Francis. "Corporate Reorganization under Chapter X: A Post Mortem," *Journal of Finance* (June 1948), pp. 19-28.

Carleton, W., and E. Lerner. "Statistical Credit Scoring of Municipal Bonds," *Journal of Money Credit Banking* (November 1969).

Clemence, R., and F. Doody. *The Schumpeterian System*. Cambridge, Mass.: Addison Wesley, 1950.

Cochran, W.G. "On the Performance of the Linear Discriminant Function," *Technometrics*, Vol. 6 (May 1964), pp. 179-190.

Cohen, J., and S. Robbins. *The Financial Manager*. New York: Harper & Row, 1966.

Cohen, K., T. Gilmore, and F. Singer. "Bank Procedures for Analyzing Business Loan Applications," in K. Cohen and F. Hammer, eds., *Analytical Methods in Banking*. Homewood, Illinois: Richard D. Irwin, 1966, pp. 218-251.

Connellys, N. "Automation and Computers in Commercial Lending," *Journal of Commercial Bank Lending* (September 1967), pp. 21-66.

Cooley, W.W., and P.R. Lohnes. *Multivariate Procedures for the Behavioral Sciences*. New York: John Wiley and Sons, 1962.

Dembitz, F. "Progress and Delay in Railroad Reorganizations Since 1933," *Law and Contemporary Problems* (Summer 1940).

Dewing, A.S. *The Financial Policy of Corporations,* 4th ed. New York: Ronald Press, 1941, Vol. 2.

――――. *Financial Policy of Corporation*, 5th ed. New York: Ronald Press, 1953, Vol. 2.

Donaldson, Gordon. "In Defense of Preferred Stock," *Harvard Business Review*, Vol. XL (July-August, 1962), pp. 123-136.

Durand, D.D. *Risk Elements in Consumer Installment Financing*, Studies in Consumer Installment Financing. New York: National Bureau of Economic Research, 1941, No. 8.

Elton, Edwin, and Martin Gruber. "An Inferential Model for Determining Stockholder Marginal Tax Brackets," *Review of Economics and Statistics* (February 1970), pp. 68-74.

Fisher, Lawrence. "Determinants of Risk Premiums on Corporate Bonds," *Journal of Political Economy*, Vol. LXVII, No. 3 (June 1959), pp. 217-237.

――――. "Some New Stock Market Indices," *Journal of Business*, Vol. XXXIX (January 1966), pp. 191-225.

Fisher, Lawrence, and James Lorie. "Rates of Return on Investments in Common Stock: The Year-By-Year Record, 1926-65," *The Journal of Business*, Vol. 41, No. 3 (July 1968), pp. 291-316.

Fisher, R.A. "The Use of Multiple Measurements in Taxonomic Problems," *Annals of Eugenics* (September 1936), pp. 179-188.

Foulke, Roy A. *Practical Financial Statement Analysis*. 5th ed. New York: McGraw-Hill, 1961.

Frank, R.E., A.A. Kuehn, W.F. Massy. *Quantitative Techniques in Marketing Analysis*. Homewood, Illinois: Richard D. Irwin, 1962.

Frank, R.E., W.F. Massy, and G.D. Morrison. "Bias in Multiple Discriminant Analysis," *Journal of Marketing Research*, Vol. 2 (August 1965), pp. 250-258.

Friedman, M., and A. Schwartz. *A Monetary History of the United States: 1867-1960*. Princeton, N.J., 1963.

Gerdes, J. "Corporate Reorganizations: Changes Effected by Chapter X of the Bankruptcy Act," *Harvard Law Review* (November 1938).

Gordon, M.J. "Towards a Theory of Financial Distress," *Journal of Finance* (May 1971), pp. 347-356.

Guthmann, H., and H. Dougall. *Corporate Financial Policy*. 3rd ed. Englewood Cliffs, N.J.: Prentice-Hall, 1955.

Hammer, F. and Y. Orgler. "Developments in Credit Scoring for Commercial Loans," *Journal of Commercial Bank Lending*, Vol. 51, No. 11 (July 1969), pp. 25-31.

Hickman, W.B. *Corporate Bond Quality and Investor Experience*. Princeton, N.J.: Princeton University Press, 1958.

Hilton, G. "The Consistency of the Interstate Commerce Act," *Journal of Law and Economics* (October 1966), pp. 87-114.

Holtzman, R. *Tax-Free Reorganizations*. Lynbrook, N.Y.: Farnsworth Publishing, 1967.

Jaffee, D.M., and F. Modigliani, "A Theory and Test of Credit Rationing," *American Economic Review* (December 1969), pp. 850-872.

Johnson, C. "Ratio Analysis and the Prediction of Firm Failure," *Journal of Finance* (December 1970), pp. 1166-68.

Karrenbrock, W., and H. Simons. *Intermediate Accounting*. 3rd ed. Cincinnati: South-Western, 1958.

Keran, M. "Monetary and Fiscal Influences on Economic Activity—The Historical Evidence," *Review, Federal Reserve Bank of St. Louis* (November 1969).

Krause, S. "Chapters X and XI—A Study in Contrast," *Business Lawyer*, Vol. 19 (January 1964), pp. 511-526.

Leavy, Harry. "Early Warning System—New Supervisory Tool," *Federal Home Loan Bank Board Journal* (September 1969), pp. 12-14.

Lewis, K. "Business Failures—Another Example of the Analysis of Failure Data," *American Statistical Association Journal* (December 1954), pp. 847-52.

Long, R., S. Overton, and J. Holt. "Automation: Guidelines for Designing An Automated Commercial Loan Information System and the Use of Computers in Loan Decision Making," *Journal of Commercial Bank Lending* (January 1969), pp. 13-31.

Loomis, Carol J. "The Jones Nobody Keeps Up With," *Fortune* (April 1966), pp. 237-247.

Loving, Jr., R. "Penn Central's Bankruptcy Express," *Fortune* (August 1970), pp. 104-109 and 164-171.

McEnally, R.W., and E. Dyl. "Risk of Selling Short," *Financial Analysts Journal* (November-December 1969), pp. 73-76.

Meltzer, A. "The Appropriate Indications of Monetary Policy," in *Savings and Residential Financing*, 1969 Conference Proceedings (Chicago 1969), pp. 11-31.

Merwin, C. *Financing Small Corporations*. New York: National Bureau of Economic Research, 1942.

Meyer, J., M. Peck, J. Stenason, and C. Zwick. *The Economies of Competition in the Transportation Industries*. Cambridge, Mass.: Harvard University Press, 1959.

Meyer, P. and H. Pifer, "Prediction of Bank Failures," *Journal of Finance* (September 1970), pp. 853-868.

Mitchner, M., and R. Peterson. "An Operations-Research Study of the Collection of Defaulted Loans," *Operations Research* (August 1957), pp. 522-545.

Modigliani, Franco, and Merton Miller. "The Cost of Capital, Corporation Finance, and the Theory of Investment," *The American Economic Review*, Vol. XLVIII, No. 3 (June 1958), pp. 261-297.

Moore, G., and J. Shishkin. *N.B.E.R. Occasional Paper #103*, New York, 1967.

Murray, Roger F. "The Penn Central Debacle: Lessons for Financial Analysis," *Journal of Finance* (May 1971), pp. 327-32.

Myers, H., and E. Forgy. "Development of Numerical Credit Evaluation Systems," *Journal of American Statistical Association*, Vol. 50 (September 1963), pp. 797-806.

Newman, W., and J. Logan. *Management of Expanding Enterprises*. New York: Columbia University Press, 1955.

Peck, M. "Transportation in the American Economy," in S. Harris, ed., *American Economic History* New York: McGraw-Hill, 1961, pp. 340-65.

Pogue, T., and R. Soldofsky. "What is a Bond Rating?" *Journal of Financial and Quantitative Analysis* (June 1969), pp. 201-228.

Rao, C.R. *Advanced Statistical Methods in Biometric Research*. New York: John Wiley & Sons, 1952.

Robichek, Alexander, and Stewart Myers. "Problems in the Theory of Optimal Capital Structure," *Journal of Finance and Quantitative Analysis* (June 1966), pp. 1-35.

Sadd, V., and R. Williams. *Causes of Commercial Bankruptcies*. Washington, D.C.: Government Printing Office, 1932.

Seligson, Charles. "Major Problems for Consideration by the Commission on the Bankruptcy Laws of the United States," *American Bankruptcy Law Journal* (Winter 1971).

Schumpeter, Joseph. *Business Cycles*. Vols. I and II. New York: McGraw-Hill, 1939.

Sharpe, William. "A Simplified Model for Portfolio Analysis," *Management Science*, Vol. 9, No. 2 (January 1963), pp. 277-293.

Silber, W., and M. Polakoff. "The Differential Effects of Tight Money: An Econometric Study," *Journal of Finance* (March 1970), pp. 83-97.

Simpson, P., and P. Anderson. "Liabilities of Business Failures as a Business Indicator," *Review of Economics and Statistics* (May 1957), pp. 193-199.

Smith, K.V. *Classification of Investment Securities Using MDA*, Institute Paper #101 (Purdue University, Institute for Research in the Behavioral, Economic, and Management Sciences, 1965).

Smith, R.F., and A. H. Winakor. *Changes in the Financial Structure of Unsuccessful Corporations*. University of Illinois, Bureau of Business Research, 1935.

Sprinkle, Beryl. "Money Matters," *Barron's* (December 1, 1969), p. 5.

Stanley, David and Marjorie Girth. *Bankruptcy: Problem Process and Reform*, (Brookings Institution, 1971).

Tamari, M. "Financial Ratios as a Means of Forecasting Bankruptcy," *Management International Review*, Vol. 4 (1966), pp. 15-21.

Ulmer, M., and A. Nielsen. *Survey of Current Business* (April 1947), pp. 10-16.

Vance, S.C. "Penn Central—A Lesson for Bank Boards and One-Bank Holding Companies," *The Bankers Magazine* (Winter 1971), pp. 77-83.

Van Horne, J. *Financial Management and Policy*. Englewood Cliffs, N.J.: Prentice-Hall, 1968.

Wall, A., and R. W. Dunning. *Ratio Analysis of Financial Statements*. New York: Harper and Row, 1928.

Walter, James. "Determination of Technical Solvency," *Journal of Business* (January 1957), pp. 30-43.

——. "A Discriminant Function for Earnings Price Ratios of Large Industrial Corporations," *Review of Economics and Statistics*, Vol. XLI (February 1959), pp. 44-52.

Westerfield, R. "The Assessment of Market Risk and Corporate Failure," unpublished working paper, Wharton School of Finance, August 1970.

——. "Pre-Bankruptcy Stock Price Performance," University of Pennsylvania working paper, Fall 1970.

Weston, J. Fred. "Economic Background of the Penn Central Bankruptcy," *Journal of Finance* (May 1971), pp. 311-326.

Weston, J. Fred, and Eugene Brigham. *Managerial Finance*, 2nd Edition. New York: Holt, Rinehart & Winston, 1966.

Williams, J.B. "Survey of Commercial Loan Charge-Offs for the Year Ending December 31, 1968," *Journal of Commercial Bank Lending* (August 1969), pp. 42-47.

Work, G. "Loan Decision Making and the Critical Assumption," *Journal of Commercial Bank Lending* (October 1967), pp. 17-23.

Wyatt, A., and D. Kieso. *Business Combinations: Planning and Action*. Scranton, Pennsylvania: International Textbook Co., 1969.

Zarnowitz, V., and L. Lerner. "Cyclical Changes in Business Failures and Corporate Profits," Chapter 12 in *Business Cycle Indicators—Volume I*, G. Moore, ed. New York: National Bureau of Economic Research, 1961.

Special Periodical Publications

Annual Report of the Federal Deposit Insurance Corporation, 1968, Washington, D.C.

"Class I Drop-Outs," *Barrons* (April 5, 1971), p. 5.

"New Railroad Era?" *Barrons* (March 29, 1971).

Dun's Statistic Review. New York: Dun & Bradstreet, Inc.

Dun's Review. New York: Dun & Bradstreet, Inc.

The Failure Records (Annual). New York: Dun & Bradstreet, Inc.

Federal Reserve Bulletin, Board of Governors, Federal Reserve System, Washington, D.C., October 1969 and April 1971.

Federal Taxes, Vol. 3. Englewood Cliffs, N.J.: Prentice-Hall, 1970.

Financial Daily Card Service. Financial Information Co., New York.

Finance Docket submitted on behalf of Bond Trustee of N.Y., New Haven & Hartford R.R. before ICC, October 21, 1968.

"From Underdog to Top Dog," *Forbes* (July 1, 1970), pp. 31-34.

"Allocation of Corporate Reorganization Between Chapters X and XI of the Bankruptcy Act," *Harvard Law Review*, Vol. 69 (December 1955), pp. 352-362.

Jessop Steel Corp., Annual Reports.

Moody's Industrial Manuals (Annual). New York: Moody's Investment Service, Inc.

"Railroads: Numbers Game," *Newsweek* (April 26, 1971), pp. 77-78.

National Income and Product Accounts of the United States and Survey of Current Business (U.S. Department of Commerce).

New York Times, September 4, 1957, p. 50:7—"Bankrupt Company Disputes Valuation."

"Peat Marwick Mitchell & Company Replies," *Fortune* (September 1970), pp. 87-88.

"SEC Corporation Release #95," June 7, 1955.

"SEC Corporation Release #105," January 24, 1957.

"SEC Corporation Release #106," February 26, 1957.

"SEC Corporation Release #107," August 26, 1957.

Security & Exchange Commission Annual Reports. Securities & Exchange Commission, Washington, D.C., 1946-1970.

Standard and Poor's Stock Guide. New York: Standard & Poor's Corp., January 1959, 1962.

Standard and Poor's Trade and Securities Statistics. New York: Standard & Poor's Corp.

"A Proposed Analytical System to Provide an Objective Basis for Supervision," in *State of California Division of Savings and Loan*. Price Waterhouse & Co., December 21, 1967.

Survey of Current Business: Business Statistics, 1965. U.S. Dept. of Commerce, Office of Business Economics, 1965.

Table of Bankruptcy Statistics. Administrative Office of the President, Washington, D.C., 1970.

"ICC Begins Study of Penn-Central Unit, Expects New Reporting, Accounting Rules," *Wall Street Journal* (July 3, 1970), p. 2.

Wall Street Journal (April 9, 1971), p. 2; March 29, 1971; March 17, 1971, p. 1; December 31, 1970; October 10, 1970, p. 3; July 30, 1970.

Index

Absolute economic value, 12
Accounts receivable management, 92–94
Accuracy:
 in classification, 67
 predicting, long-range, 71–79
Acts of God, business failure and, 23
After-tax expected earnings, capitalized, 101
Age factor, in failures, 21–22
American assets, foreign appropriation of, 1
AMTRAK, 158
Anderson-Jordan study, 44
Assets:
 foreign government appropriation of, 1
 reorganization and, 6
 See also Total assets.
Assignment, defined, 12

Bankruptcy, 105–124
 action in, initiating, 8
 alternatives to, evaluating, 95
 classification of, 70
 defined, 2
 effect of, analyzing, 127
 financial arrangements, 97–98
 insolvency in, 3
 investing in entities, 136
 involuntary, 7
 laws regulating, 4
 merger prior to, 105
 in perspective, 1–24
 railroad, history of, 175–178
 receivership in, 5
 second order effects, 1
 statements prior to, 68
 statistics, 14–24
 stock market risk, 139–141
 types of, 3
 See also Corporate bankruptcy, Railroad bankruptcy
Bankruptcy Act (1898), 4, 5
Bankruptcy Act (1933):
 liquidation under, 12
 See also Chandler Act of 1938
Bankruptcy Act (1934), 7
Bankruptcy Act (1938):
 proposed changes in, 13–14
 See also Chandler Act of 1938
Bankruptcy case, illustrative, 25–36
Bankruptcy costs, 1
Bankruptcy filings, 18
Bankruptcy implication model, accuracy in, 73

Bankruptcy laws, study recommendations, 13
Bankruptcy merger, security holders and, 112–113
Bankruptcy potential, share valuation and, 125–138
Bankruptcy price behavior, 78–81
Bankruptcy procedure, review of, 8
Bankruptcy process:
 evolution of, 4–14
 voluntary/involuntary, 7
Bankruptcy reorganization, 95, 98
 under Chandler Act, Chapter X, 7–12
 defined, 3
 merger under, 107
Bankruptcy statistics, aggregate, 17–21
Bankrupt entities:
 investing in, 136–138
 results with, 142
 secondary sample, 69, 70
Banks:
 merger suggestions, 121
 size of, and loan policy, 88
Baskin, 136
Baxter, Nevins, 126, 127
Beaver, William H., 71, 79, 80
Beaver study, bankruptcy price behavior, 79
Bias, potential, 68
Boeing Aircraft, 120–121
Brigham, E., 8, 9–11
Burglary, business failure and, 23
Business cycles, changes in, evolution, 44
Business failure:
 age factor in, 21–22
 analysis of, 37
 causes of, 22–24
 costs of, 53
 cyclical turning point, 42
 fundamental, immediate, 38
 influences on, 37–57
 in perspective, 1–24
 portents of, 58
 post World War II, 38
 predicting, 83–104
 sources of, 57
 statistics, 14–24
 types of, 2n
 See also Failure
Business loans:
 credit-scoring procedures, 91
 credit-scoring techniques, 84

Calkins, Francis, 102, 127, 136
Capital charges, business failure and, 23

196

About the Author

Edward I. Altman was born in 1941 in New York City and obtained the Ph.D. in Finance from the University of California, Los Angeles, Graduate School of Business in August 1967. He has been with New York University since September 1967. During the academic year 1971-72 Professor Altman is a Visiting Professor of Finance at the Institut Superieur des Affaires in France. He has published numerous articles in academic and professional journals and has served as a referee for the *Journal of Finance, American Economic Journal* and the *Western Economic Journal*. Since 1968, he has served as the Proceedings Editor of the *Journal of Finance* and is currently on the Advisory Board to the University of Puerto Rico, College of Business Administration. Professor Altman is also an advisor to the Presidential-Congressional Commission on the National Bankruptcy Laws of the United States.

HIEBERT LIBRARY

3 6877 00122 7940

Date D